Centerville Library
Washington-Centerville Public Library
Centerville, Ohio
DISCARD

D1195449

BAG OF BONES

Also by J. North Conway

Nonfiction

The Big Policeman: The Rise and Fall of America's First, Most Ruthless, and Greatest Detective

King of Heists: The Sensational Bank Robbery of 1878 That Shocked America

The Cape Cod Canal: Breaking Through the Bared and Bended Arm

Head Above Water

Shipwrecks of New England

New England Visionaries

New England Women of Substance

American Literacy: Fifty Books That Define Our Culture and Ourselves

From Coup to Nuts: A Revolutionary Cookbook

Fiction

The Road to Ruin

Zig Zag Man

Poetry

Life Sentences

My Picnic With Lolita and Other Poems

DISCARD

BAG OF BONES

——◆◆◆◆◆——

The Sensational Grave Robbery of the Merchant Prince of Manhattan

J. NORTH CONWAY

LYONS PRESS

Guilford, Connecticut

An imprint of Globe Pequot Press

To buy books in quantity for corporate use
or incentives, call **(800) 962-0973**
or e-mail **premiums@GlobePequot.com**.

Copyright © 2012 by J. North Conway

ALL RIGHTS RESERVED. No part of this book may be reproduced or transmitted in any form by any means, electronic or mechanical, including photocopying and recording, or by any information storage and retrieval system, except as may be expressly permitted in writing from the publisher. Requests for permission should be addressed to Globe Pequot Press, Attn: Rights and Permissions Department, P.O. Box 480, Guilford, CT 06437.

Lyons Press is an imprint of Globe Pequot Press.

Text design: Sheryl Kober
Layout artist: Justin Marciano
Project editor: Kristen Mellitt

Library of Congress Cataloging-in-Publication Data is available on file.

ISBN 978-0-7627-7812-6

Printed in the United States of America

10 9 8 7 6 5 4 3 2 1

This book is dedicated to my mother and father.

TABLE OF CONTENTS

Hotel, the Stewart estate's resort in Saratoga Springs, New York. Hilton's actions lead to a boycott of Stewart's stores by the Jewish community. Hilton also reneges on building the "Working Women's Hotel," causing a furor among New York City women, who also threaten a boycott.

In which ghouls steal the body of A. T. Stewart from its grave at St. Mark's Cemetery in November 1878. Despite several clues, a twenty-five-thousand-dollar reward offered by Henry Hilton, and an extensive investigation by the New York City Police Department, no leads are found in the mystifying case. Hilton does not immediately inform Mrs. Stewart of the ghastly deed for fear that it might send her into shock. He subsequently accuses the church sextons of the appalling crime in an effort to close the unnerving case.

In which the theft of A. T. Stewart's remains causes a national media sensation and expends the resources of the entire New York City Police Department, as well as private detectives hired by Henry Hilton. While several suspects are apprehended and then released, new clues in the case are uncovered and followed but only lead to a series of dead-ends. Hilton receives hundreds of letters from unnamed sources claiming to be in possession of the body and demanding ransom payment for its return.

In which the motive for the theft continues to elude the police while clues suggest it is the handiwork of professional grave robbers, most notably George Christian, a notorious "resurrectionist" who steals bodies for medical research. Yet, neither Christian nor the flood of mysterious letters claiming to know the location of A. T. Stewart's body lead the police to the culprits. Stewart's body remains missing.

In which the noted investigator, New York City Police Captain Thomas Byrnes, makes a breakthrough in the sensational case and arrests two men, Henry Vreeland and William Burke, charging them with the heinous crime. The two men lead the police on a merry chase through parts of New Jersey where they claim the body is buried.

management style, and a series of egregious public relations blunders ultimately led to the liquidation of the company. Hilton refuses to accept any blame for the company's demise.

In which, in 1881, Mrs. Stewart, without Henry Hilton's approval, makes arrangements with men claiming to be the grave robbers for the return of her husband's remains. On a deserted road in New York's Westchester County, two wagons cross paths, one containing an emissary from Mrs. Stewart with a twenty-thousand-dollar ransom and the other driven by unidentified men who exchange a burlap bag of bones for the ransom money and ride off. The bones are taken by train to Garden City, where they are placed in the crypt at the Cathedral of the Incarnation.

In which one thousand people travel to Garden City, Long Island, to take part in the April 1885 dedication ceremony of the Gothic-style Cathedral of the Incarnation—the huge, ornate, and costly memorial Cornelia Stewart has built for her husband. Construction of the cathedral takes nine years and costs approximately three million dollars. On May 22, 1885, Cornelia Stewart signs over the deed of the great cathedral and all of its adjacent buildings and schools to the Episcopal church for one dollar.

In which Cornelia Stewart dies on October 25, 1886, leaving behind a will that bequeaths nearly half of the remaining Stewart estate to Judge Henry Hilton. Stewart heirs seek to have the will voided, claiming fraud by Hilton. The case lingers in the courts for the next seven years before being resolved. In the end, Hilton's attempts at replicating his benefactor's retail business success all fail. Hilton dies, and the once great Stewart fortune is gone.

Introduction

BONES OF CONTENTION

The tale surrounding the theft and ransom of department store magnate A. T. Stewart's body—told here in *Bag of Bones*—would be magnificent fodder for today's "cold case" entertainment industry were the remains those of a contemporary man of Stewart's astounding wealth. But this crime took place long before co-ed detective units and lab-coat forensics. It remains one of America's great and enduring mysteries.

Bag of Bones is the third and final installment of my trilogy about New York City during the Gilded Age. *King of Heists* (2009) told the story of the greatest bank robbery in American history, carried out in 1878 by George L. Leslie, dubbed "King of the Bank Robbers." *The Big Policeman* (2010) details the career of Thomas Byrnes, a colorful, sometimes ruthless police officer who rose through the ranks to become superintendent of the New York City Police Department and who is credited as the father of American detective work.

Byrnes is a key player in the A. T. Stewart drama. He is the head cop in the investigation of the gruesome, sensational crime at the heart of the story. I think of the Stewart case as a classic whodunit, yet it weaves together elements of true crime, biography, and Manhattan history and culture, all set against New York City's decadent social order—the Gilded Age.

Running parallel to the grave-robbing narrative is the story of the Stewart family's rise and fall, and how the family fortune fared under the questionable stewardship of one of Stewart's most trusted friends, Judge Henry Hilton. Any reader will be quick to conclude that Bernie Madoff had nothing on Judge Hilton. The tragedy of A. T. and Cornelia Stewart serves as a cautionary tale, one that reinforces how vital study of the Gilded Age is to our understanding of contemporary American society. The Gilded Age was a term coined by Mark Twain and used as the title of a book he wrote with Charles Dudley Warner in 1873, *The Gilded Age: A Tale of To-Day*. It encapsulates a period in American history (1870–1890) of enormous greed, the accumulation of great wealth by the so-called robber barons—people who made their great fortunes through ruthless and uncontrolled business practices—and the vulgar display of that wealth.

Gilded Age figures occupy the top tier of the list of the richest Americans in history according to both *Forbes* and the *New York Times*. Among them are John D. Rockefeller (1839–1937), America's first billionaire, ranked number one with approximately $190 billion by early twenty-first century currency standards, followed by Cornelius Vanderbilt (1794–1877), who was estimated to be worth about $140 billion, and John Jacob Astor in the number three spot at nearly $115 billion. Andrew Carnegie (1835–1919) reached sixth place, and A.T. Stewart (1803–1876), who is considered the father of the American department store, was in the seventh position. The Gilded Age yielded five of the top ten richest men in American history. During this period it was estimated that the richest 2 percent of the people owned one-third of the nation's wealth, while the richest 10 percent owned three-quarters. If, as stated in the Sermon on the Mount, "the meek shall inherit the earth," then the celestial courts will surely be clogged with litigation. According to Robert Frank of the *New York Times*, during the "New Gilded Age" of the 1990s and the early 2000s, "today's rich barely hold a candle to the Gilded Age titans. ... This is partly a measure of the astounding wealth accumulated by Rockefeller, Vanderbilt, Astor, and Carnegie." Count A. T. Stewart among these notable Gilded Age billionaires.

At the time of his death in 1876, before Rockefeller had completed his ascent, Alexander Turney Stewart was considered the third richest man in America behind only Vanderbilt and Astor. He left his wife, Cornelia, an estate estimated at more than forty million dollars, a vast fortune that he had made in the retail sales business and that had earned him the title of the "Merchant Prince of Manhattan."

An Irish immigrant, Stewart began his career in New York City in 1823, selling linens from the old country. By 1862, he had built the largest department store in the world, the "Cast Iron Palace." Stewart's store was six floors tall and located on the corner of Broadway and Ninth Street. It had a cast-iron front and a glass dome skylight.

The immense store employed more than two thousand people and had nearly twenty departments, selling everything from burlap bags to women's calf gloves. He later established department stores overseas, including in London and Paris.

In 1869, Stewart completed his ornate mansion on the corner of Fifth Avenue and Thirty-fourth Street in New York City. Unlike the other luxurious brownstone mansions owned by the Astors and Vanderbilts, all located along what was referred to as "Millionaires' Row," Stewart's was made entirely out of Italian marble, cut exclusively for him and shipped to the United States. Costing approximately two million dollars, it took seven years to build. Constructed in Parisian Empire design, the building had three main floors, an attic with a mansard roof, and a ballroom that ran the full length of its Fifth Avenue frontage. A lighted moat separated the residence from the sidewalks. Stewart filled the mansion with expensive furniture and antiques and a large and valuable art collection. There was no home like it in America.

Stewart's attempt to outdo his multimillionaire neighbors, like William and Caroline Astor, did not endear him to New York City's powerful and affluent society. He and his wife found themselves ostracized by high class circles, viewed as millionaire upstarts. Still, their exclusion did nothing to damage his retail empire. Following the death of Cornelia Stewart in 1886, the Marble Mansion was sold, and in 1901 it was torn down.

Stewart did not spend all of his fortune on himself and his wife. Although he was not known as a philanthropist among the ranks of Andrew Carnegie, he was still very generous to those in need. During the Irish potato famine of 1848, Stewart sent a shipload of provisions to his native Lisburn and invited young people to take free passage to America, where he found them jobs within his vast department store complex. He also sent fifty thousand dollars to the victims of the 1871 Chicago fire.

His most lasting philanthropic endeavor was the building of Garden City, New York. In 1869, Stewart bought more than seven thousand acres on the Hempstead Plain on Long Island, where he established the first planned workers' community in the United States. Garden City included sixteen miles of streets and avenues, a central park, affordable homes, stores, and a hotel. Stewart even built a railroad into the city so his employees could take the train to work at one of his many retail, wholesale, or manufacturing businesses. Stewart had nearly thirty thousand trees planted in his development. He did not, however, offer home ownership. Instead he acted as landlord of the community. Today, Garden City remains one of the country's most sought after residential locations.

In November 1878, A. T. Stewart's body was stolen from its resting place at St. Mark's Churchyard in New York City and held for more than two hundred thousand-dollar ransom. Advised by family friend Henry Hilton,the executor of Stewart's will, Cornelia Stewart did not comply with the grave robbers' demands. Several suspects were arrested but were soon released after it was discovered that either a desire for fame or heavy-handed police tactics had motivated their false confessions. The gruesome crime created a media frenzy as newspapers tried to outdo each other in their sensational coverage. The American imagination was captivated. In just one example, the incident was depicted in Mark Twain's humorous story "The Stolen White Elephant," published in 1882.

Not only did the grave robbing cause a national sensation, it also led to one of the most notoriously bungled police investigations in New York City's history.

Finally, in 1881, nearly three years after the body of her husband was stolen, Cornelia Stewart reportedly regained her husband's remains. The Merchant Prince of Manhattan, now just a burlap bag of bones, was handed over on a dusty road in Westchester County. Cornelia buried her husband for the last time in the family crypt at the Episcopal Cathedral of the Incarnation in Garden City—a structure completed in 1885 by Cornelia as a lasting memorial to her husband.

Two great mysteries surround that crypt today. There is no way to know if the bones buried there are truly those of A. T. Stewart. A century before DNA testing, bones were just bones and there was no method to accurately identify if they were Stewart's or not. The children of Cornelia and A. T. Stewart preceded them in death, and no one has ever sought to exhume the bones for identification. They remain laid to rest in the family crypt on the orders of Cornelia, who claimed without a doubt that the bones belonged to her husband. If it was good enough for her, it appeared to be good enough for everyone connected with the case.

The other enduring mystery is who actually stole the bones? The grave robbers? They were never caught.

But there is much more to this mystery than the gruesome theft of A. T. Stewart's bones and their questionable recovery. There is Judge Henry Hilton. How did this man get his hands on the forty-million-dollar Stewart fortune? And how was he able to manipulate the grieving widow into allowing him to continue the A. T. Stewart retail business, despite explicit instructions in Stewart's will to sell the business and give the proceeds to his wife? Hilton's inexplicable hold over Cornelia Stewart extended even beyond her death in 1886, when she bequeathed him approximately $9.5 million, half of her estate. And there is another head-scratching mystery—how did Hilton, the executor of the vast A. T. Stewart retail empire, manage to run the business into the ground and spend all of the Stewart fortune by the time of his death in 1899?

Except for Garden City and the Cathedral of the Incarnation, there is nothing that remains of the once great and successful A. T. Stewart department store, considered the first such store in America. The unique buildings Stewart constructed to house his retail empire, the Marble Palace and the Cast Iron Palace, are gone. Even his luxurious white marble mansion on Fifth Avenue is gone. His entire forty-million-dollar fortune was depleted at the hands of Hilton. The A. T. Stewart story disappeared along with it. The man who practically invented the American department store has for too long been lost in the annals of American history. *Bag of Bones* attempts to unravel some of the mysteries surrounding Stewart. Throughout the book, I have included headlines and portions of newspaper articles from the period. These pieces are replicated exactly as they appeared. The typos and misspellings are just as they were in such newspapers as the *New York Times,* the *Brooklyn Eagle,* and other historical sources.

1

COUNTER CULTURE

In which Alexander Turney Stewart, New York City's "Merchant Prince of Manhattan," dies, leaving his widow, Cornelia, a forty-million-dollar fortune and naming Judge Henry Hilton as the executor of his estate. From his humble beginnings in Ireland, Stewart rises to wealth and power, and constructs a series of landmark buildings, including his two retail outlets—the Marble Palace and the Cast Iron Palace—and his lavish domicile, the Marble Mansion.

To paraphrase the great Charles Dickens from *A Christmas Carol*, A. T. Stewart was dead to begin with—dead as a doornail. Alexander Turney Stewart died on April 10, 1876, at seventy-two years of age in his palatial home, dubbed the "Marble Mansion," located on the corner of Fifth Avenue and Thirty-fourth Street, in the heart of New York City. At the time of his death, Stewart was one of the wealthiest men in America. He left behind a fortune worth approximately forty million dollars. His real estate holdings in New York alone were assessed around four million dollars but were more likely to bring in more than ten million dollars. His personal wealth ranked third in the nation behind William B. Astor Sr., who made his fortune in real estate holdings, and Cornelius Vanderbilt, who became rich through his railroad investments.

Among the properties Stewart owned were the "Cast Iron Palace," his giant retail department store that occupied the block bordered by Broadway, Fourth Avenue, and Ninth and Tenth Streets; the Metropolitan Hotel; his wholesale store on Broadway, Chambers, and Reade; the "Marble Mansion;" the Globe Theater property on Broadway; and four city lots valued at ninety-six thousand dollars collectively.

His private art collection, including paintings and statuary on display in his home, was estimated to be worth more than $600,000. Among the paintings was Meissonier's *Charges des Cuirassiers*, for which Stewart paid approximately $75,000. His personal property was assessed at three million dollars. Yet, personal property and Big

Apple real estate represented only a portion of his immense wealth. Besides stocks and bonds, he owned millions of dollars worth of mill property near Fishkill, New York; Garden City in its entirety; the railroad connecting the planned community to Hunter's Point; the Grand Union Hotel in Saratoga Springs, New York; stores and businesses in London, Paris, and other European cities; and manufacturing mills throughout the United States and abroad. An enormously successful retail merchant, he was the largest importer of goods in America and he owned more real estate in the country than any other person, with the exception of William B. Astor.

DEATH OF A.T. STEWART
CAREER OF THE MERCHANT PRINCE
He Dies At His Residence In Fifth Avenue Surrounded By His Friends— Mr. Stewart's Birth And Early Life— The Secret Of His Success—Incidents Of His Business Life—Wealth And Personal Habits

At 1:50 o'clock yesterday afternoon Alexander Turney Stewart died, at his residence at Thirty-fourth Street and Fifth avenue, in this city, in the seventy-third year of his age. ... While it is true that it was chiefly as a merchant that Mr. Stewart was eminent, it was not that alone, nor even his great wealth, that made him conspicuous. It cannot be said that he was noted as a public philanthropist, or that he used any part of his fortune, which is estimated at from $40,000,000 to $50,000,000 for the benefit of the City where he acquired it. The only monument of this kind which he has left behind him is the Women's Home at Thirty second street and Fourth avenue, which is yet uncompleted. ... So also is Garden City, on Long Island, where he furnished comfortable homes to poor men at rates which, indeed, gave him fair returns, but also enabled them to live far more decently than ever before. ... In March 1869 President Grant appointed him Secretary of the Treasury, and it is understood that he would have accepted had not his confirmation been prevented by the law of 1742, which excludes from that office all who are interested in importations. ... As his fortunes increased, Mr. Stewart made his domestic arrangements keep pace with it, until several years ago he removed to the house in which he died, and which is perhaps the most palatial private residence on the Continent. ... The funeral services will take place at St. Mark's Church, at Second avenue and Stuyvesant street.

—*New York Times*
April 11, 1876

A. T. Stewart, who was frequently referred to in print as the "Merchant Prince," is credited with developing the first department store. That honor actually belongs to Aristide Boucicaut, whose Paris store, Bon Marché, began in 1838 and developed into the first department store in 1852. There, for the first time, a great quantity of merchandise was sold in various departments all under one roof. Boucicaut established fixed prices and a money-back guarantee—policies that Stewart later incorporated into his business. By 1855, Bon Marché employed nearly four thousand workers and had sales of approximately $300,000 daily.

Still, A. T. Stewart can be credited with starting the first American department store. That title is undisputed. In 1846, Stewart built the country's first department store on 280 Broadway, between Chambers and Reade Streets. The store was dubbed the "Marble Palace," because of its size and ornate marble façade. In 1862, Stewart built an even larger, more ornate store. The huge six-story structure took up a full city block bounded by Broadway, Fourth Avenue, and Ninth and Tenth Streets, and had a dome skylight and emporium. It is thought to be the first building in New York City with a cast-iron front. It was appropriately enough dubbed the "Cast Iron Palace."

———•••••———

A. T. Stewart was born in Lisburn, Ireland, on October 12, 1803. Lisburn, in Ulster Province, six miles from Belfast, is located along the banks of the Lagan River. John Turney, a Lisburn farmer, had one daughter, Margaret. His wife died while Margaret was still a child. When Margaret reached the age of eighteen, she married farmer Alexander Stewart, a native of Scotland, who had settled in the north of Ireland on Red Hill in Lisburn, not far from where Margaret's father ran his farm. Alexander Stewart contracted tuberculosis shortly after his marriage to Margaret and died, leaving his pregnant widow to fend for herself. A few months after her husband's death, she gave birth to a son. He was christened Alexander Turney Stewart, in honor of his father and grandfather. John Turney took his daughter and grandson into his home to care for them and subsequently remarried a younger woman who had a child of her own. The relationship between Margaret and her stepmother was intolerable. Still a beautiful woman, Margaret remarried a man named David Bell in 1804. They emigrated to America, leaving her baby son in the care of his maternal grandfather.

John Turney wanted his grandson to become a Protestant Episcopal minister of the Church of England and set in motion the apparatus to have young Alexander admitted to Trinity College in Dublin. In the meantime, the boy attended a local school, and in 1814 began his studies at Neely's English Academy. After Neely's he spent two years at Trinity College. In 1816, John Turney died, and a guardian, Thomas Lamb, an Irish Quaker, took in the boy. Alexander Turney Stewart was studious and received an excellent classical education, becoming proficient in Greek and Latin. He passed all his examinations with honors, but long before he had completed his second year at Trinity and even before his grandfather died, he had discarded the notion of ever becoming a clergyman, a decision he never revealed to his grandfather while he was alive. It was only after his grandfather's death that he expressed his feelings to his guardian.

"I have not the qualities a clergyman ought to possess, indeed, I have not the least desire to enter the ministry, I rather shrink from it. So long as I feel so, it seems to me unwise to go on with my preparation for sacred orders," Stewart told Lamb.

Lamb responded: "Perhaps you are right; I am not prepared to say that your views are wrong. I am quite sure that no young man should enter the ministry against his own judgment and wishes; but we need to give the subject serious consideration, that we may settle it wisely."

With his desires now known, Stewart continued his formal education while setting his sights on a different career choice. He wrote frequently to his mother, who was then living in New York City, and the correspondence between them led Stewart to yearn to travel to America—New York, specifically—to try to make his fortune in the retail business. It was an odd choice of careers for a young man schooled primarily in the classics, urged to enter the ministry, trained as a teacher, and lacking any education or training in the field of retail business.

Thomas Lamb, who willingly acquiesced to Stewart's desire, insisted that the boy gain some experience in the retail trade before trying to launch his career overseas in America.

He set the young Stewart up with a job as a grocer at a small store in Belfast, where he could not only learn the retail business firsthand, but also earn some money.

Still, Stewart longed to begin his career in the New World, to leave Ireland, reunite with his mother, and begin a new life. Long and arduous days and nights laboring as a Belfast grocer were merely a hindrance, he thought, to his true vocation awaiting him in America.

———————

In the spring of 1818, Stewart packed his bags, along with the money he had earned working as a grocer in Belfast, and left for America. He landed in New York City six weeks later and joined his mother and stepfather. Stewart now had two half-siblings, James and Mary, and they all lived as one family for a brief time before Stewart struck out on his own.

Lamb had supplied the young Stewart with letters of introduction to a number of his Quaker friends living in New York, and Stewart wasted no time calling on them. Having studied two years at Trinity College, Stewart was more than capable in teaching the classics and math. He obtained a temporary position at a wealthy private school, Isaac N. Bragg's Academy on Roosevelt Street, then a very fashionable part of the city. He was paid a yearly stipend of three hundred dollars, a more than comfortable amount for a young man during that era, but Stewart had other ambitions. He wanted to begin a retail business, and although he had no immediate idea what type of retail enterprise he would open, his life's path spread out before him when he made a monumental and life-changing loan to a friend.

While still teaching school, Stewart loaned eighty dollars to a friend who wanted to open a small dry-goods store. Because of an emergency in his life, the friend was unable to continue with his enterprise. Stewart saw his chance. He resigned his teaching position and began his life's work, albeit on a small scale, at a storefront on Greenwich Street, a location he occupied from roughly 1819 to 1823. Stewart launched his full-blown retail career in 1823 when he moved to a small rented store at 283 Broadway.

The America to which Alexander Turney Stewart immigrated in 1818 had a population of 9.6 million people. About 124,000 people were living in New York City when he arrived.

Like much of the rest of the country, New York City was not able to support major retail stores, relying instead on what was and remains known as the "country store," which, like the later department stores, carried all kinds of goods and supplies, including clothes, food, tools, and household necessities.

One of the first "country stores" was begun by Jedediah Barber, who opened his "Great Western" store in 1811 in one room of his home on Main Street in Homer, New York. Much of Barber's business was conducted in trade or bartering. Still, he built his business from one small room to an establishment with three floors of merchandise and ten employees. The store remained in business until 1856.

———•••———

Stewart's retail genius was immediately demonstrated by his ability to identify trends in women's fashion. He was quick to become aware of what many of New York City's most fashionable women were wearing and noted that many of the dresses had lace trim. This type of needlework was an expensive enterprise in the United States, which added to the cost of the dresses, but lace was an inexpensive commodity in Stewart's homeland, especially in Belfast, where Irish lace was cheaply and abundantly made. Stewart immediately struck on an idea. He returned to Ireland and invested what little money he had in importing Irish lace, the kind used in trimming expensive dresses. Stewart discovered he could sell the Irish lace from his small storefront on Greenwich Street for more than ten times the price he bought it. Despite the huge markup, it was still half as much as the going price of the same lace trimmings in New York. Buying Irish lace low in Ireland and selling it high in America brought the young Stewart his first retail success.

In 1823, Stewart opened the first of his Broadway stores at 283 Broadway, a very modest place that became known as "Stewart's little store." The store, with a twenty-five-foot frontage, took up merely one-half of the building, which also housed the Washington Hotel. The rent for the new store was just $250 per year. It consisted of one large front room with a smaller room in the rear, where Stewart lived and slept.

In 1824, he returned to Ireland, where he received an inheritance of approximately $3,500 from his grandfather. He used a large amount of this money to buy Irish lace scallop-trimmings used on women's dresses and shipped them back to New York, where he sold them from his small storefront. The tiny store was a one-man operation with Stewart working as his own buyer, salesman, and bookkeeper. He became adept at all three roles. Stewart was the first to introduce the radical retail idea of a one-price-for-all-customers rule.

Before the introduction of Stewart's system, shoppers often haggled with merchants about prices, trying to beat down the cost of various items. Merchants in turn would try to sell inferior goods for more than they were worth or misrepresent the products they were selling as new when they were anything but fresh. Stewart promised his customers that he would not sell anything in his store for more than its value in the open market. He also vowed to his customers that, if a particular product went down in worth, he would lower the price of the merchandise accordingly. If the value of certain goods rose, he would increase the price accordingly as well, without fail. Thus, Stewart proved his business acumen.

Stewart negated all the previous haggling that retail shopping had entailed with his one-price rule. Although the one price—no haggling rule was unpopular at first, Stewart soon became known as an exceptional and honest judge of the value of goods. His price was almost always lower than the price of the same goods anywhere else.

Stewart was able to sell his items at a lower cost because he always paid cash for the merchandise he bought from suppliers— another of what would become his long-standing rules for his retail business. Paying cash gave him the advantage of buying goods and materials in large quantities at the best price. Stewart bought much of his merchandise at auctions, not relying on credit. His cash-only policy also made him the buyer of choice with sellers and distributors who were trying to sell off their merchandise quickly. By paying only cash, Stewart often realized a 2 percent discount. In the beginning Stewart dealt with a limited amount of merchandise, which made the 2 percent discount seem inconsequential, but as Stewart increased his volume, the discount produced substantial profits. Moreover, when sellers were intent on liquidating a product, they knew that turning to Stewart first would supply them with an immediate infusion of funds. And Stewart tended to pass his savings onto his customers, always maintaining a minimal markup, preferring instead to profit from volume.

"In that way I limit competition and increase sales; and although I realize only a small profit on each sale, the enlarged area of business makes possible a large accumulation of capital and assures the future," Stewart said.

His formula for retail success was sound, simple, and successful. Soon, most of the women in New York City became faithful and loyal customers.

He, in turn, served them fairly and honestly. Along with his one-price and cash-only rules, Stewart prided himself on another important rule, which was absolute integrity when selling merchandise in his store. He never let any merchandise be misrepresented in order to sell it at a higher price, such as mislabeling domestic merchandise as imported. No damaged or faulty items were sold without full disclosure to the customer. And regardless of the shopper's station in life, from the wealthiest heiress to the poorest household servant, no one was taken advantage of or overcharged. Word of mouth spread quickly through the city. Only one year went by before Stewart's store became too small to accommodate all the business he enjoyed and he made plans to move.

In September 1825, a small advertisement appeared in the *Daily Advertiser* announcing the sale of "a general assortment of fresh and seasonable dry goods," at A. T. Stewart's on Broadway.

In 1826, Stewart moved his base of retail operations to a larger store at 262 Broadway and began to hire salesmen and saleswomen to handle the vast number of customers. He interrogated each of his salespeople personally, to make sure they lived up to his highest expectations of honesty and integrity. Stewart was keenly aware that one bad salesperson could reflect poorly on his business, and he was not averse to firing those who did not meet his expectations. Despite how quickly his business grew, Stewart gave every aspect of his retail operation his personal attention, and his enterprise prospered accordingly.

———

Short in stature and lean, A. T. Stewart had watery blue eyes and a reserved demeanor. He dressed plainly, although fashionably, and shunned personal extravagances such as rings, stickpins, watch chains, or any other form of jewelry. He was known for being practical in his dress and his habits. He awoke early and worked well into the evening. He seldom celebrated holidays and spent little time on leisure or recreation. He was religiously devoted to the day-to-day operations of his business, a trait that did not diminish even as his empire spread throughout New York City and the world.

In 1823, he married Cornelia Mitchell Clinch, a young woman he had met while he was a member of St. Mark's Episcopal Church. A mutual friend from the church had introduced them when Stewart first arrived in New York in 1918. Cornelia was one of nine children of Jacob and Susanna Clinch, a modestly wealthy and well-connected New York City family. Jacob Clinch was a partner in the ship chandler firm of Jones and Clinch. The Stewarts had two children, John and May. John was born in 1834 and died as an infant. May died at birth in 1838. The Stewarts had no other children and no heirs to the growing family fortune.

———

The retail business of A. T. Stewart expanded, making the establishment of a wholesale arm mandatory. While many retail concerns set their course by establishing specialty markets, Stewart gambled on providing a wide assortment of wholesale and retail products. He sold everything from his store, especially as it related to women's fashion and household needs.

Stewart became a major importer, personally developing a series of business relations throughout the world in order to replenish his retail stock with only the finest and most up-to-date goods. Although these various arrangements were suitable for a time, they did not meet Stewart's needs in the long run. The manufacturers he dealt with often could not provide Stewart with the correct merchandise he was looking for—either the color, quantity, or quality of the various stock he desired would be unavailable. He subsequently turned to manufacturing, allowing him to create for his stores unique product lines, including fabrics that no other seller in the city could reproduce.

His business acumen led him to realize tremendous profits within a short span of time and compelled him to move his base of operations again within just a three-year period, from 262 Broadway to a larger venue at 257 Broadway. There, the operations would remain for more than fifteen years, until he purchased a city lot at Broadway and Chambers Streets in 1846 and built his famous Marble Palace.

The Marble Palace became the retail hub of Stewart's vast department store empire. The new building had a distinctive white Tuckahoe marble that set it apart from the otherwise drab sandstone structures surrounding it. This crisp, bright look alone was astonishing in a city otherwise dominated by sandstone and earth tones, and gave the Stewart store a landmark identity that other establishments lacked. The Marble Palace was four stories high. The ornate Italian style of design incorporated by the architects, Trench & Snook, gave the building an air of social majesty.

Inside the store were two ornamental columns representing the twin pillars of "Commerce and Plenty." There was a seventy-foot-wide rotunda with a balcony gallery overhead. High atop the building was a glass dome. Stewart planned his store so that it included distinct departments, with a vast and varied inventory from which to choose.

The Marble Palace sold imported European merchandise to women, provided fashion shows displaying the most recent styles and trends, and featured a lushly ornate "Ladies Parlor" on the second floor, where women could lounge, talk, and refresh themselves. The parlor was replete with full-length mirrors—another department store first initiated by Stewart.

exquisitely chaste, classic and tasteful ... the most splendid dry goods store in the world.
—JAMES G. BENNETT, *New York Herald,* 1846

When we visited the store ... we found a line of carriages drawn up in front reaching from Chambers to Reade streets. Crowds of fashionable people were passing in and out, and

*all were warm in their expressions of gratifications of all the
beautiful and tasteful arrangements and architecture of this
whole building.*

—*New York Herald*, 1846

*"our aunt's availing herself of the relative proximity to go and
shop at Stewart's and then come back for us; the ladies' great
shop, vast, marmoreal, plate-glassy and notoriously fatal to the
female nerve (we ourselves had wearily trailed through it, hang-
ing on the skirts, very literally, of indecision) which bravely
waylaid custom on the Broadway corner of Chambers Street."*

—FROM "A SMALL BOY," BY HENRY JAMES

*The marble palace of A.T. Stewart & Co. has lately been
enlarged, and it is now probably the most spacious and the
handsomest store of the kind in the world. With its dimensions
thus extended, it is 175 feet deep and 165 feet wide. 350 men
are employed in it; 100 sewing machines are kept constantly
busy, and 150 women earn their daily bread by taking work
from the establishment. Carpets from Persia, England and
France, shawls from Cashmere and from China, silks from all
the celebrated manufactories of Europe, curtain draperies and
ormolu furniture from Paris, and exquisite laces from Brussels
and Mechlin are here brought together as if by a fairy wand
... the multitudinous assemblage of humanity,—men, woman,
and children,—numbering between five and six thousand,
who daily throng the immense bazaar, and weary the attentive
salesmen with their various errands of business or of fashionable extravagance and pleasure.*

—SUPPLEMENT TO THE *Hartford Courant*, SEPTEMBER 18, 1858

Stewart was one of the first American retail merchants to understand that a department store was a public institution and more so that
shopping was a civic event that entailed a degree of pomp and circum-

stance. The Marble Palace was built with these two ideas in mind. The store included a dome and a rotunda, two types of structures that had previously been used almost exclusively in public buildings like libraries and government offices. In fact, City Hall, located southerly from the new Stewart department store, served as a model for his store, since it too was constructed of marble and had a dome and a rotunda. According to Mona Domosh, in her book, *Invented Cities: The Creation of Landscape in Nineteenth-century New York and Boston,* Stewart intended his new store to add "cultural legitimacy to the commercial impulse." According to Domosh, "the Marble Palace was not only a functionally designed merchandizing structure but also a cultural adornment to the city."

Stewart desired his new store to be an appropriate setting for commercial enterprise: a suitable, safe, and comfortable place for women shoppers to spend their time. The store included organized displays of merchandise and a host of facilities designed specifically for women. The walls and ceilings were adorned with elaborate frescoes. A huge, flamboyant chandelier hung over the vast grand hall, and on the farthest wall on the first floor were huge imported mirrors, which made the room appear much larger than it truly was. A flight of stairs led to a shopping gallery on the second floor, where a range of marble and mahogany shelves displayed an array of new merchandise. Stewart showcased his goods in the building's giant plate-glass windows. By 1850, the Marble Palace was the largest store in the city and known not only for its merchandise and selection, but also its distinctive style.

There had been other high buildings but none so stately and simple. And even now there is, in its way no finer street effect than the view of Stewart's buildings as seen on a clear blue brilliant day, from a point low of Broadway.
—Harper's Magazine, 1854

"I have known persons who always bring in luck. I sometimes open a case of goods and sell the first from it to some person

who is unlucky, and I am sure to lose on it in the end. I fre-
quently see persons to whom I would not sell at all if I could
avoid it."

—A. T. Stewart, 1848

An anecdote about retailer extraordinaire A. T. Stewart conveys that he was so superstitious that, when he decided to move his flourishing mercantile store from one location to another, he paid the old woman who sold apples and peanuts outside of his original store to relocate to the front of his new store. The old woman, Stewart contended, had brought him luck, and Stewart was a firm believer in luck, despite his vast business acumen. The street vendor, who had stood in front of Stewart's store for years, dressed in layers of rags, smoking an old clay pipe in the corner of her weathered, toothless mouth, was astonished to learn that Stewart wasn't glad to be rid of her. On the contrary, Stewart considered her such a good luck charm that he went so far as to carry the old wooden box in which she kept her wares to the location in front of his new store on Chambers Street. He made her promise to continue her business there on the sidewalk and vowed to supplement her income if she agreed to remain there. To no one's surprise, the wizened old woman maintained her point of sale in front of Stewart's new store. Stewart was not the first businessman to amass a fortune in America through the development and growth of his department store empire, but his surely was one of the most lucrative. By 1848, Stewart was a multimillionaire. He was only forty-five years old.

———

Although A. T. Stewart's Marble Palace was considered the first real American department store, in point of fact, it was a transitional model since it did not include the variety of merchandise so readily associated with the modern American department store. Still, it was a first and remains one of three major developments in the overall growth of the retail business in America, along with Montgomery Ward's creation of the mail order catalog business (1872) and the F. W. Woolworth low-cost 5 and 10 cent store (1889).

But it was Stewart who changed the concept of the specialty store into a general merchandise outlet, and it was Stewart who first built a specially designed store from which to sell his merchandise. The result was that Stewart made shopping easy, expedient, and enjoyable—in other words, he created the concept of the one-stop shopping venue.

Another of Stewart's innovations was maintaining the principle of selling in volume. He sustained a small markup on his merchandise because he was able to sell so much. "I study to put my goods on the market at the lowest price I can afford and secure a reasonable profit. In that way I limit competition and increase my sales," Stewart said.

Dishonesty by any of his sales staff was punished with immediate dismissal, while customer and company loyalty, integrity, and ability were rewarded with promotions and increases in wages. According to Stewart's policies, a young man who began work at one of his stores as an usher at a mere five dollars a week could earn, within a short period of time and through his own initiative and honesty, twenty-five dollars a week as a sales clerk. And there were opportunities well beyond those available to industrious employees. Meanwhile it became widely circulated that, if any sales clerk within Stewart's employ was caught misrepresenting the intrinsic value of any merchandise, they would be fired. News of this traveled fast within the buying public and served as a great notice for the store. Word of mouth among customers spreading the high standards employed at Stewart's was advertising that Stewart couldn't dream of paying for. Stewart would regularly line up his salesmen and lecture to them on the way they should conduct themselves.

"You will deal with ignorant, opinionated, and innocent people," he told his employees. "You will often have an opportunity to cheat them. If they could, they would cheat you, or force you to sell at less than cost. You must be wise, but not too wise. You must never actually cheat the customer, even if you can. If she pays the full figure, present her a hank of dress-braid, a card of buttons, a pair of shoestrings. You must make her happy and satisfied, so she will come back."

Cultural historian Harry Resseguie's extensive examination of the development of the American department store during the period 1860 to 1880 identifies eleven characteristics that are associated with the retail department store. They are:

1. A central location
2. Many departments under a single roof
3. A variety of free services, including the return of merchandise for a refund or exchange
4. One price for all patrons
5. Low markup
6. Cash sales
7. Aggressive, specialized advertising
8. Large volume
9. Centralized nonselling functions
10. Purchasing inventory for cash
11. Selling of old stock though bargain sales.

A. T. Stewart adhered to many of these as early as 1846. On the issue of the one-price-for-all policy, Stewart was a leader often credited with originating such policies within the network of department stores. Once again, as far back as 1846, Stewart had adopted the one-price for everyone policy within his store.

"He was, I believe, among the first to establish the one-price principle," Thurlow Weed, an intimate friend of Stewart's told the *New York Tribune,* following Stewart's death in 1876.

According to Resseguie, "One of the most important and least appreciated policies on which the American department store system is based is the unrestricted right of the would-be customer to enter the store, inspect the merchandise, price it and purchase it or not without being inopportune to do so, and without interference from clerks or store executives."

Stewart's "open door" policy for customers truly changed the American retail business. In effect, Stewart gave birth to the concept of "browsing." Prior to Stewart's innovative policy of free entrance, shoppers would be hounded by salespeople and seldom ever left to peruse the store unattended. A sale was expected, and customers were often browbeaten into making a purchase. According to Stewart, his free entrance policy allowed shoppers to "gaze upon a million dollars' worth of goods and no man will interrupt either your meditation or admiration."

Stewart was also credited with being the first retailer to incorporate the clearance sale. During the various economic downturns beginning in 1837, when his business was housed in the Broadway location, Stewart put his high-priced inventory on sale in order to liquidate his old stock and make room for the new. But Stewart did not use clearance sales in his stores only during economic crises. Stewart himself checked his inventory daily, and slow-moving products were reduced in price.

"Let us see if people will take them at that," Stewart was noted as saying when he ordered markdowns on his products.

Retail history indicates that Stewart was not the originator of clearance sales. They were first put into effect in Paris at Bon Marché and other department stores. Still, it can be clearly stated that Stewart was the first American retailer to adopt the policy as part of the overall operation of his retail business.

Stewart sold his merchandise for cash and allowed for a limited amount of purchases on credit, with customer credit extended at most for six months. He also had a liberal, although seldom advertised, return policy that allowed customers to return unsatisfactory merchandise for exchange or refund. Unique to Stewart's return policy was that a reasonable discount would be given for returned merchandise, meaning if five yards of fabric was returned, he would give the customer credit for four yards, and if the price of the merchandise had been lowered since the purchase, the customer would be given credit at the new reduced price, not the original cost. Accordingly, as all of A. T. Stewart's retail innovations caught on with New York's shoppers, his empire and personal wealth grew exponentially.

2

THE CAST IRON PALACE

In which A. T. Stewart expands his wholesale, retail, and manufacturing businesses, employing two thousand people and earning himself approximately two million dollars a year. Stewart undertakes one of his grandest philanthropic gestures by planning a "Working Women's Hotel" in New York City, so working women will be able to find safe, comfortable, and reasonably priced accommodations. He buys more than seven thousand acres of land in Hempstead, Long Island, where he intends to build a model community—Garden City.

To accommodate his expanding empire, in 1862, Stewart bought part of the old Randall Farm, which was bounded by Ninth and Tenth Streets, Broadway, and Fourth Avenue. There, he erected a six-story, cast iron building that included a great emporium and glass dome skylight. This store covered two and a quarter acres and cost nearly three million dollars. It was quickly dubbed the Cast Iron Palace, and it became the centerpiece of all of Stewart's business in New York City. The Marble Palace on Broadway was used for his wholesale operations.

Stewart's sales staff grew accordingly. He had begun his small business in 1823 with one or two salesmen, and by the time the Cast Iron Palace was built, he employed more than two thousand people in his stores. The personnel logistics of the Cast Iron Palace were massive. According to one contemporary magazine estimate, in this single retail store, one general superintendent had nineteen assistants. Each assistant was the head of a particular department. More than a dozen cashiers within the various departments received and paid out money, while more than two dozen bookkeepers kept the record of the day's transactions. About thirty ushers directed shoppers to their desired departments in the store; two hundred boys received the customers' money and brought back their change from their purchases. There were four hundred and seventy sales clerks (some of whom were women) and fifty porters. And nine hundred seamstresses were employed to make alterations for merchandise purchased at the huge store.

The average daily number of customers visiting Stewart's Cast Iron Palace was twenty thousand. During the store's busiest season, Christmas, more than thirty-five thousand people were estimated to visit in a single day. Customers ranged from the very wealthy, who might spend thousands of dollars during their visit, to the lowly charwoman, who might buy a single piece of cloth that she would later use to sew a dress.

By 1870, it was estimated that the Cast Iron Palace brought in an average of sixty thousand dollars daily, while on some days the store's cash receipts reached almost one hundred thousand dollars.

Stewart earned an income of two million dollars in the first year that the Cast Iron Palace was open. In 1865, he earned nearly four million dollars. From the Cast Iron Palace retail business and the Marble Palace wholesale business, as well as all his international and domestic manufacturing concerns, Stewart earned an average of three million dollars a year over the course of the next six years. Using the Consumer Price Index based on relative value, Stewart's earnings would equal forty-one million dollars by today's currency standards.

———◦—◦———

Stewart wasn't the only innovative retailer to establish himself in New York City. An array of retail businesses burst on the scene. Stores such as Macy's, Lord & Taylor, and Brooks Brothers were launched along Broadway and Sixth Avenue, between Ninth and Twenty-third Streets. The area became known as "Ladies' Mile," because of the profusion of clothing and dry-goods stores dedicated to the growing needs and desires of women. Besides the department stores, there were a multitude of concert halls, theaters, art galleries, furniture stores, and piano showrooms.

Henry Sands Brooks had long before begun to address the clothing needs of New York City men when he opened H. & D. H. Brooks & Co. in April 1818 at Catharine and Cherry Streets. In 1833, his son Henry

Jr. took control of the business and in 1845 introduced the first ready-to-wear suits for men. His three sons, Daniel, John, and Elisha, took over the business in 1850 and began their trademark "Brooks Brothers" for selling boys' and men's clothing.

In 1826, Samuel Lord opened his first small dry-goods store at a Catherine Street location. In 1838, his wife's cousin, George Taylor, became a partner. In 1859, Lord & Taylor moved to Broadway and Grand Street, establishing itself as one of the most prized women's fashion stores.

In October 1858, a former Nantucket sea captain and whaler, Captain Rowland H. Macy, opened Macy's department store in New York City on the corner of Fourteenth Street and Sixth Avenue. Macy, a Quaker, had failed at the retail business several times before starting this successful enterprise. He sold his merchandise like Stewart, at a fixed price, advertised his store in the city's newspapers, and discounted his merchandise to move product. From his days as a young boy sailing on the *Emily Morgan* whaling ship, Macy had a red star tattooed on his hand. He used the red star as the symbol for his store, and it remains part of the Macy's logo to this day. The store sold men's and boys' clothing including coats, vests, and pants and women's coats, cloaks, raincoats, dresses, skirts, blouses, and hats. Macy was one of the first retail merchants to hire women executives, and in 1866 he expanded his store by purchasing several adjoining buildings. Ultimately, he owned nearly a dozen buildings. When he died in 1877, he was reported to be worth close to two million dollars. In 1924, Macy's Herald Square location in Manhattan became the largest store in the world.

In 1872, Joseph and Lyman Bloomingdale opened Bloomingdale Brothers Great East Side Bazaar at 938 Third Avenue in New York City. The completion of the Third Avenue elevated railroad connected lower Manhattan to this newly established uptown store. In 1886, the brothers built a new store that took up an entire city block at Third Avenue and Fifty-ninth Street.

———•◦•———

In 1865, Benjamin Altman opened his first store on Third Avenue. He later bought his brother's store on Sixth Avenue, where his business, B. Altman & Company, remained for the next thirty years. In 1906 the store moved to Fifth Avenue and Thirty-fourth Street. Altman's became one of the most stylish stores on Ladies' Mile.

———•◦•———

All along Ladies' Mile, department and dry-goods stores flourished, their attractive display windows overflowing with merchandise, the wide sidewalks packed with eager shoppers, and the streets lit by gas and eventually electrical lights. Besides Stewart's Cast Iron Palace, and B. Altman & Co., there were Adams & Co., H. O'Neill & Co., Stern Bros., James McCreery & Co., and a multitude of smaller emporiums catering to every need of New York City women.

Every store had its specialty. B. Altman & Co. was widely known for the best ladies' attire. H. O'Neill & Co. was renowned for its millinery, and Stern Bros. was known for its silks and laces. Ladies' Mile was in its heyday in the Gilded Age.

But it wasn't just in New York City that the phenomenon of the department store and retail merchandising was blossoming. In Philadelphia, John Wanamaker started his Oak Hall Clothing Bazaar in 1861. Wanamaker was a master of advertising and even earned himself the dubious title of "The Father of Modern Advertising." Huge posters, balloons, and full page newspaper ads all contributed to Wanamaker's success. In 1876 he built a new store replete with skylights and gas chandeliers and heralded it as "the largest space in the world devoted to retail selling on a single floor." In 1896, Wanamaker would buy the Cast Iron Palace.

———•◦•———

And there was the enormously successful Marshall Field in Chicago. Marshall Field joined Levi Leiter in 1865 and opened a store in the Windy City's downtown. The store's slogan was, "Give the Lady What She Wants," and it offered fashionable merchandise at low fixed costs. After the Chicago Fire in 1871 gutted their original store, Field and Leiter opened a new one. Field ultimately bought out his partner and built a new twenty-story store that covered an entire Chicago block, and by 1914, it became the largest department store in the country.

———

Also in Chicago in 1872, an enterprising retail merchant named Aaron Montgomery Ward mailed the first general merchandise catalog, a single sheet of fifty items, beginning the era of the catalog mail order business. By 1876 the catalog had grown to 150 pages, and by 1888 the company's annual sales reached one million dollars. When Ward died in 1913, annual sales for the company were approximately forty million dollars.

———

With the advent of department stores came other innovations in New York City life and style. The use of plate glass windows originated with the department store. They were introduced as a source of light to allow shoppers to adequately view merchandise, but soon they became an integral part of marketing. Windows on the ground floors of department stores became a prime location to show off wares. Department stores could put all their most important merchandise on display, and women shoppers gained the advantage of being able to browse a variety of merchandise without ever entering the store.

As window shopping became the accepted custom, sidewalks had to be widened to accommodate shoppers. The new wide, paved sidewalks assured fashionable women walking, browsing arm in arm and side by side along Ladies' Mile, that they would not get their dresses dirty as they crossed paths with other shoppers or stopped to eye the products on display.

Another innovation aimed primarily at women shoppers was the addition of streetlights to allow shopping into the evening, while ever increasing public transportation options—elevated trains, trolleys, and buses—provided shoppers with easy, reliable, and safe means of access to the stores.

As Mona Domosh writes in *Invented Cities: The Creation of Landscape in Nineteenth-century New York and Boston,* "The department store, then, helped turn the private domestic world into a realm of publicly purchased and appraised commodities; it was integral in the association of women with consumerism, thus making continuous consumption ideologically acceptable; and it was by and large responsible for feminizing the downtown."

Of all the growing retail concerns in America, A. T. Stewart's was the most successful. He established a worldwide business not only in retail but also in wholesale and manufacturing. He had branch offices in Philadelphia and Boston, as well as in Manchester, Nottingham, and Bradford, England; Paris and Lyons, France; Belfast, Ireland; Glasgow, Scotland; and Berlin, Germany.

All English merchandise was bought and shipped from Stewart's Manchester offices. In Belfast he had a plant where linens were bleached. At the branch in Glasgow, Scottish goods were bought and shipped to the American store. In Paris, merchandise from France, Germany, and East India was bought and sold. In Lyons, Stewart established an enormous network of warehouses for silk. In Berlin, there was a woolen factory and warehouse. In America, Stewart established manufacturing enterprises at factories such as the Mohawk Mills in Little Falls, New York; the New York Mills in Holyoke, Massachusetts; the Woodward Mills in Connecticut; and the Yantico Mills, in New Jersey. All of these businesses kept Stewart's Cast Iron Palace stocked with the most fashionable new merchandise. The annual expenses were more than one million dollars. The value of the merchandise sold was estimated at fifty million dollars. And his overall payroll, worldwide, included more than seven thousand employees.

"The advantages we possess are so superior that competition of small dealers is out of the question, and the moment they feel the pressure they cry out against monopoly, and attribute all kinds of vindictiveness to the firm. But, after all, the public at large are benefited. We are enabled to offer them the largest stock at the smallest cost, with all the guarantees that are inseparable from a responsible house, whose name and honor are part of the business."

—Alexander Turney Stewart, 1862

"People come to me and ask me for my secret of success; why, I have no secret, I tell them. My business has been a matter of principle from the start. ... If the golden rule can be incorporated into purely mercantile affairs it has been done in this establishment. ... The customers are treated precisely as the seller himself would like to be treated were he in their place ... nothing is misrepresented, the price is fixed, once and for all, at the lowest possible figure, and the circumstances of the buyer are not suffered to influence the salesman in his conduct in the smallest particular."

—Alexander Turney Stewart, 1862

At an estimated cost of nine million dollars a year, Stewart's custom fees were higher than any other importer's in New York City. Most ships carrying textiles from distant ports, destined for New York, could be counted on to be bringing over Stewart imports. The cost estimates of imports for his combined retail and wholesale businesses were approximately fifty million dollars yearly. According to one congressional report (1872), Stewart's imports totaled about one-tenth of all imports arriving in the port of New York.

Stewart's domestic manufacturing enterprises made him the largest contractor for military uniforms and other accessories during the Civil War. His manufacturing concerns continued to produce a variety of garments and accessories for women, including cloaks, underwear, dresses, and fur wraps. His companies also produced housewares such as tablecloths, napkins, and sheets, as well as household items not readily available in other stores. Carpets and mattresses were another of his key product lines. At the time of his death in 1876, Stewart had begun work on constructing a carpet factory in New York that was to be the most sophisticated and largest carpet manufacturing enterprise in the country.

"More than anyone else in America probably Alexander T. Stewart is the embodiment of business. He is emphatically a man of money—thinks money; makes money; lives money. Money is the aim of his existence, and now at sixty-five, he seems as anxious to increase his immense wealth as he was when he sought his fortune in this country forty years ago."
—JUNIUS HENRI BROWNE, *The Great Metropolis*, 1869

According to Michael Klepper and Robert Gunther, authors of the 1996 book *The Wealthy 100: From Benjamin Franklin to Bill Gates— A Ranking of the Richest Americans, Past and Present*, A. T. Stewart ranked seventh among the top ten all-time wealthy Americans with an estimated fortune of $46.9 billion based on the country's gross national product at the time compared with an equivalent fortune in today's economy.

Among the top ten are eight men who made their fortunes during the Gilded Age and two who did so in the retail business, Stewart and Marshall Field. With figures based on billions of dollars in the economy of 1996, the top ten are:

1. John D. Rockefeller, $189.6 billion
2. Andrew Carnegie, $100.5 billion
3. Cornelius Vanderbilt, $95.9 billion
4. John Jacob Astor, $78 billion
5. Bill Gates, $61.7 billion
6. Stephen Girard, $55.6 billion
7. A. T. Stewart, $46.9 billion

8.   Frederick Weyerhaeuser, $43.2 billion

9.   Jay Gould, $42.1 billion

10. Marshall Field, $40.7 billion

A. T. Stewart could have become as grand a philanthropist as the other richest men in American history, but it was really not his nature. He and his wife were childless, his children having died in infancy, and so he spent all of his time engaged in his business enterprises. He was not against giving to charity but instead preferred to make investments in enterprises that showed a profit as well as being of a public benefit. One example was his idea of building a hotel in New York City exclusively for working women. Although construction began with the best intentions, the hotel was not completed before Stewart died. When it finally opened, the idea of using it as a working women's hotel was soon abandoned. It became instead an ordinary profit-making business.

WORKING WOMEN'S HOTEL
GRAND LEGACY FROM
MR. STEWART
The Splendid Building On Fourth-Avenue
Nearly Ready To Be Opened—The
Best Of Everything Within The Means
Of Every Working Woman—Less Than
$5 Per Week Expected To Pay For
Board And Room—Full Descriptions
Of The Purposes And Facilities

The "Women's Hotel" on the corner of Fourth-avenue and Thirty-second and Thirty-third streets, founded by the late Alexander T. Stewart, is now almost completed and will soon be formally opened by a grand reception. ... There are 502 private rooms in the hotel. Of these 115 are double rooms. ... The 387 single rooms are half the size of the double ones. All these rooms are furnished in the most comfortable and elaborate style. ... The entire building is the model American hotel; the best constructed, the most elaborately furnished, the best appointed, and with the most perfect culinary department of any hotel in the world. Besides all this, the Women's Hotel is by almost 200 rooms the largest in the Metropolis and it is intended to furnish women who earn their livelihood the best possible living for the least possible money. ... Mr. Stewart, after much reflection upon the subject, concluded that all the necessaries and domestic luxuries of life were within the reach of even those who earned but small incomes. ... The Women's Hotel has cost to build and finish just $2,000,000.

—*New York Times*
November 12, 1877

Stewart provided money and assistance during several national and international disasters. In 1848, when the great potato famine hit Ireland, he sent over a ship full of provisions and instructed his agents there to pick decent men and women who were able to read and write to bring to the United States, where he would find them work in his store or with other employers. One hundred and thirty-nine men and women were brought over and found jobs.

At the start of the Civil War in 1861, Stewart gave generously to the Union cause. He contributed one hundred thousand dollars to the United States Sanitary Commission and later, in 1862, as the war took an economic toll on the English cotton manufacturing industry, he gave ten thousand dollars to help workers in England who had lost their jobs because of the cotton famine during the Civil War.

Stewart realized that the war would cause an increase in the price of cotton, since cotton was grown in the Southern states and manufactured into cotton goods in the Northern industrial states. To circumvent the economic disaster that the rise in cotton prices might cause to his business enterprises, or worse, the inability to buy cotton at all, he heavily invested in every cotton product he could get his hands on. This allowed him to continue selling products, and he was able to maintain a monopoly on cotton during the war. Although he lost much of his business in the South he more than made up for this loss through his sale of uniforms, blankets, and other military goods to the Union army.

At the beginning of the war, the Union forces had trouble outfitting troops, so Stewart bought several woolen mills in New York and New England where he manufactured uniforms and other necessities for the troops, which he sold to the government at an extremely low cost. Stewart ultimately received huge numbers of government contracts for goods, generating a giant profit for his business.

In a letter to a Tennessee cotton supplier who had repudiated Stewart for his support of the Union cause, Stewart did not mince words:

Dear Sir—Your letter requesting to know whether or not I had offered a million of dollars to the Government for the purposes of the war, and at the same time informing me that neither yourself nor your friends would pay their debts to the firm as they matured, has been received. The intention not to pay seems to be universal in the South—aggravated in your case by the assurance that it does not arise from inability; but whatever may be your determination or that of others at the South, it shall not change my course. All that I have of position and wealth, I owe to the free institutions of the United States, under which, in common with all others, North and South, protection to life, liberty, and property have been enjoyed in the fullest manner. The Government to which these blessings are due, calls on her citizens to protect the Capital of the Union from threatened assault; and although the offer to which you refer has not in terms been made by me, I yet dedicate all that I have, and will, if need be, my life, to the service of the country—for to that country I am bound by the strongest ties of affection and duty. I had hoped that Tennessee would be loyal to the Constitution; but, however extensive may be secession or repudiators, as long as there are any to uphold the sovereignty of the United States, I shall be with them supporting the flag.

Yours, &c, Alexander T. Stewart. New York, *April 29th, 1861.*
—*Frank Leslie's Popular Monthly,* Vol. 1, 1876

Stewart was a favorite of First Lady Mary Lincoln, who spent thousand of dollars on various merchandise including expensive clothes and accessories. According to the Smithsonian Institution's First Ladies Hall, "She vented her frustrations in an orgy of spending—buying handsome clothes and beautiful accessories for herself and elegant furnishings for the White House."

And according to the documentary *Abraham and Mary Lincoln: A House Divided,* "She bought new dresses, hats ... it was said that in three months, she purchased 300 pairs of gloves. Many of her purchases were never even unpacked."

Stewart displayed his usual marketing savvy when he gave Mrs. Lincoln a $2,500 lace shawl. The gift made headlines across the country: "At the last levee at the White House, Mrs. Lincoln wore a lace shawl, presented her by A. T. Stewart of New York, which cost $2,500," a *New York Times* article declared.

At the time of her husband's assassination in 1865, Mrs. Lincoln owed Stewart close to thirty thousand dollars on her line of credit.

Stewart became a close friend of General Ulysses S. Grant and became an ardent supporter of Grant's campaign for the presidency. Aside from his friendship with Grant, Stewart had tremendous respect and admiration for the general, who had contributed so much to the Union cause and its ultimate success. When Grant became president in 1869, he nominated Stewart as secretary of the treasury. The Senate unanimously confirmed the nomination, but it was brought to light that a merchant in active business was legally disqualified from accepting the position. Stewart asserted that he would be willing to donate the profits from his business ventures to the underprivileged of New York City during his term of office, but opposition remained. Grant asked Congress to repeal the law that prohibited Stewart's appointment but could not muster enough votes to do it. Stewart ultimately had to withdraw his nomination.

After the great Chicago Fire in 1871, Stewart gave fifty thousand dollars to the relief fund. He also donated to various churches and instituted a policy that gave clergy and teachers a 10 percent discount on all their purchases at his stores. One of Stewart's salesmen was reported to have said, "Over half of the people in New York are now clergymen or teachers."

But the crowning triumph of Stewart's generosity was the building of Garden City.

Stewart himself conceived of the idea of building a town that would be an affordable model community for employees and others. The goal was to build comfortable homes at a reasonable cost, far enough from New York City to keep away uninvited guests and yet close enough that his employees who were living there could easily make it to work. He planned to establish his own railroad line, the Central Railroad of Long Island, to transport residents to and from the city. Stewart envisioned that the land would be the property of his corporation and could not be sold outright. Even the homes would be built by the corporation and only leased to those living there. Stewart intended it to be a self-governing community where its inhabitants would enact their own laws. His plans called for the construction of a large hotel, wide roads, schools, and churches, with hundreds of trees and shrubs and initially, more than fifty homes built on spacious lots. More homes would be built later as the town grew in population.

Stewart intended his planned community to be private and fashionable. It would be, for all intents and purposes, a Garden of Eden for his employees and their families. Stewart named his planned community Garden City.

Hempstead Plains, L.I.

The town of Hempstead L.I. owns about 7,500 acres of unimproved land lying on the Long Island Railroad, about twenty miles distant from this City. It is of the character of the prairie land of the West, being exceedingly level, and the soil, never yet turned by the plow, is as black as the prairie lands of Illinois. ... Mr. A.T. Stewart has since made an offer of $412,500 for the whole tract, with a view to building a village for workingmen on the site. ... Exactly what he intends to do, Mr. STEWART explains in the following letter to the editor of the Hempstead Sentinel:

Having been informed that interested parties are circulating statements to the effect that my purpose in desiring to purchase the Hempstead Plains, is to devote them to the erection of tenement-houses and public charities of a like character. I consider it proper to state that my only object in seeking to acquire these lands is to devote them to the usual purposes for which such lands, so located, should be applied—that is, open them by constructing extensive public roads; laying out the lands in parcels for sale to actual settlers, and erecting at various points attractive buildings and residences, so that a barren waste may speedily be covered by a population desirable in every respect as neighbors, tax-payers and as citizens. In doing this I am prepared and would be willing to expend several millions of dollars.

Very respectfully yours,

Alex. T. Stewart

—New York Times, July 9, 1869

In 1869, Stewart purchased a plot of land, more than 7,000 acres, on the Hempstead Plains on Long Island. Hempstead Plains was a flat, treeless tract of land running from New Hyde Park to Farmingdale. Stewart bought the land from the Town of Hempstead, which was more than willing to get rid of what it viewed as a wasteland, for $55 an acre. Stewart paid a total of $394,350 for it all. Over the next six years, the property was surveyed and divided into wide streets and roadways; the grand hotel was built and surrounded by a magnificent park in the center of the town; trees were planted; the railroad was built, as was a water and gas works; and homes were constructed. It was a model suburban community. Stewart died before he saw his planned Garden City reach its full potential, and if it wasn't for the efforts of his widow, Cornelia, the planned community might never have become a reality.

After Stewart's death in 1876, Garden City was practically a ghost town. While homes rented for a mere one hundred dollars a month, almost no one had moved into the town. A reported seven commuters rode Stewart's Central Railroad of Long Island for the daily trip into Manhattan.

The Hempstead Plains property is about twelve miles long and two and a half wide. 'Garden City,' as it is called, is four miles from the western end, and has upon it 102 houses, renting from $150 to $1,200 each. At present its population is about 300. In the centre is, a large brick hotel, tastefully constructed, which cost, furnished, $100,000. ...

Nine thousand acres of this land were bought in 1868, from the town of Hempstead, for $450,000 and to this area 1,000 acres have been recently added. A contract has also been made for waterworks, to cost $125,000 ... to pump 2,500,000 gallons a day, if required. That part of the Central Railroad of Long Island running from the western end of Garden City, four miles to Farmingdale, was owned by Mr. Stewart, and leased to the Central Railroad Company, together with the road of one mile to Hempstead.

—Frank Leslie's Popular Monthly, VOL. 1, 1876

It was Cornelia Stewart who turned Garden City into a bustling and much sought after community. As a monument to her husband's memory, she commissioned the building of the Cathedral of the Incarnation, an enormous and elaborate Gothic-style church, with a two hundred-foot spire, marbled interior and exterior, flying buttresses, and pinnacles. She also built an ornate home for the bishop, a seminary, a rectory, and two preparatory schools, St. Paul's for the boys and St. Mary's for the girls.

She ultimately persuaded the Episcopal Church to move its seat from Brooklyn to Garden City. Cornelia agreed to deed the cathedral and other church buildings and schools to the Episcopal Church of Long Island with the condition that her husband would be buried in the cathedral. It was an offer the church couldn't refuse. After Cornelia's death in 1886, her heirs formed a new corporation, the Garden City Company, in 1893 for the purpose of continuing the development of the community. In 1919 Garden City was incorporated into a public village, and it ultimately became an exclusive, upper-crust, and much desired community of large, expensive homes. It was A. T. Stewart's sense of vision and planning that forever altered the face of Long Island.

While the Working Women's Hotel and Garden City may have been built on altruistic intentions, there is little doubt that Stewart's Marble Mansion was calculated to impress and outdo his wealthy, illustrious neighbors. It was one of the most ornate and elaborate private homes in America. The designer of Stewart's mansion was John Kellum, who designed all of Stewart's buildings, including the Cast Iron Palace, the women's hotel, and the buildings and homes at Garden City. In their book *Stately Homes in America: From Colonial Times to the Present Day* (1903), Harry W. Desmond and Herbert Croly write, "In the case of the old Stewart mansion, the palatial idea made an early and obvious appearance. The location, the character of the design, the choice of the material, everything about the house, inside and out, showed that the old Irish merchant wanted to make a grand impression; and he undoubtedly succeeded in doing so—upon his contemporaries."

The location of the mansion was across the street from the home of the multimillionaire William Backhouse Astor Jr., the oldest son of William Backhouse Astor Sr. and the wealthiest member of the Astor family in his generation. William Sr.'s father, John Jacob Astor, made his fortune in the fur trade and real estate, and when he died in 1848, he left behind an estate estimated at more than twenty million dollars. He is considered America's first multimillionaire. In 1859, Astor Jr. erected the magnificent home at 350 Fifth Avenue, where he lived with his wife, Caroline.

In 1869–1870, when Stewart completed his mansion, the average lot size in New York City was twenty-five feet wide by one hundred feet deep. Stewart's mansion extended 150 feet on Thirty-fourth Street and nearly 112 feet on Fifth Avenue. He had purchased the land, upon which already stood a large brownstone mansion, in 1861. At first Stewart had his architect draw up plans to remodel the existing home, but he subsequently changed his mind and had the building torn down so he could erect a new one, which became his Italian and Tuckahoe (Westchester County) marble mansion. The main entrance on the Thirty-fourth Street side included a wide flight of steps, each more than thirty feet long. Huge marble posts were erected at the foot of the staircase, and a marble balustrade was built on either side to enclose the ground around the mansion. The huge white marble used as the base for the steps leading to the main door was rumored to have been the single largest piece of marble ever dug from any quarry in the country.

According to historian Junius Henri Browne, the main role of the new rich in New York City during the Gilded Age was to "annoy and worry the Knickerbockers, who have less money and are more stupid."

The nickname "Knickerbocker" derived its origins from American author Washington Irving (1783–1859), who in 1809 published

A History of New-York from the Beginning of the World to the End of the Dutch Dynasty, a satirical account of the Dutch colonists who settled New York. Irving wrote the book under the pseudonym "Diedrich Knickerbocker," and afterward the assumed surname became the nickname for native residents of New York.

Browne wrote that he viewed these wealthy native New Yorkers (Knickerbockers) as the "narrowest and dullest people on the island." And he further ridiculed them as having "done much to induce the belief that stupidity and gentility are synonymous terms."

Browne was no more kind in this regard to the newly rich, those like Stewart. He derided people who were social and economic upstarts, who came from a poor background and had earned their fortune, rather than inherited it, and who had not gained acceptance by the socially superior and wealthy Astor and Vanderbilt class. According to Browne, Stewart and his ilk "generally manage to render themselves very absurd."

"They outdress and outshine the old families, the cultivatedly comfortable, the inheritors of fortunes and everybody else, in whatever money can purchase and bad taste can suggest."

Surely Stewart's two-million-dollar, three-story, French-style mansion next to the Astor home was a marble testament to Browne's observation.

"From the beginning, Stewart was determined to create a domicile that was different from, and implied greater wealth than, the Astor brownstone across the street, with which it invited constant comparison. There were few ways in which the upstart new millionaires could outdo the Astors, but they quickly learned that one means was through architecture—by building something of higher fashion, more costly, connoting European sophistication and aristocracy more than Knickerbocker sedateness. In that sense Stewart succeeded."

—WAYNE CRAVEN, *Gilded Mansions: Grand Architecture and High Society,* 2009

The Astors and the Stewarts lived opposite each other where Fifth Avenue met Thirty-fourth Street. According to Eric Homberger, author of *Mrs. Astor's New York: Money and Power in a Gilded Age* (2002), "Mrs. Astor acted as though Stewart and his wife did not exist."

Caroline Astor was the doyenne of American high society in the latter half of the nineteenth century, the very symbol of New York City's "old money" and values. She clearly delineated what was and was not deemed acceptable in New York's high society, and despite his vast fortune, Alexander and Cornelia Stewart were not among those deemed socially acceptable.

Caroline Schermerhorn was the daughter of a wealthy Dutch merchant and had colonial Dutch aristocracy on both sides of her family tree. She married William Backhouse Astor Jr. in 1854.

"I have been insane on the subject of moneymaking all my life. I won't sue you for the law is too slow. I will ruin you. What do I care about the law? Hain't I got the power?"

—CORNELIUS VANDERBILT, (1794–1877)

NEW-YORK MILLIONAIRES

The founders of the great New-York fortunes of the present century JOHN JACOB ASTOR, ROBERT LENOX, ALEXANDER T. STEWART and CORNELIUS VANDERBILT—have all passed away. ... At the time of JOHN JACOB ASTOR'S death in 1848 his fortune was estimated at from $30,000,000 to $40,000,000 and he was counted fifth on the list of rich men, Baron De Rothschild, Louis Philippe, the Duke of Devonshire, and Sir Robert Pell only exceeding him. The late Mr. ROBERT LENOX like Mr. ASTOR was a self-made man. ... The Lenox Farm to-day without a brick in it would be worth $8,000,000. ... The fortune of A.T. Stewart—of quicker growth than that

*of ASTOR—was accumulated in one lifetime. At Mr. STEW-
ART'S death in 1876, it was estimated at $80,000,000, or twice
the amount of the highest estimate of JOHN JACOB ASTOR'S
fortune when he died in 1848. ... Mr. WILLIAM H. VANDER-
BILT is to-day the richest man in New York. He inherited the
bulk of Commodore VANDERBILT'S fortune, who at the time
of his death was accounted a richer man than either of the
present ASTORS."*

—New York Times, DECEMBER 26, 1878

Q: *"Mr. Stewart you are a very rich man, why do you bother
yourself building this immense place?"*
A: *"That is the very question I asked myself this morning,
when I took a look at that big hole in the ground. The worst of
it is my neighbors don't like it."*
*"Mr. S. is a man of progress—of the modern time—he is a man
for improvement and enjoyment. ... When he builds a house
for another—as his marble palace on Fifth Avenue—to use his
own words, 'a little attention to Mrs. Stewart'—it is a different
matter. That is to please her."*
—The Rich Men of the World and How They Gained Their Wealth,
JESSE HANEY & CO., 1867

*Mr. Stewart's marble palace, built on the site of the large struc-
ture formerly the residence of Dr. Townsend is perhaps the
handsomest and most costly private residence in the country.
The building, elegantly furnished, constructed with lofty and
spacious rooms, has been an object of curiosity to sight-seers
ever since it was completed. ... Certainly the most interesting
feature of the building, however, is the art gallery in the rear,
where are located a large number of important and valuable
works. ... Mr. Stewart's collection surpassed in importance
and value any other in the country and is estimated to be
worth at least $600,000.*
—Frank Leslie's Popular Monthly, JUNE 1876

THE ART GALLERY
A List Of The Pictures In Mr. Stewart's Collection—Works Valued At Over Six Hundred Thousand Dollars

The collection of works of art possessed by the late Mr. Stewart far surpassed in importance and value any other in this country, for not only did it comprise many pictures of great artistic merit, but many of the master-pieces of the respective artists represented, as, for instance, those of Gerome, Meissonnier, Fortuny, Knaus, Dubuffe, Erskine Nicol, Hiram Powers, Church and Huntington.

—*New York Times*
April 12, 1876

Among the artworks in the vast Stewart collection were: *A View in the Park at Versailles* by Giovanni Boldini (1842–1931); *L'Aumone* and *La Sentinelle* by Jean-Louis-Ernest Meissonier (1815–1891); *The Chariot Race, Pollice Verso* and *La Collaboration* by Jean-Léon Gérôme (1824–1904); *The Snake Charmers* (a replica) by Mariano Fortuny (1838–1874); *Court of Fools*, by Eduardo Zamacois (1841–1871); *The Horse Fair* by Rosa Bonheur (1822–1899); *The Children's Feast* by Ludwig Knaus (1829–1910); a painting by Adolphe Yvon (1817–1893) allegorically representing the Union of the States painted for Stewart at a cost of twenty thousand dollars; *Niagara* by Frederic Edwin Church (1826–1900); and *Lady Washington's Reception* by Daniel Huntington (1816–1906).

"It is hard to conceive that any one surrounded by works of art, as was Mr. Stewart, could have had so little understanding of what constituted a work of architecture."
—PETER B. WRIGHT, ARCHITECT, 1876

The Stewart mansion was fully detailed on all sides. It rose three stories from the basement and was crowned with a mansard roof with projecting dormer windows. The ceilings were more than eighteen feet high. The mansion included massive-size drawing rooms, a music room, a reception hall, a dining room, a library, and the art gallery. A picture gallery extended the full length of the house while paintings hung throughout the mansion ornamenting the walls and ceilings. The ceiling and wall paintings included garlands, flowers, and classical figures. The Stewarts enjoyed the most expensive European furnishings, including gilt and onyx furniture and chandeliers, and two $10,000 vases.

The entrance on Thirty-fourth Street led into an immense hall, and off the hall were four huge rooms: the music room, a dining room, a breakfast room, and a reception room, all elaborately and ornately furnished. The painted walls were covered with framed paintings, the floors were richly carpeted, and an abundance of sculptures were scattered throughout.

The entrance on Fifth Avenue opened onto a main drawing room that ran parallel to the main hall. The library on the second floor mimicked the size of this grand room. The second floor contained eight rooms, including the main bedrooms, lavish affairs with dressing rooms, a sitting room, and a billiard room.

The third floor was equally divided into eight rooms, including a central hallway and a main sitting room. The vast structure was lit with twelve bronze gas chandeliers surrounded with porcelain and etched glass shades.

Huge fluted Corinthian columns were built in the entrance to the main hall, coming in from the Thirty-fourth Street side, and giant mirrors hung on many of the walls reflecting the gas light from the chandeliers.

"All the interior was sculptural in detail and commanding in effect. Window and door surrounds were cased with marble framing carved in Italy, and the walls of the entrance hall were paneled with marble," according to Jay Cantor's 1975 article, "A Monument of Trade: A. T. Stewart and the Rise of the Millionaire's Mansion in New York."

"It is a huge white marble pile; has been four or five years in the process of erection, and has already cost $2,000,000. It is very elaborate and pretentious, but exceedingly dismal, reminding one of a vast tomb. Stewart's financial ability is extraordinary, but his architectural taste cannot be commended."
—JUNIUS HENRI BROWNE, *The Great Metropolis*, 1869

"At the corner of Thirty-fourth Street and Fifth Avenue stands a large white marble mansion, utterly devoid of architectural merit, built by a leading local celebrity, who died some ten years ago, A. T. Stewart. Mr. Stewart was an Ulster man, hard as nails, who put his patrimony of about $1,000 into dry goods, and started a shop in New York. He was honest and able, but grasping, unsympathetic, and oppressive to those in his employ, out of whom, with the aid of a lieutenant even harder and harsher than himself, he squeezed a maximum of labour with a minimum of remuneration. He died unregretted and childless, leaving vast wealth, and his remains were stolen by body-snatchers in hopes of a ransom."
—*Good Words*, 1887

It was in this often much maligned and equally heralded, palatial estate on Fifth Avenue that A. T. Stewart, the multimillionaire "Merchant Prince" died. Stewart had always superstitiously avoided the number thirteen and would shy away from a business transaction if that number appeared in any form. He reportedly preferred to be ridiculed for his superstitions rather then tempt fate. He would also never sit and eat at a table that had thirteen people at it. He fought to overcome this superstition, ultimately giving in during one dinner party when he was coaxed to sit down at a table of thirteen guests. Approximately thirteen weeks afterward, he was dead.

3
CAVEAT EMPTOR

In which vast tributes are paid to the life of the "Merchant Prince" upon Stewart's death, lavish funeral, and interment in St. Mark's Cemetery. Although Stewart bequeaths all his assets to his wife, Cornelia, and names his friend and confidant, Judge Henry Hilton, only as executor of his estate, Hilton seizes upon the opportunity, incorporating a new firm to run Stewart's wholesale, retail, and manufacturing concerns. The new head of all operations: Henry Hilton.

A. T. Stewart died on April 10, 1876, at seventy-two years of age from a bladder infection and peritonitis—an infection caused by an inflammation of the lining of the abdominal cavity.

His funeral was an elaborate event, befitting a man of his wealth and stature. The pomp and circumstance surrounding it was equal to that of the death of an American statesman, and Stewart had become a statesman of sorts—a leading light in the development of an American economic institution: the department store.

> STEWART has been a moral power in the commercial history of the United States, whose value it would be difficult to overestimate. The success of his system of plain dealing produced so many imitators that it is to-day the rule instead of the exception among the leading dry-goods merchants of our great cities.
>
> —*New York Times* editorial, April 11, 1876

If Stewart's funeral was a lavish event, he had no hand in planning it. That honor fell to others, including his widow, Cornelia, and his closest business and personal friend, Judge Henry Hilton. His final resting place—the family vault in St. Mark's Churchyard—was an obscure and humble spot, devoid of any extravagant trappings, an undistinguished grave in the Bowery section of New York City. He was buried in the family vault alongside his two children and his mother. The vault was inconspicuous and close to a dozen feet underground.

THE DEAD MILLIONAIRE
MR. STEWART'S LIFE
AND DEATH.
The Funeral To-Morrow—The Remains To Lie In State—Mr. Stewart's City Property—His Art Gallery—Scenes About The Family Residence.

All yesterday the remains of the late Alexander T. Stewart lay in the Lace Room, in which he died, at the family residence in Fifth avenue. The preparations for the funeral have not yet been completed, but the services will be held to-morrow at 11 A.M. in St. Mark's Protestant Episcopal Church, and will be conducted by the Pastor, Rev. J. H. Rylance, assisted by Bishop Potter. The remains will then be deposited in the family vault, in St. Mark's Churchyard.

—*New York Times*
April 12, 1876

Stewart's body was placed on ice and lay in state in the Lace Room at the Marble Mansion. Several photographs were taken, and a plaster cast of his face was made. Cornelia Stewart remained in seclusion for much of the day under a doctor's care. Judge Hilton and George Hamill, the undertaker, made the funeral arrangements. It was decided that Stewart would be buried in a plain oak casket with gold handles and moldings. The interior of the casket was lined with white satin, and on the lid was a large silver plate inscribed with the words:

ALEXANDER T. STEWART

Born Oct 12th, 1803

Died April 10th, 1876

The casket was enclosed in a cedar box and lined with a thick sheet of lead. It would be buried in the Stewart family vault at St. Mark's Church located on the corner of Second Avenue and Stuyvesant Street. The churchyard contained the family vaults of many of New York City's most well-known families, including that of the city's most illustrious citizen, Peter Stuyvesant, who died in 1675 and was known as the "late Captain General and Governor in Chief of New Amsterdam."

The Stewart family vault was on the same eastern side of the churchyard, a dozen or so yards from Stuyvesant's vault, and was marked by a small, flat stone with the names of the deceased and the number 112, hardly a notable or recognizable resting place for the "Merchant Prince of Manhattan."

Despite his great wealth, Stewart remained an unassuming figure to the end. His million-dollar mansion on Fifth Avenue and his two enormous and lavish stores were, it seemed, for him a lasting testament to his wealth, fame, and good fortune. In death he sought humble, eternal obscurity.

1. Full name of the deceased, Alexander Turney Stewart; 2. Age, seventy-two years, five months, twenty-nine days; color, white; 3. Married; 4. Occupation, merchant; 5. Birthplace, Lisburn, Ireland; forty-six years in the United States; How long resident in this City, forty-six years; 7. Father's birthplace, Ireland; 8. Mother's birthplace, Ireland; 9. Place of death, Thirty-fourth street, corner of Fifth avenue, Twenty-first Ward; 10. If a dwelling, by how many families living separately occupied, One, (second floor) 11. I hereby certify that I attended deceased from March 19, 1876 to April 10, 1876; that I last saw him alive on the 10th day of April, 1876; that he died on the 10th day of

April, 1876, about 1:30 o'clock P.M., and that the cause of his death was: First, (primary) Cystitis; second, (immediate) Peritonitis; place of burial, St. Mark's Church; date of burial, April 13, 1876; undertaker, G.W. Hamill, No 26 Third avenue.

—A. T. STEWART'S DEATH CERTIFICATE, SIGNED BY DR. E. E. MARCY AND RECEIVED BY THE DEPUTY REGISTER OF VITAL STATISTICS, APRIL 12, 1876

A.T. STEWART'S FUNERAL SERVICES AT CHURCH AND HOUSE

The Body Lies In State At The Fifth Avenue Residence—A Magnificent Floral Display—The Short Service At The House—An Imposing Funeral Procession.

—*New York Times*
April 14, 1876

Since St. Mark's could not accommodate what Hilton and Hamill projected would be an enormous crowd, it was decided that mourners would need tickets to attend the service. The tickets would be distributed to dignitaries, associates, and employees first, while others wishing to attend would be required to file an application for whatever was left over after the initial distribution. The front pews of the church were reserved for family, relatives, business associates, and prominent guests, including Governor Samuel Tilden of New York, who would also serve as a pallbearer.

Stewart's funeral was conducted in accordance with the rituals dictated by the Episcopal Church. There was a service at the house followed by a church service. There was a display of flowers at the house, where the body lay in state, and at the church. Some of the most distinguished men and women in New York and from across the country attended the service at Stewart's palatial home.

Around 8 a.m. on the day of the funeral, a long line of current and former employees came to the house to pay their respects. Some were assigned various duties in the house and were identified by an armband of black and white rosette on their left arms. Two employees were stationed at the foot of the stairs leading into the house. Two more were stationed halfway up the staircase and others at the entrance itself.

A crowd of thousands congregated outside the Stewart mansion, along both sides of Thirty-fourth Street. A police squad of forty uniformed officers lined the street leading to the main entrances. No one was allowed to pass through the police line without a ticket issued by the Stewart family.

At 9 a.m. the doors to the mansion were opened, allowing those who came to pay their respects to enter in single file, orderly and quiet, with the police and ushers checking tickets. For more than an hour, the crowd streamed through the doors of the mansion, filling it to capacity. The floral display adorning the coffin measured seven feet long and four feet wide. The mass of flowers included fresh white roses, lilies, orchids, and ivy. At the base of the arrangement were the initials, A.T.S., spelled out in violets on top of a bed of pure white lilies. At the head of the coffin was a four-foot-high harp made of flowers with a floral cross next to it.

The coffin was covered with purple velvet and lined with white satin. The edges of the velvet drape were hemmed with a four-inch band of gold. Gold-plated rods were affixed to both sides of the coffin along with gold handles on the sides and end. A bouquet of white flowers rested on top of the coffin at the base of a plain gold cross.

Bishop Horatio Potter held a brief solemn service, after which mourners filed past the coffin, paying their respects. The coffin was then removed from the house and transported by hearse to St. Mark's Church.

The hearse was a long black carriage with gilded edges, drawn by a team of black horses in gold harnesses. The plain, dark carriages of the mourners followed the hearse. Altogether, there were about sixty-five carriages in the procession from the Stewart mansion to St. Mark's.

The ticketed mourners were allowed inside the church, quickly filling eight hundred seats among the pews and standing in rapt attention along the back of church once the seats were all occupied. Four hundred tickets had been issued to employees. President Grant, who had been scheduled to attend, sent his regrets and offered his condolences to Mrs. Stewart. Pressing matters of state took precedence for the chief executive.

Bishop Potter and his assistants met the cortege at the front door of the church around 12:15 p.m. Stewart's coffin was taken to the front of the church, where it was once again placed in a great sea of flowers and wreathes. Among the pallbearers, besides Governor Tilden, were Governor Alexander Rice of Massachusetts, former Governors John Adams Dix and Edwin Morgan of New York, U.S. Secretary of State Hamilton Fish, and several prominent New York judges. The pallbearers were seated in the first pew. Once they were seated, Judge Hilton escorted Mrs. Stewart down the center aisle. She wore a black dress and cloak, and her face was covered in a dark veil. Hilton and the widow Stewart were followed down the aisle by other family members, including her brother, Charles Clinch, and his wife.

When the funeral cortege had completely settled into their seats, the service was begun by the Rev. Dr. Joseph Rylance, followed by Bishop Potter and finally the Rev. Dr. Stephen Tyng Jr. As part of the Episcopal service, the church sexton threw a handful of dirt onto the coffin.

What was startling to those in attendance was the absence of any sermon. Most expected an oration about Stewart, his life, and his many accomplishments, even if a brief one. But no sermon was given. Following the service, the congregation sang the hymn "Rock of Ages," and the illustrious cadre of pallbearers took Stewart's coffin from the church. Judge Hilton stepped from his pew holding his arm out for the widow Stewart to take, but she didn't move. Everyone waited. Mrs. Stewart sat frozen in her pew for several moments until finally she rose to her feet, took Hilton's waiting arm, and followed the coffin out of the church. Stewart's remains were taken to the family burial vault in the nearby churchyard cemetery. There, Bishop Potter said a short benediction before the pallbearers and family mourners dispersed. Mrs. Stewart, still leaning on Hilton's arm, was the last to leave.

ALEXANDER T. STEWART

The dramatic completeness of a successful mercantile career has never been better exemplified than in the life of A.T. Stewart. There is very little romance about it, and through all its stages there run the homely qualities of shrewdness, thrift, and perseverance, mingled with just enough of boldness and original enterprise to raise the man above the rank of the plodding and cautious merchant who bears a competency instead of a magnificent fortune. ... His life is a standing proof of the efficacy of honesty, industry, and well-directed intelligence in laying the foundation of vast wealth. The man who has amassed the largest fortune ever accumulated within the span of a single life was simply a hard-working, careful merchant, with a decided talent for organization and a somewhat rare faculty for taking a firm grasp of petty details as of broad and general principles. ... There was no gambler's luck in the methods of actions which expanded the five thousand dollars of 1822 into the forty or fifty millions of 1876. ... His dealings with opponents have been characterized as harsh and pitiless, but that was because he looked on commercial competition as a system of warfare in which the longest purse and the best directed energy were as much entitled to their reward as the most skillful strategy or the most approved weapons of destruction. If the few suffered from such a system, the many were the gainers.

—*New York Times* EDITORIAL, APRIL 11, 1876

TRIBUTE FROM GARDEN CITY

A meeting of the citizens of the town of Hempstead, Long Island, in which Garden City is included, was held yesterday afternoon in the Town hall in the village of Hempstead. Resolutions of regret at the death of Mr. Stewart were adopted, and a deputation to attend his funeral was appointed.

—*New York Times* APRIL 13, 1876

Sympathy and regrets at the death of Stewart were tempered with the sobering reputation he had among many New York City businessmen who viewed him as a monopolist. An editorial appearing in the April 12 edition of the *New York Times,* simply titled "Monopoly and Competition," depicted Stewart as a ruthless monopolist who was merciless when dealing with his competitors and believed in cornering every market in which he had dealings. According to the editorial, "… he seemed to regard business as a species of warfare, in which the strongest was the surest of winning, and he realized keenly the advantage of having full control of so much of the field as he could occupy …

"Those who came in conflict with him in his endeavors to carry out his plans could expect no mercy, and received none, and his successes were not embittered, or at least they were not prevented, by the fact that they involved the necessity of the failure of others."

At the time of his death, Stewart's only partner in his great retail and wholesale empire was William Libbey, who had been with him for longer than twenty years. Although a partner, Libbey did not share in the profits but merely drew a salary—a generous salary, but just a salary nonetheless.

Stewart left nothing in his will for charity, a surprising and disappointing revelation to many New Yorkers. Stewart named his widow, Cornelia, Libbey, and Hilton as executors of his great estate. The will, dated March 27, 1873, instructed the executors to liquidate his massive business concern. Hilton was bequeathed one million dollars for the purpose of carrying out these final wishes. The will directed Hilton to "exercise a sound discretion in bringing my said partnership affairs to termination." Stewart had been prompted to prepare his will because of his failing health. Three years later, the liquidation of the massive retail empire was not carried out as Stewart had directed. It was ultimately liquidated, many years later, but by then, the business was a mere skeleton of its former self. Stewart left all his property to his wife and her heirs. He left a variety of gifts and legacies, totaling one hundred thousand, to twelve people who served him in his business, and he bequeathed a total of $15,500 to be shared among his household servants. He left a twelve-thousand-dollar annuity to his sisters-in-law, Sarah and Rebecca Morrow, and free use of the home they lived in at 30 East Thirty-ninth Street. He left an equal sum of ten thousand dollars to Charles Clinch, Anna Clinch, Julia Clinch, Emma Clinch, and Sarah Smith, all relatives of his wife. He also left to Anna, Julia, and Emma Clinch, the maiden sisters of his wife, the free use of the house they lived in at 115 East Thirty-fourth Street. He requested that all employees who had been with his company for twenty years receive one thousand dollars and those with ten years of service, five hundred dollars. Although he alluded to his intention to fund various charities, he made no mention of which charities he meant and left the selection and amounts to be determined by his wife. All and all, Stewart's will was a general disappointment to everyone, except of course his widow and one Judge Henry Hilton.

"The will of Mr. Stewart, which was filed in the Surrogate's Office on the day after, the funeral:

1. Bequeathed all the property and estate of the testator to his wife, Cornelia M. Stewart, her heirs and assigns forever.

2. Appointed Henry Hilton to act for the testator, and in behalf of his estate, in managing, closing, and winding-up his partnership business and affairs, and empowered him in respect thereto as fully as the testator was authorized to do by the articles of copartnership of the firm of Alexander T. Stewart & Co.

3. It bequeathed to said Henry Hilton $1,000,000.

4. It revoked and annulled all other wills, and appointed as executors, Cornelia M. Stewart, Henry Hilton, and William Libbey. This was signed March 27th, 1873, and witnessed by William P. Smith, of Thirty-fourth Street and Fifth Avenue; W. H. White, of 228 Fifth Avenue; E. E. Marcy, M.D., of 396 Fifth Avenue."

This was followed by a codicil bearing the same date, in which the following legacies were bequeathed:

"To George B. Butler, the sum of $20,000; to John M. Hopkins, the sum of $10,000; to A. R. P. Cooper, the sum of $10,000; to Edwin James Denning, the sum of $10,000; to John B. Green, $10,000; to George H. Higgins, $10,000; to Henry H. Bice, $5,000; to John De Bret, $5,000; to Robert Prother, $5,000; to Henry Dodge, $5,000; to Hugh Connor, $5,000; to William Armstrong, $5,000; 'each of whom have long and faithfully served me in my business affairs.' Also to William P. Smith, $5,000; to William Lynch, $2,500; to Martha Turner, $2,500; to Rebecca Turner, $2,500; to Sarah Turner, $500; to James Cummings, $1,000; to Edward Thompson, $1,000; to Michael Riorden, $500; 'all faithful servants of my house.'"
—*Frank Leslie's Popular Monthly*, Vol. 1, 1876

In a letter he left for his wife, Stewart directed her to rely on Hilton in all matters regarding his estate as well as any contributions to charities he neglected to include in his will. Because the letter to his wife was not a binding legal document, no vast contributions to charities ever materialized, at least not immediately.

Cornelia Stewart had relied on her husband's good judgment for her whole life and had no mind or inclination toward his business concerns. Knowing full well the trust her husband placed in Hilton, she conveyed her own trust to Hilton. For the remainder of her life, she relied on Hilton in all matters, both business and personal; that is, except for one—the recovery of her husband's stolen body.

Besides being Stewart's legal advisor, Hilton had been Stewart's closest friend and confidant. Although there were few who didn't surmise that Hilton would become the executor of Stewart's will, no one ever suspected that he would become the heir to Stewart's fortune.

———•—••••••—•———

Henry Hilton's career was founded on his friendship with Alexander Stewart and the vast fortune Stewart accrued through his visionary business acumen. Hilton proved to have none of Stewart's business savvy, and in fact, his lack of business and public relations know-how and his reckless management ultimately led to the demise of Stewart's once great retail empire and the total dissipation of his fortune.

Except for his close relationship with Stewart, Hilton had an unremarkable career. He was born in Kingston, New York, in 1821, eighteen years after Stewart was born. After being admitted to the bar, he went to work in the law offices of Judge W. W. Campbell, a firm that Stewart used as part of his growing business concerns. But it wasn't his association with Campbell's law firm that led to Hilton's long and close relationship with Stewart. It was his marriage. In 1849, Hilton married Ellen Banker, the second cousin of Cornelia Stewart. Through this marriage Hilton made the acquaintance of Stewart and his wife.

Hilton's role in the affairs of Alexander Stewart began early in his life, as Stewart came to view the attorney as much more than just legal counsel. Stewart and his wife often expressed their view that Hilton was more of a son than an advisor, a role Hilton was more than happy to assume. In both public and private affairs, Hilton made himself indispensable to the aging merchant and his wife. He became the master of ceremonies for the Stewart family's social endeavors. Despite all his wealth, Stewart had never been able to master the fine art of social graces expected from a man of his means, and he relied on Hilton's expertise in these matters.

On his deathbed, Stewart reportedly told his wife that the entire extent of his business interests should go to Hilton.

I especially appoint Henry Hilton of the City of New York to act for me and in behalf of my estate in managing, closing, and winding up my partnership business and affairs, and I empower him in respect thereto as fully as I may or can, or am authorized to in and by the articles of co-partnership of the firm of Alexander T. Stewart & Co. I further authorize and direct the said Hilton, while so acting in behalf of my estate and in my place and stead, to exercise a sound discretion in bringing my said partnership affairs to a termination and discharging all obligations connected therewith, trusting to his judgment that he will so act in respect thereto as to avoid in so far as can be avoided any unnecessary loss to those connected with me in business. For which service, and as a mark of my regard, I give to aid Hilton $1,000,000.

—FROM THE LAST WILL AND TESTAMENT OF ALEXANDER TURNEY STEWART

In a letter attached to the will, Stewart wrote to his wife: "Our friend Judge Hilton will, I know, give you any assistance in his power, and to him I refer you for a general understanding of the various methods and plans which I have at times with him considered and discussed."

———

Henry Hilton had served as a judge of the Court of Common Pleas. He had a commanding presence, which more than made up for his lack of knowledge pertaining to the law. He was striking in appearance and in possession of the finest of manners.

This was in stark contrast to the man who had called upon him as his closest and most trusted advisor, Alexander Stewart. What Stewart had in great business acumen, he completely lacked in outward appearance and social graces. Stewart was modest and unassuming in dress. Quiet, polite, even shy in most social circumstances, he lacked confidence in his manners and in dealing with the social etiquette of the times. Hilton was tall and robust, flamboyant in his dress and demeanor. Stewart was short in stature, thin, and pale. Hilton sported a shock of wavy chestnut hair and a dark mustache, while Stewart was balding and wore wispy tuffs of muttonchop sideburns. Where Hilton relied steadfastly on a gold pocket watch that hung from his vest pocket on an exquisite gold chain, Stewart preferred to rely on public timepieces, mantle pieces, and publicly displayed clocks throughout the city to keep track of the hour. In the worlds of business, finances, social graces, and appearance, Alexander Turney Stewart and Henry Hilton were exact opposites. And so they were inseparable.

The only thing the two men did have in common was their ancestry. Stewart was born in Lisburn, Ireland, on October 12, 1803. Hilton was born in October 1821 in New York to a Scottish-Irish father and a Scottish mother.

Hilton had three brothers, all of them professionals. His oldest brother, James, was a lawyer and later became a judge in Iowa. His brother Joseph was a doctor and served as the New York City coroner. His brother Archibald became a prominent lawyer in New York. Henry Hilton was admitted to the New York bar in 1846 and established a meager practice in the city.

After serving five years as a judge, Hilton was defeated in his reelection bid. He resumed his law practice, starting the firm of Hilton, Campbell, and Bell. Hilton maintained an office within the firm and also had an office within Stewart's retail business.

Following the Civil War, when Stewart threw his support behind the presidential campaign of Ulysses S. Grant, Hilton served as his political intimate, working behind the scenes to help elect Grant. It was during this period that Stewart and Grant became close friends.

Hilton slowly began to involve himself in the day-to-day operations of Stewart's retail business. In 1873, he accompanied Stewart to Europe to assist in the reorganization of the overseas operations. During this time Stewart awarded Hilton full power of attorney, allowing him to act on his behalf in all matters pertaining to his national and international operations.

It was not merely Stewart's will that caused a sensation in social and business circles in New York and beyond. On April 14, 1876, less than a day after Stewart's magnificent funeral, Cornelia Stewart announced that she had signed over her husband's entire business to Henry Hilton in exchange for the one million dollars that her husband had bequeathed to Hilton. Hilton and William Libbey then agreed to carry on the business of the late Merchant Prince under a new partnership. The stunning announcement flew in the face of Stewart's explicit written wishes that Hilton liquidate the businesses. The news of the new partnership and subsequent continuation of A. T. Stewart & Co. sent shockwaves through the business, legal, and social communities.

Know all men by, &c., that I, Cornelia M. Stewart, of the City of New York, widow, have made, constituted and appointed, and by these presents do make, constitute and appoint Henry Hilton, of said City, my true and lawful attorney, for me and in my name, place, and stead, with full power and authority to do all and every act or thing that I might or could do in reference to my estate, real or personal; to make, sign, seal, and execute and deliver any covenant, deed, or other instrument in writing for me and in my name, that I might or could do; to transfer any stocks, bonds, securities, or other real and personal property, as fully as I might or could do; to make and execute any agreement or contract relating to or affecting any of my estate, real or personal, as fully as I might or could do; to collect, demand and receive all sums of money due to me, and to compromise any such claim or demand, and, on such composition or receipt of the same, full acquittance and discharges to give and grant in my name, and to appoint agents or attorneys under him, and to revoke the same when necessary. And generally to do all and every act or thing relating to or concerning my real or personal estate that I may or could do, giving and granting unto my said attorney full power and authority to do and perform all and every act, anything whatsoever requisite and necessary to be done in and about the premises, as fully to all intents and purposes as I might or could do if personally present, with full power of substitution and revocation, hereby ratifying and confirming all that my said attorney or his substitute shall lawfully do or cause to be done by virtue hereof in witness whereof I have here unto set my hand and seal the 14th day of April, in the year of one though sand eight hundred and seventy six.

    Cornelia M. Stewart.

    —DOCUMENT FILED WITH THE NEW YORK CITY REGISTRAR'S OFFICE,

        APRIL 14, 1876.

It was obvious to anyone that Hilton's arrangement was in direct conflict with Stewart's last wishes. Still, no one protested. What wasn't obvious was that Hilton would drain Stewart's business dry and obliterate its mark on New York City.

Meanwhile, most people assumed that Hilton had readily turned over his one-million-dollar inheritance to Cornelia Stewart. However, there was never any record of Hilton doing so. In essence, he not only kept the one million dollars left to him by Stewart, but he managed to take control of Stewart's entire forty-million-dollar empire.

At the time of his death, the value of Stewart's wholesale and retail enterprises was approximately twelve million dollars doing approximately forty million dollars worth of business annually. The sale and liquidation of the Stewart empire would have brought in twice as much as the twelve million it was worth, but the sale never materialized. Instead, Hilton assumed operational control over a national and international business.

If Cornelia Stewart had any misgivings, she did not express them. But the arrangement left her bereft of cash, and all her future personal expenditures had to come from Hilton. There was never any indication that Hilton refused any of her requests. However, it is important to note that all her expenses were charged to interest-bearing loans. In other words, Cornelia Stewart was borrowing her own money, at a price.

Hilton announced to the press that it was his intent and the intent of Mrs. Stewart to carry on with those charitable works started by the late Alexander T. Stewart and to finance others. The only two charities Hilton publicly committed to were the Working Women's Hotel in New York City and an undisclosed religious project planned for Garden City. There was a public outcry over the lack of specifics regarding the potential charitable works being considered by Hilton and the widow Stewart, and in an effort to stem the tide of criticism, Hilton announced the distribution of the paltry sum of about $120,000 in total donations to a variety of charitable organizations in the city. This merely fanned the flames. One hundred twenty thousand dollars was a negligible amount considering the vast fortune Stewart had left behind. Soon, the plans for the religious project at Garden City grew into a full-blown charitable enterprise calling for the construction of an ornate Episcopal cathedral along with boarding schools for boys and girls and a rectory for the Episcopal bishop. The cathedral would cost millions, and for the time being, news of the endeavor quelled any further outrage regarding the size of the charitable contributions Hilton and Cornelia Stewart had made.

A. T. STEWART & CO.
The New Firm—Articles Of Copartnership Between Judge Hilton And Mr. Libbey.

This is to certify, 1. That we, Henry Hilton and William Libbey, both of the City and State of New York, have this day formed a copartnership for the purpose of conducting a general mercantile business in the City of New York and in the cities of Boston, Philadelphia, Paris, Lyons, Manchester, Bradford, Nottingham, Belfast, Glasgow, Berlin, Chemnitz, and elsewhere in the United States and in the Kingdom of Great Britain and Ireland, and on the Continent of Europe and in other foreign countries. 2. That the principal place of said partnership will be in the City of New York. 3. That said business will be conducted under the firm name of A. T. Stewart & Co., which firm name it is hereby certified, will be continued in use by Henry Hilton and William Libbey, of the City and State of New York aforesaid; the said Henry Hilton being the assignee and grantee of Cornelia M. Stewart, devisee and legatee under the last will and testament of Alexander T. Stewart, late of the City of New York, now deceased, as to all the interest of said Alexander T. Stewart in the late firm of A. T. Stewart & Co., which firm had business relations with foreign countries.

Witness our hands and seals this 14th day of April, A.D. 1876.
HENRY HILTON
WILLIAM LIBBEY

—*New York Times*
April 16, 1876

THE BUSINESS TO BE CONTINUED
An Important Statement By Judge Hilton— The Various Employees Resume Work This Morning

The TIMES reporter called last evening on Judge Henry Hilton, one of the Executors of the late Mr. A.T. Stewart's will, for the purpose of ascertaining to what extent the business and various enterprises of the deceased merchant would be conducted hereafter. Judge Hilton said there would be no change whatsoever in the extent or manner of carrying on the business in the two dry-goods stores and their various branches. He had visited the retail establishment yesterday, and given instructions to the various heads of departments to proceed with the transactions of business in their several departments precisely as they did before Mr. Stewart's death. "To-morrow," said he, "9,600 employes will resume work where they left off last Monday." In connection with his business Mr. Stewart had fourteen factories in operation, which will not be limited in their functions.

Along with maintaining the entire retail operations, Hilton continued on with work started by Stewart at the Grand Union Hotel in Saratoga. Hilton awarded contracts for the reconstruction of the hotel.

—*New York Times*
April 15, 1876

Alexander Stewart was dead and buried, and Henry Hilton was on his way.

4

A PROBLEM WITH HOTELS

In which Henry Hilton, as head of the A. T. Stewart business empire, commits the first of his many public relations blunders by refusing accommodations to Jewish banker Joseph Seligman and subsequently banning all members of the Jewish community from the Grand Union Hotel, the Stewart estate's resort in Saratoga Springs, New York. Hilton's actions lead to a boycott of Stewart's stores by the Jewish community. Hilton also reneges on building the "Working Women's Hotel," causing a furor among New York City women, who also threaten a boycott.

Within months of the new partnership organized between Judge Henry Hilton and William Libbey to continue A. T. Stewart's businesses, the enterprise proved profitable for the new owners. Under Hilton and Libbey's leadership, the company earned a cash profit of more than six hundred thousand dollars within a mere two-month period, a sum the two men split between themselves, with Hilton receiving the lion's share at 80 percent. But even with Libbey receiving just 20 percent of the profits, it was far more than he would have received if Stewart were still alive. Throughout his business relationship with the late retail magnate, Libbey, although a partner in the business, drew a hefty salary but did not share in the overall profits.

Hilton was a better friend of Stewart's, however, than he was a manager of Stewart's retail empire. Despite the early profits, his leadership of A. T. Stewart & Co. was marred by one dubious blunder after another, beginning with his decision to enter the retail market in Chicago, a market dominated by the business icon Marshall Field. In July 1876, Hilton leased space in several buildings in downtown Chicago. The move proved disastrous. Clearly the refrain in real estate is now and was then, "location, location, location." The sites that Hilton was able to rent were far outside the retail district for most Chicago shoppers. Following the Chicago Fire in 1871, Field and other retailers established their operations on the west side of the city, creating a whole shopping district. By the time Hilton ventured into the market, west side commerce had been fully established. Since Hilton was unable to rent or buy retail space in the district, he opted to lease outside of it, hoping the Stewart name would attract shoppers. It didn't. Hilton opened his Chicago store with approximately $1.3 million worth of inventory displayed within a dozen departments. During his lifetime, Stewart had kept his distance from Chicago rather than go head to head with the established retailers like Marshall Field, and conversely, Field knew he would be no match for Stewart on his own turf of New York City. This standoff benefited both men, but Hilton had other ideas.

Although a shrewder businessman than Hilton, Field offered to share the wealth in the Chicago market by proposing to Hilton that the two retail giants agree to an arrangement that would avert a price war, which would prove disastrous for both concerns. Hilton did not agree to the arrangement, and so a price war ensued, with Hilton receiving the worst of it. Within four years the Chicago branch of A. T. Stewart & Co. was operating at a loss. In 1882, the branch was closed for good as part of the company's overall liquidation.

If the Chicago foray proved to be a huge business mistake, Hilton's handling of the Grand Union Hotel in Saratoga Springs, New York, was a devastating public relations blunder that accelerated the downfall of A. T. Stewart & Co.

Work on Garden City continued just as Stewart had planned, including the laying of some fourteen miles of water pipe. Hilton told newspapers that additional homes would be built and streets laid out. The railway line to and from Garden City would be completed, allowing residents to travel to Wall Street in a matter of twenty minutes.

Hilton also promised that work would continue on the Working Women's Hotel on Thirty-second Street and that affordable, clean, and safe living conditions for working women would be completed strictly according to Stewart's original plans and intentions. The hotel would be fireproof and have a steam-driven elevator. When asked by reporters to provide specifics regarding other intended charitable works using Stewart's fortune, Hilton said, "Actions will show for themselves. Mr. Stewart despised alms-giving and preferred to assist people to maintain themselves by their own industry."

Indeed, Hilton's actions did speak for themselves but ultimately produced a firestorm of condemnation.

Following Stewart's death and Hilton's takeover of the company, Hilton decided to replace the previous manager of the Grand Union Hotel in Saratoga Springs. James Breslin, who had successfully operated the hotel under Stewart, was asked to leave. Stewart had never found fault with Breslin's management of the place, but because the 1876 season at Saratoga was so poor, Hilton decided that Breslin had to go.

Saratoga was a summer resort; its mineral springs, spas, and the Saratoga Race Course—the oldest thoroughbred racetrack in America—attracted scores of the rich and famous every year. They came to gamble, relax, and vacation surrounded by the gay, rich Victorian elegance of the town. Saratoga was chockablock full of ornate mansions, which the wealthy owners referred to lovingly as their "summer cottages." Stewart's Grand Union Hotel, regarded as the largest hotel in the world, and the United States Hotel were the two most elegant and massive buildings in the town.

During the late spring of 1877, Hilton noted that despite the many improvements made to the Grand Union Hotel, more and more of Saratoga's wealthy visitors were checking into the United States Hotel down the street. Through some wrong-headed process of deduction, Hilton attributed the competitive disadvantage to the large number of Jewish visitors who frequented the Grand Union Hotel. Looking for someone to blame for the hotel's terrible performance and without Breslin at the helm to be a scapegoat, Hilton conveniently decided to prohibit the many members of the New York Jewish community who frequented the hotel. Hilton's actions were unnecessary and deplorable, only further propelling the downfall of the company.

In June 1877, New York City banker Joseph Seligman, who had been a frequent guest at the Grand Union, was refused accommodations. Despite his protests, Seligman was told that under Hilton's orders, all Jewish guests were being excluded from the hotel. Hilton's actions and refusal to withdraw his orders produced a firestorm of protest that spread not only throughout New York's Jewish community but through other religious groups as well. It was a stunning blow to Hilton and his hotel, but there was more: The protest carried over to A. T. Stewart & Co.'s retail and wholesale businesses.

A SENSATION AT SARATOGA
NEW RULES FOR THE GRAND UNION

No Jews To Be Admitted—Mr. Seligman, The Banker, And His Family Sent Away— His Letter To Mr. Hilton—Gathering Of Mr. Seligman's Friends—An Indignation Meeting To Be Held

On Wednesday last Joseph Seligman, the well-known banker of this City and a member of the syndicate to place the government loan, visited Saratoga with his wife and family. For ten years past he has spent the summer at the Grand Union Hotel. His family entered the parlors and Mr. Seligman went to the manager to make arrangements for rooms. That gentleman seemed somewhat confused and said: "Mr. Seligman, I am required to inform you that Mr. Hilton has given instructions that no Israelites shall be permitted in the future to stop at this hotel."

Mr. Seligman was so astonished that for some time he could make no reply. Then he said: "Do you mean to tell me that you will not entertain Jewish people?" "That is our orders, Sir," was the reply.

—*New York Times*
June 19, 1877

Seligman and his family had spent their summers at the Grand Union Hotel for a decade. There was no reason for him to imagine that registering at the hotel in June 1877 would be any different. When told that Jews were now being barred admittance, Seligman demanded to know why.

"Are they dirty?" he asked the manager at the front desk. "Do they misbehave themselves, or have they refused to pay their bills?"

The manager told him that it had nothing to do with those things.

"The reason is simply this: Business at the hotel was not good last season and we had a large number of Jews here. Mr. Hilton came to the conclusion that Christians did not like their company, and for that reason shunned the hotel. He resolved to run the Union on a different principle this season and gave us instructions to admit no Jew."

The outraged banker returned to New York City and immediately wrote a letter to Hilton demanding to know why Jews were being excluded from the hotel. In the letter he said that if Hilton did not see Jews worthy to enter his hotel, then it would be wise for him to send a circular to all Jews informing them not to make purchases at his stores. He charged Hilton with bigotry and said Hilton was not worthy of and lacked the ability to run a hotel like the Grand Union.

In his letter Seligman wrote, "A little reflection must show you that the grievous falling off in your business is not due to the patronage of any one nationality, but to the want of patronage at all, and that you, dear Judge, are not big enough to keep a hotel nor broad enough in your business views to run a department store."

According to Hilton, Seligman had been spoiling for a public fight because A. T. Stewart & Co had previously done nearly all of its foreign banking business with Seligman's bank but had discontinued the arrangement. Hilton claimed that Stewart himself had intended the Grand Union Hotel to be a family home during the summer where his 2,500 guests expected security and satisfaction. The concerns of these guests, Hilton said, had to be considered. The hotel, according to Hilton, was run for them and not for those for whom they have expressed dislike. Mr. Seligman, according to Hilton, represented not a class of Hebrews, but of Jews, with whom many of his other guests, especially the female guests, did not wish to associate. These other guests, Hilton claimed, did not wish to be forced to engage with this class of Jew.

"It is the fault," Hilton said in the *New York Times,* "of this class of 'Jews' themselves that they are discriminated against. ... Families like the Hendricks and Nathans are welcome everywhere, while those Jews (not Hebrews) of whom Joseph Seligman is a representative are not wanted any more at any of the first-class Summer hotels. They have brought the public opinion down on themselves by a vulgar ostentation, a puffed-up vanity, an overweening display of condition, a lack of those considerate civilities so much appreciated by good American society, and a general obtrusiveness that is frequently disgusting and always repulsive to the well-bred."

A group of Seligman's friends and business acquaintances met to discuss the ugly affair and determine what action they might take. The group decided that New York's Jews, or for that matter Jews from across the country, could not afford to let the matter rest. Something had to be done.

JUDGE HILTON'S STATEMENT

In the evening a reporter of the TIMES called upon Judge Hilton at his residence and found him willing to speak upon the subject. He said that Mr. Seligman was not ejected from the Grand Union. He had been boarding at the Clarendon up to the time of the opening of the Grand Hotel. He then came over and "in an ostentatious manner," it seems, demanded the best apartments. ... Judge Hilton does not consider Mr. Joseph Seligman a Hebrew. Years ago, he said, Mr. Seligman absolutely threw overboard the Hebrew Bible and Moses ... he but plays the mountebank if he attempts to arouse the prejudices of the Orthodox Hebrew Church by circulating any stories or insinuations to the effect that he was turned out of the Grand Union Hotel simply because he belonged to that ancient faith. ... Mr. Seligman is a "Jew" in the trade sense of the word, and the class of Jews he represents, while they are not forbidden to come to the Grand Union are not encouraged.

—*New York Times*
June 19, 1877

The refusal of the Grand Union Hotel at Saratoga to admit Mr. Joseph Seligman and family as guests and Judge Hilton's explanation of it ... have created a profound sensation in this City and in all sections where there are Summer hotels or people who patronize them. ... The general position taken is decidedly opposed to that of Judge Hilton although there are a few hotels in this City where Jewish custom is openly discouraged on grounds similar to those stated by Judge Hilton.

—*New York Times*
June 20, 1877

When asked whether he would clarify his order excluding Jews, Hilton said that the new rules were adopted after a great deal of deliberation and for purely business reasons alone. According to Hilton, his action had the approval of a majority of "the better class" of Americans and many first-class hotel proprietors. Hilton said many of his hotel associates were glad to be rid of a "ruinous evil."

Addressing the controversy, the *New York Times* ran an article that included interviews with local hoteliers who generally disputed Hilton's claims that many, if any, hotels approved of Hilton's behavior.

According to the *Times*, Mr. Waite, the general manager of the Windsor Hotel, was asked if the hotel discriminated regarding the admission of guests.

"We have not the slightest possible objection to Hebrews as guests at this hotel," Waite said. "We have always found them, as a class, the promptest paying customers and have never had an account outstanding against them on our books."

The management at the Grand Central Hotel stated that "a great mistake had been made at Saratoga."

According to the management at the Metropolitan Hotel, "If persons apply for accommodations who are undesirable, there are ways of letting them know they are unwelcome without offending them."

At the Hotel Brunswick, Mr. E. R. McCarty said that Jews were "good customers and were not hard to please."

Lewis Leland, the general manager of the Sturtevant House, told reporters, "No one was ever excluded from the Sturtevant on account of religion or race."

At the Gramercy Park Hotel, management noted that many Jewish guests had stayed there and further noted, "It was never observed that they were unlike other persons living in the hotel in their manners. No complaint had ever been made against any of them."

At the Hotel Devonshire, Mr. Livermore, the proprietor, said, "The Hotel Devonshire makes no discriminations against Hebrews, nor do I see how it could if it complied with the laws under which hotels conduct their business."

Ferdinand Earle, owner of Earle's Hotel, said he thought that the policy of Judge Hilton "seemed suicidal."

But not every New York City hotel owner disputed Hilton's new orders in Saratoga.

According to the *Times*, "Major Field, manager of the Albemarle Hotel said he would not have Jews come to the establishment at any price because they killed a good class of customer wherever they were allowed. They rendered themselves obnoxious to other guests by their egotism and love of display and never settled their bills."

But in general, the hotel industry did not support Hilton's outlandish claims. Yet, despite public and industry opinion, or the potential long-term cost of it, Hilton stuck militantly to his discrimination policy at the Grand Union Hotel in Saratoga.

The repercussions of Hilton's published response regarding Joseph Seligman's "class of Jews" was immediate not only on the Grand Union Hotel but also on the Hilton-run A. T. Stewart & Co. stores. Within a day of Hilton's comments, one hundred Jewish mercantile accounts at the wholesale and retail Stewart businesses were closed and Jewish women throughout the city vowed not to shop at A. T. Stewart's any longer. According to a report published on June 20, 1877, in the *New York Times*, these actions by the city's Jewish community would cost "from $3,000,000 to $5,000,000 a year from Jewish traders alone." Nearly two-thirds of A. T. Stewart customers were Jewish, the article claimed.

JEWISH MERCHANTS COMBINING
They Are Determined To Deal No More With A.T. Stewart & Co.—The Race Proscribed Through Mr. Seligman— Representative Views From Prominent Clotheirs—No Public Meeting Sought

There was less general interest yesterday in the Grand Union Hotel discrimination. Among the Hebrews however, there is apparently a deep-seated determination to do no more business with the house of A.T. Stewart & Co. There is said to be a paper circulating containing a pledge to have no further dealings with this firm. Interviews with several Jewish merchants are given herewith, which express the opinions of the many whom our reporter conversed. One of them says that Judge Hilton has proscribed the Jewish race through Mr. Seligman and that the race as a body will resent the insult. Few if any are in favor of any public indignation meeting, Mr. Seligman's friends being satisfied with the expression already made in a private and semi-public way. Judge Hilton compares his manner of rejecting Jewish people with that of some other hotel keepers who, he claims, make just as rigid discrimination in less open manner; he thinks that his method is fairer and that he has done his duty.

—*New York Times*
June 22, 1877

Jewish clothiers banded together in their boycott of A. T. Stewart & Co. A majority of Jewish-run businesses agreed that Stewart's would lose the patronage of Jewish clothing merchants throughout the country. According to the merchants, there would be no further dealings with Stewart's, certainly no buying anything from it, and only under extraordinary circumstances, selling anything to it. Jewish-run operations comprised three-fourths of the clothier trade.

According to Mr. Hoffman of Hoffman, Goldsmith & Co., located at 139 Duane Street in the city's clothier district, although Mr. Seligman did not represent all Jews, "The Jews cannot help feeling that their race has been proscribed through Mr. Seligman and resent it for all time." Hoffman said, "It is idle for Judge Hilton to try to split the hair by an attempted discrimination between the Jew and the Hebrew on the score of religion. ... As a race they are united against the outrage upon one of their fellows. ... The Jews all know Mr. Seligman and his life and they are satisfied with him as a splendid American citizen."

"We are unanimously and absolutely resolved to avoid Stewart and Co. henceforth in all business. The line is drawn now not between American and Jew, that is impossible socially and commercially, but between the Jew and ex-Judge Hilton, and the line will never be wiped out," Hoffman concluded.

JEWISH CLOTHIERS OF ONE MIND
They Will Trade No More With A.T. Stewart & Co.—The Race Proscribed Through Mr. Seligman—Opinions Of Prominent Firms.

Mr. Seligman may or may not be Hilton's social equal, but I know personally ... that the gross description of Seligman's personal habits given by Hilton has evolved from his inner knowledge of his own self and is considered by those who know him best to be a perfect photograph of the nature of the artist himself. He thought he was describing Mr. Seligman but he was, in a fit of absent-mindedness looking in a mirror at a reflection of himself and painting it for mankind. ... Watch the result. I hope Judge Hilton can stand it—we can.

—*New York Times*
June 22, 1877

Jewish women throughout the city and the country were even more indignant than their male counterparts about Hilton's order banning Jews from his hotel. And they were determined to take out their own form of retribution on Hilton and A. T. Stewart & Co. It was well known that Jewish women spent large sums annually at Stewart's store, some speculated upward of ten thousand dollars in some cases and one thousand dollars per year in other cases. Regardless of the sums, Jewish women closed their accounts at Stewart's store, in droves. It was projected that the loss of this patronage would be four million dollars in one year alone, a staggering amount.

It was not merely the Jewish community that boycotted A. T. Stewart & Co. A large number of other nationalities, in sympathy with the Jewish victims of Hilton's discrimination, also joined the boycott. Hilton underestimated the impact the boycott would have. In a June 23, 1877, issue of the *New York Tribune*, Hilton proclaimed, "I can stand it if they can. A man will buy goods where he can buy them most advantageously ... no one—least of all a Jew—is going to bite his own nose off."

> *"When we are poor and ignorant we are Jews.*
> *When we are well to do we become Israelites.*
> *When we are rich and influential we are called Hebrews."*
> —Baron James Rothschild (1792–1868)

Jesse Seligman, the brother of Joseph, told reporters, "I am at a loss what to think concerning Judge Hilton. In view of his extraordinary statements in to-day's *Times*, it would be charitable to suppose that the warm weather had affected his brain."

According to the brother, the late A. T. Stewart held no opinions as audacious as Henry Hilton's.

Jesse Seligman told reporters, "Mr. Stewart was a man of great talent, of enlarged and liberal views and of great business foresight. He never for one moment countenanced such silly notions as those of Judge Hilton. If he could realize the gross indiscretion in a business point of view which Mr. Hilton is committing, it would be enough to make him turn in his grave."

According to Jesse Seligman, Americans weren't buying any part of Hilton's prejudicial beliefs.

"The American public were too broad and liberal in their principles to entertain such vulgar and exploded prejudices, and that Judge Hilton would realize his mistake to his cost before the Summer was over," he said.

Seligman's brother was not the only outraged party to voice his contempt of Hilton's behavior. Seligman received letters of support from a vast array of indignant citizens.

"You can well afford to stand for social principle and I hope you will fight it out on the line which Judge Hilton has chosen to assume," one unidentified supporter wrote.

From Philadelphia, Seligman received a correspondence stating: "We would like to know the truth of the statements which we see in the newspapers. We are dealing largely with the house of A.T. Stewart & Co., and would like to know whether such bigotry really exists with the chief of such an honorable establishment."

About fifty businesses, from New York City and beyond, all longtime customers of A. T. Stewart & Co., immediately closed their accounts with Stewart's. Among them were Coleman Brothers and Neustadter Brothers of San Francisco, Kohn & Co. of Chicago, and a host of city establishments, accounting for tens of thousands of dollars in lost revenue. Those buying from Stewart's were not the only ones who withdrew their patronage. Sellers who for decades had sold their goods to Stewart's began withdrawing their business as well, accounting for even more financial losses.

Regardless of the public furor, Hilton refused to back down and took great pains to inform reporters of the public support he had received for his actions. He told the *Times* that he was firmer than ever in his position and was receiving scores of letters and telegrams from across the country commending his exclusion policy. He told reporters that no discrimination against Jews was exercised in any way in the wholesale and retail side of A. T. Stewart & Co., desperately trying to distance the department store side of his affairs from the hotel side. It did little good. Hilton was seen as a bigot, and nothing he could do or say would change what was quickly becoming a widely accepted view of the man who had taken over Stewart's vast empire.

Yet despite the public outrage and the Jewish boycott, Hilton didn't even try to make amends. In a letter dated July 9, 1877, written to a friend in Chicago, Hilton boasted, "If they do not wish to trade with our house, I will be perfectly satisfied, nay, gratified, as I believe we lose much more than we gain from their custom. Should the Jews under these circumstances want to draw a sharp line, I might determine not to deal with or purchase from them and then they might possibly find greater reason than ever for feeling bad. Every dollar we sell them is set off by at least $500 purchased from them. ... It has not heretofore been my nature to back out or hedge when I have deliberately taken a stand, and I am now too well on in years to begin. ... Possibly the Jews may yet regret having made such a fuss about a matter in which they had no cause for complaint. The laws yet permit a man to use his property as he pleases and I propose exercising that blessed privilege, notwithstanding Moses and all his descendants may object."

As the Jewish boycott hobbled the Grand Union Hotel in Saratoga, where business fell off even more in succeeding years, the boycott of Stewart's retail and wholesale businesses caused profits to decline so much that Hilton was forced to suspend operation of the wholesale branch and combine it in space at the retail location. Hilton refused to publicly acknowledge that the Jewish boycott had anything to do with either financial loss.

The Saratoga incident was best summarized by New York City Rabbi Gustav Gottheil of Temple Emanuel during his sermon on June 23, 1877: "The absurdity of the attack becomes more apparent if you put the case in legal form: Judge Henry Hilton vs. Jews and Judaism. When that purse-proud man and his 'model hotel' at Saratoga and even his Broadway stores shall be all swept away and buried in oblivion, the race which has given the world some of its most highly prized treasures, and which has fought more battles for truth and for the triumph of liberal principles amid Christian civilization than any other, will continue its great historical mission."

REMOVAL OF THE STEWART WHOLESALE STORE

Judge Hilton says that the rumors of the probable removal up town of the wholesale store of A.T. Stewart & Co. are true, and that the downtown store may be closed by the 1st of December. The process of removal to the up-town store has been going on for some time and about one-half of the wholesale department has been transferred.

—*New York Times*
November 13, 1878

Between the debacle of his foray into the Chicago market and the boycott of his hotel, retail, and wholesale businesses by the Jewish community, it would seem as if Hilton's troubles couldn't get any worse. But the straw that appeared to break the camel's back—and another prime example of Hilton's ineptitude—was the closing of one of Alexander Stewart's major and most visible acts of philanthropy, the Working Women's Hotel, on May 26, 1878.

Stewart had intended the Working Women's Hotel to be a philanthropic gesture. He had wanted to build an affordable hotel for working women in New York where they could live in a secure, clean, comfortable, and upscale environment at a reasonable cost.

The building was begun in January 1869 and took nine years to complete at a cost of $3.7 million. Stewart, who had checked in on the construction of his grand experiment almost daily, said of it, "That hotel will make 1,000 working women happy and independent. If it succeeds the example will be imitated. It will be a woman's kingdom, where those of them that wish to be alone can be so. It will prove whether or not the sexes can live apart, and whether or not it will be better for them to do so, whether or not they will choose to."

At the time of Stewart's death in 1876, the hotel, on the corner of Fourth Avenue and Thirty-second and Thirty-third Streets, had not been completed. The grand gesture by Stewart was welcomed by thousands of working women in New York and notably by members of the growing feminist movement, who saw Stewart's hotel as another major foothold for women in the working environment. Even before Stewart's death, though, Hilton had openly expressed his doubts about the project, calling it impractical. And so it was with a great deal of elation that women throughout the city read in the newspapers that Hilton fully intended to complete the Working Women's Hotel. Their elation was, however, short-lived.

The hotel had the capacity of one thousand patrons and guests. The building covered sixteen lots formerly owned and occupied by the locomotive shops of the Hudson River Railroad. It was approximately two hundred feet square and seven stories high, constructed as a square to let the maximum amount of light and ventilation into the rooms. In the center of the lobby was an elaborate fountain surrounded by an assortment of plants and vases of flowers. Aside from its magnificent cosmetics, the building was fireproof, built almost entirely of brick, iron, and stone. On its roof were two enormous iron tanks holding thirteen thousand gallons of water to be piped throughout the hotel. There were numerous wide staircases throughout the hotel and five elevators that ran from the basement to the roof. Two of the elevators were in the rear of the hotel, to be used as freight elevators; two were located in the front for patrons and guests; and a main central elevator was located at the very front of the building.

Of the 502 private rooms in the hotel, 115 were double rooms, measuring approximately thirty by sixteen feet. The remaining 387 rooms were designed for single occupancy and were half the size of the double rooms. They were furnished with heavy, expensive, custom-made marble-topped black walnut furniture and decorated with paintings from Stewart's collection. The rooms were indeed small, and more than half had no clothes closets or wardrobes—a glaring oversight, or perhaps intentional, considering what Hilton ultimately did.

Every floor was covered with plush, expensive carpeting. Each room was supplied with gas and hot and cold water and was heated by the giant boilers in the basement. Semiprivate bathrooms were available on every floor with attendants to assist boarders. There was also a huge laundry room for dropoffs. The main dining room had a seating capacity of six hundred people and was under the supervision of a French chef who had previously worked at the Grand Union Hotel in Saratoga. There were several spacious reception rooms for guests and entertaining and a fifty-five-by-one-hundred-foot parlor. A library, with 2,500 volumes, and a reading room were also available. Throughout the library, reception rooms, parlor, dining room, and hallways, a number of paintings were hung and sculptures placed on display.

Women had to adhere to a plethora of rules and restrictions, including no guests in their rooms, a ban on additional furniture, a cost of ten cents imposed on baths, and no pets. None of these were deal breakers for most working women longing to stay. It was, by all Gilded Age standards, an elegant and luxurious hotel. It was also the largest hotel in New York City.

When he was alive, A. T. Stewart stipulated that the $3.7 million enterprise would not be required to ever produce a profit. He intended it to be self-supporting, and if not, the Stewart estate was to supplement any deficiency in its revenues. If, according to Stewart, the hotel did show a profit, then that profit was to be applied to the rates of guests in proportion to the surplus. Under no circumstances was any woman to be charged more than $5 a week for her board and single room lodging. According to the *New York Times,* Stewart intended to "give the working women of New York the best hotel accommodations, the best rooms, best furniture, best food, best attendance, best living for less than $5 per week."

THE WOMEN'S HOTEL OPEN
A GREAT ENTERPRISE BEGUN.
The Most Brilliant Reception Ever Held In New York—Twenty Thousand People Surging Through The Building— The Magnificient Appointments Inspected In Detail—Mrs. Stewart Congratulated By Thousands.

The great Women's Hotel, projected by, and finished according to the expressed wishes of the late Alexander T. Stewart, was formally opened last night. The occasion was probably the most brilliant of the kind in the history of the country. ... The hotel was brilliantly illuminated from cellar to the topmost floor, and the tiers of light were visible for blocks in every direction. ... Every apartment was found to be complete, comfortable, even luxurious. ... It is estimated that nearly 20,000 persons visited the new hotel last night. ... Mrs. Stewart was abundantly congratulated upon the consumption of the plans of her husband and Judge Hilton was overwhelmed with compliments as it was well known that many of the details were directed by his taste and carried out under his personal supervision.

—*New York Times*

April 3, 1878

It took Judge Henry Hilton less than sixty days to close the hotel. On May 26, 1878, Hilton announced that as a charity for working women, the hotel was a failure. Hilton also announced that it would be remodeled and reopened on June 8, 1878, as a commercial hotel called the Park Avenue Hotel. Although Hilton had claimed that more than one thousand applications for admission to the hotel had been filed and that nearly seventy-five women had moved into the hotel on the first day, he then claimed, at the announcement of its closing, that the hotel had never had more than fifty registered guests and that the enterprise had lost five hundred dollars a day over the fifty-three days it had been in operation.

Hilton told the press that Cornelia Stewart was heartbroken by the failure of her late husband's pet project. "The women for whom the hotel was built have not patronized it liberally, and it has been run at a loss," Hilton said. "Mrs. Stewart has therefore determined to end the experiment at once."

He went on to say, "A hotel on an extensive scale for women is an impossibility. Women want to associate with the other sex and the restrictions imposed upon them in this house were so severe that many who would gladly have taken advantage of its benefits declined for that reason."

NOT ONLY FOR THE WOMEN
A WHITE ELEPHANT TO BE MADE PROFITABLE
Mr. Stewart's Woman's Hotel To Be Thrown Open For All—The Original Plan Unsuccessful—What Judge Hilton Says

Mrs. A. T. Stewart, bitterly disappointed, has made up her mind, after two months' experience, that the Woman's Hotel experiment is a complete failure. She has, therefore, concluded to abandon it. ... Mrs. Stewart was very much grieved at the failure. She had expected grand results from the enterprise, had taken a room in the hotel for her own exclusive use ... and had hoped to spend the remainder of her days in the midst of those of her sex whom her husband's philanthropy had surrounded with all the comforts of life. But after all that had been done and after the enormous expenditures that had been made, the women could not be brought to appreciate the hotel and patronize it in sufficient numbers to warrant running it any longer for the exclusive benefit of women.

—*New York Times*
May 26, 1878

According to Hilton, as the manager of the Stewart estate, it fell upon him to save the estate from the financial burden of the Working Women's Hotel and to find some profitable use for it. He concluded that structural changes would allow him to open it as a commercial hotel.

"The richest woman in this country have not better parlors or bedrooms and no place in the world can produce better cooking or service. But it is a failure," Hilton said.

"Women will not be kept from the other sex," he said. "You can run a hotel for men exclusively—but for women you can't. I am not greatly surprised at the failure. But I have done my full duty in the face of a conviction of inevitable failure."

A WOMAN'S HOTEL NO MORE
The Park-Avenue Opened
Its Formal Opening By The Managers Of The Stewart Estate

Owing to its lack of patronage and its consequent failure as a hotel for women exclusively, the late Woman's Hotel was thrown open to the general public yesterday at noon, under the name of the Park-Avenue Hotel. ... $50,000 have since been expended upon it in making such alterations as the change in its character necessitated. ... The store room on the ground floor, on the corner of Thirty-second-street and Fourth-avenue, has been converted into a large and elegantly fitted up bar-room, with a 38-foot bar backed by tall, broad plate mirrors. ... On the Fourth-avenue side it is adjoined by three large lounging and smoking rooms. ... On the Thirty-second-street side the bar adjoins the cigar stand and two large billiard rooms.

—*New York Times*
June 9, 1878

The firestorm of protest caused by Hilton's closing of the Working Women's Hotel only added to his already damaged reputation. Far worse than the damage to his reputation was the damage heaped on the Stewart business. A flood of public denunciation rolled in from feminist groups, working women, and the press.

It is said that those ladies who took board while the establishment was the Women's Hotel will be welcome to remain as long as they please at the rates on which they entered.

—*New York Times*
June 9, 1878

Hundreds of women gathered at Cooper Institute on the evening of June 4, 1878, to protest Hilton's closing of the hotel. One speaker after another condemned Hilton's actions and comments. Again Hilton managed to offend an enormous percentage of his patrons. And, similar to the protests of the Jewish community, Hilton refused to accept blame or apologize.

JUDGE HILTON AND THE LADIES
A Public Meeting Of Women To Be Held To Protest Against Alleged Wrongs

On Friday afternoon a number of prominent ladies who feel aggrieved at the statements given to the press by Judge

Hilton in reference to the failure of the Woman's Hotel, met at the residence of Mrs. C.S. Lozier, M.D. for the purpose of protesting against the position taken by Judge Hilton. The ladies, after debating as to the best course to pursue in the matter, determined to hold a public meeting at the Cooper Institute.

—*New York Times*
June 2, 1878

We the undersigned appeal to the honest, noble-hearted working women, to all true women who sympathize with them, and to all fathers and brothers who possess a sense of justice to unite with us at Cooper Institute, Tuesday, June 4, in a public protest against the insult Judge Hilton has put upon all womanhood by insinuations which he permits to be circulated as an excuse for the wrong he has perpetrated in appropriating to mercenary and selfish purposes what he has extensively advertised as a noble charity.

—public notice,
—*New York Times*
June 2, 1878

The women at the Cooper Institute meeting read and approved a series of resolutions. Among the resolutions was an affirmation that the intentions of the late A. T. Stewart to provide safe and comfortable living accommodations for working women had been "effectually and shamefully thwarted."

They called upon Mrs. Stewart to intervene on the closing of the hotel, entreating her to remain steadfast to her late husband's plan, and to ensure that "what was intended for working women shall not be taken from them."

Further resolutions exonerated Mrs. Stewart from any blame for the closing of the hotel. But more explicit was a resolution that would have a dramatic and immediate impact on Hilton and the A. T. Stewart business enterprise. It read: "*Resolved*, That until the evil genius of sordid gain that presides over Stewart's vast commercial enterprise shows signs of true reform, every self-respecting woman should withdraw her patronage therefrom and that that which was built up by women chiefly, be taken away by women."

The Woman's Hotel had never been open to women. It was not open to those who earned their living by manual labor, as they did not receive wages enough. Among this class were Judge Hilton's own employees. Lady physicians or students were not allowed to have libraries or working desks in their rooms. Lady artists were not allowed to have easels. No sewing machines were permitted in rooms. The management turned pale when musical instruments were mentioned. Literary women were not allowed to take books from the library and that was closed at 10 P.M. The inmates were thus presided over as though they were schoolgirls. ... Judge Hilton ought to know that he does not rule this country, that it is not a kingdom and that if it was, he would not be selected King.

—Mrs. Matilda Fletcher,
—*New York Times* June 5, 1878

Printed cards were distributed for women and men to sign, pledging that they would no longer shop at Stewart's store.

The card read: "Until five years after the date, we shall not buy anything at Stewart's store, in consequence of the unmanly insinuations regarding the management and failure of the Woman's Hotel, hoping that in that time the managers thereof may better learn the characteristics of American women."

Thousands of these pledge cards were signed in Manhattan and Brooklyn. The boycott by the women took effect immediately. Thousands of women transferred their patronage from Stewart's to other merchants.

SCOLDING JUDGE HILTON
THE WOMEN'S GREAT
MASS-MEETING

Cooper Institute Packed—An Evening Of Uproarious Merriment—A Code Of Rules Provided For The Reconstructed Hotel— Resolutions That Delighted The Audience— Speeches On All Sorts Of Subjects, Music, Recitations, And A Collection

Fun was evidently anticipated at the mass meeting called to protest against Judge Hilton's action in diverting the Women's Hotel from its original purpose and his published reasons therefore. At 7:30 last evening the great hall of Cooper Institute was full. At 7:45 it was jammed in every part. ... Until five years after date, we shall not buy anything at Stewart's store, in consequence of the unmanly insinuations regarding the management and failure of the Women's Hotel, hoping that in that time the managers thereof may better learn the characteristics of American women.

—*New York Times*
June 5, 1878

"Thus ends in bigotry and cant
Stewart's divinest dream."
—POEM BY MATILDA FLETCHER, COOPER INSTITUTE,
—*New York Times* JUNE 4, 1878

The condemnation of Hilton for abandoning Alexander Stewart's dream of a hotel for working women, and the subsequent feminist-led boycott of the Stewart retail store, coupled with the Jewish boycott, irrefutably damaged the Stewart brand. Hilton was forced to liquidate the business four short years later in 1882 because of the boycott-led atrophy of the enterprise. Considering the enormity of the retail empire Alexander Stewart left behind in 1876, its liquidation six years later represented one of the fastest mercantile declines in American business—all at the hands of the incompetent Judge Henry Hilton.

Despite the controversy surrounding the closing of the Working Women's Hotel, Hilton's newly reincarnated Park Avenue Hotel became a successful enterprise and one of the most popular hotels in New York City.

Hilton's public relations blunders with the Jewish community and the feminist movement and his failed foray into the Chicago retail marketplace paled in comparison, however, to Hilton's handling of the next gruesome debacle—the theft of the remains of Alexander Turney Stewart between midnight and sunrise on November 7, 1878, from St. Mark's Churchyard in the Bowery. In this ghoulish matter, Hilton once again displayed his inimitable ineptness and recklessness.

THE GHOULS STRIKE

In which ghouls steal the body of A. T. Stewart from its grave at St. Mark's Cemetery in November 1878. Despite several clues, a twenty-five-thousand-dollar reward offered by Henry Hilton, and an extensive investigation by the New York City Police Department, no leads are found in the mystifying case. Hilton does not immediately inform Mrs. Stewart of the ghastly deed for fear that it might send her into shock. He subsequently accuses the church sextons of the appalling crime in an effort to close the unnerving case.

An hour before dawn on November 7, 1878, Frank Parker, the assistant sexton of St. Mark's Church in the Bowery, stumbled on a gruesome sight—a mound of freshly dug dirt at the opening to A. T. Stewart's family vault.

According to George Washington Walling, the superintendent of the New York City Police Department, Parker cried out, "My God. They've done it at last!" Exactly who "they" were was unclear.

In his book, *Recollections of a New York Chief of Police*, published in 1887, Walling wrote that Parker was one of only two or three people who knew the exact location of Stewart's grave. Stewart's burial site had been shrouded in mystery since his elaborate funeral held two years previously. According to Walling, Parker knew "the horrible crime would convulse the city; and that he would be suspected of participating in it by those who did not know him."

Parker briefly examined the pile of fresh earth and then raced out of the graveyard to find the church sexton, George Hamill, who lived nearby on Tenth Street. Parker and Hamill returned to the churchyard where they opened the door to Stewart's tomb and climbed down the twelve steep stairs to the vault below. There, according to Walling's account, "Surrounded by the foulest stench imaginable, they saw for themselves that the tomb had been violated and Stewart's body removed."

GHOULS IN NEW YORK CITY
A.T. STEWART'S BODY STOLEN.
Removed From The Family Vault In St. Mark's Graveyard And Successfully Carried Away—An Unprecedented And Ghastly Crime—No Positive Clue To The Identity Of The Grave Robbers—The Corpse Probably Stolen To Obtain A Reward—What Judge Hilton Broadly Hints.

The grave of the late Alexander T. Stewart was successfully robbed between midnight and sunrise yesterday morning, and his remains carried off, evidently in the hope of obtaining a large ransom for their return. The scene of the outrage was in the old St. Mark's churchyard, which occupies the irregular end of the block bounded by Second-avenue, Stuyvesant and East Eleventh streets. The church edifice facing on Stuyvesant-street, divides the yard into two strips of green turf, dotted with small square marble slabs. These slabs indicate the vaults, which form a perfect honeycomb underneath the ground. The Stewart family vault is situated about the centre of that portion of the yard which lies on the eastern side of the church.

—*New York Times*
November 8, 1878

The front of St. Mark's Church stood about twenty-five feet from Stuyvesant Street. A ten-foot spiked iron fence surrounded the churchyard, and two iron gates on either side of the church led into the graveyard. There were no paths leading through the yard and no monuments aside from the tablet bearing the inscription:

IN THIS VAULT LIES BURIED

PETRUS STUYVESANT

LATE CAPTAIN-GENERAL AND GOVERNOR IN CHIEF

OF AMSTERDAM IN NEW NETHERLANDS,

NOW CALLED NEW-YORK,

AND THE DUTCH WEST INDIA ISLANDS.

DIED IN A.D. 167–, =

AGED, 80 YEARS.

171

The number 171 identified Stuyvesant's vault. The other small slabs marking burial vaults were sunken into the grass. The names and numbers of the vaults were barely visible to the naked eye in daylight, much less in the dark, when it was surmised the grave robbery took place. Stewart's vault was no different from the rest.

Stewart's underground crypt was made of arched brick about ten feet wide, fifteen feet long, and twelve feet high. The top of the tomb was covered with three feet of grass and sod. Three stone slabs covered the opening. Beneath the slabs was a flight of a dozen stone stairs leading down into the burial chamber. A series of pedestals ran along the rear of the chamber where the coffins rested.

The grave robbers dug the dirt from the stone slabs covering the opening to Stewart's vault, removed the stone slabs, descended the staircase, and headed straight for the cedar box that encased his coffin. The other coffins were not disturbed. Two of the coffins in the chamber contained the remains of the Stewarts' infant children and other Stewart family members. The robbers unscrewed the cover of the cedar box, cut through the lead top of the encasement within the cedar box, and forced open Stewart's coffin by breaking the locks and hinges. Inside the coffin lay the unembalmed body of Stewart. It was surmised that the robbers slipped Stewart's remains into a bag and left. They also took a silver nameplate that had been inside the lid of the coffin, several screws, and a strip of velvet lining cut from inside the casket. They left behind a small shovel, a lantern, some rope, and a copy of the September 24, 1878, issue of the *New York Herald*. After exiting the vault the thieves replaced the slabs covering its opening and left behind a mound of freshly upturned earth that Parker stumbled upon the next morning. They made their escape without leaving a single footprint to follow.

After examining the defiled vault himself, George Hamill told Parker to wait at the churchyard. There are varying accounts of exactly what happened next. According to Wayne Fanebust's account of the gruesome robbery, *The Missing Corpse*, "Instead of immediately informing the police, Hamill returned to his office and remained there until he was visited by a real estate agent, who convinced him the awful event should be reported."

According to George Walling's account, Hamill "ran over to the great store, a block up Fourth Avenue, rushing breathless into the glass office, only to find that Judge Hilton had not yet arrived. The sexton did not wait. He at once called a cab and drove to the judge's house, next door to Stewart's marble palace on Thirty-fourth Street. He gave the butler a message that his business was of extreme urgency, and the master of the house soon made his appearance."

According to newspaper accounts, Hamill ran to Hilton's office.

"The vault has been robbed, sir," Hamill told Hilton. "Mr. Stewart's body has been taken away! I am sorry."

Hilton didn't respond. He stared quizzically at the distraught sexton, then fell back down into a chair without saying a word.

"All gone. No traces left as I can see," Hamill said, fidgeting with his hat as he stood before Hilton.

"You say you are sorry such a thing should happen?" Hilton suddenly asked. His tone and demeanor were prosecutorial in nature and made Hamill uncomfortable.

"Why, yes, sir. Very sorry, of course," Hamill said.

"Sorry?" Hilton repeated acerbically. "That's singular."

"Singular?" Hamill replied. He had an idea what was running through Hilton's mind, and he didn't like it one bit.

"Will you come over and look for yourself, sir?" Hamill asked.

"No. I'll go down to police headquarters," Hilton snapped.

Hilton grabbed his coat and top hat, called for a coach, and left Hamill standing alone in the room. After Hilton bolted out the front door, Hamill made his way back to the churchyard.

Meeting up with Parker outside the vault, Hamill reportedly muttered, "Sexton right here for twenty years and a member of the church and living an upright life, to be suspected now of this horrid thing!"

———•••••———

Hilton raced into police headquarters calling loudly for Superintendent George Walling, but Walling was not there. Instead Hilton was met by New York City Police Commissioner Sidney P. Nichols.

"Someone has robbed the Stewart vault," Hilton exclaimed.

Nichols seemed indifferent to the news and to the angry and disconcerted Hilton. "Well, they've made a good haul then," Nichols said.

Hilton tried to explain that it wasn't Stewart's money that was stolen, it was his body—out of the grave at St. Mark's.

It took a minute for the gruesome account to set in with Nichols. When he realized what Hilton was talking about, Nichols began shouting out orders to the men stationed at headquarters. He would, he informed Hilton, take charge of the investigation himself. Nichols assigned two of his top detectives to the case—William Murray and George W. Dilks—both veteran investigators.

But Hilton had more to tell. He was positive in his suspicion that one of the sextons was somehow involved in the grave robbery. And he had some history to tell.

"You don't know, I suppose, that an attempt was made to steal the body last month? Yes. On October 9th, just four weeks ago," Hilton said.

Hilton went on to explain, "The sexton discovered that the Stewart slab had been lifted from its bed and put back again. It had been done clumsily, and one end of the marble had been dropped on the grass; perhaps the intruders had descended to the vault, but neither the casket nor the brick pedestal on which it rested had been tampered with. I discovered clay on the lock of the Eleventh-Street gate, like that over the vault, and I had new patent locks put on the gate, and the name-slab, which was before exposed, taken up and removed to a vacant spot some ten feet south-west and sunk in the grass to mislead other ghouls. The old place was carefully sodded over. I then hired Michael Bruton, night-watchman of the livery stable across the street, to visit the churchyard every hour and warn trespassers from the enclosure, without saying anything to him about Stewart's vault. There was no disturbance, and Burton's services were dispensed with three days ago."

Nichols was immediately drawn into the intrigue that Hilton described.

"I can't imagine how anybody knew where that stone was. Its approximate location was known to three of us only, and even I, who knew it best, couldn't have gone straight to it the first time, on a dark night, as these villains seem to have done. They must have obtained perfect measurements of the place. Perhaps they were watching from a convenient nook when we took up the name stone and hid it," Hilton said.

It had been raining the night of the robbery, and a light snow had fallen around midnight. No one in any of the houses that bordered the churchyard reported seeing anything suspicious. The grave robbers had come in the middle of the night and went straight to Stewart's vault in the pitch dark. Nichols entertained the idea that perhaps Hilton was onto something. Maybe it was an "inside job." He sent for George Hamill.

In the meantime, Inspector Dilks issued a police bulletin.

To All:—The remains of A. T. Stewart were last night stolen from the family vault, St. Mark's Churchyard. The casket was found broken and the body removed. The decomposition of the remains is so offensive that they cannot be concealed.

This is apparent from standing at the opening of the vault this morning; consequently the body cannot be taken across the ferries or placed anywhere above ground without discovery. Cause diligent search to be made in your precinct, as the remains were evidently stolen in hope of reward.

—POLICE BULLETIN, NOVEMBER 7, 1878 BY GEORGE W. DILKS

As Hilton had told Nichols, it was not the first time robbers had tried to steal Stewart's body. On the morning of October 9, 1878, St. Mark's sextons Hamill and Parker discovered that the slab covering Stewart's burial vault had been tampered with during the night. Someone had lifted the slab and dropped it. Hamill and Parker found the slab laying upright, one end stuck in the grass as if it had been suddenly dropped. When informed of the attempt, Hilton examined the vault and, after inspecting the churchyard, discovered clay similar to the kind found on the gate leading out of the churchyard onto Eleventh Avenue. Hilton surmised that the thieves had somehow been thwarted in their attempt and escaped over the gate. He immediately ordered new locks installed on all the gates. As he had informed Commissioner Nichols, he hired a night watchman to stand guard over the vault. Hilton had taken great pains to instruct Hamill not to reveal to the night watchman the identity of whose vault he was guarding. He also instructed Hamill and Parker to tell no one about the attempted robbery. Hilton left Hamill explicit instructions to keep the watchman on until near the end of the month, but Hamill discharged the watchman nearly a week early claiming that there was no further need to stand guard since no further robbery attempts had been made and that he and Sexton Parker would take turns checking on the vault.

THE GHOUL'S FIRST ATTEMPT

On the morning of Oct. 9 the sexton of St. Mark's, George W. Hamill, and his assistant, Francis Parker, discovered that the Stewart slab had been tampered with during the preceding night. Somebody had lifted it from its bed in the grass and had evidently let it drop in a hurry, as one end of it lay upraised on the grass and the other was sunk down into the soil. There seems to be no doubt, in the light of yesterday's discoveries, that an attempt was then made to steal the body, and that the robbers were frightened away just as they had got fairly to work.

—*New York Times*
November 8, 1878

According to testimony provided to the police by Hamill and Parker, they had been in the habit of opening the churchyard grounds at 8 a.m., and each would spend part of their day on duty at the church or patrolling the grounds. Neither Hamill nor Parker reported seeing anyone suspicious in or around the churchyard the previous day. At dusk, the police were informed, the gates to the churchyard were locked and both sextons went home.

Three police foot patrols passed the churchyard the night of the grave robbery. They were regularly scheduled patrols, and no one reported seeing anything out of the ordinary that night. One patrol covered Fourteenth Street to Houston. Another went along East Tenth and Stuyvesant Streets. And the third patrol covered East Eleventh Street, from Avenue B to Fourth Avenue. If there was anything to be seen, it was assumed one of the patrols would have seen it.

The shift for the patrols ran from 6 p.m. until midnight and from midnight until 6 a.m. Police officers Maurice Reed, John Leddy, Henry Buckers, and Daniel McInerney were on duty the night of the robbery and, when questioned by their supervisors, said they saw nothing suspicious the night before. St. Mark's was surrounded by rows of large and well-appointed homes, and almost none of the residents reported seeing anything strange the night before, with one exception. Dr. William Rausch, a dentist whose home was on the corner of Tenth Street and Second Avenue, told the police that he returned home around midnight the night before. It was a stormy night with rain and sleet. He told the police that he rushed from his carriage to his doorstep, where he fumbled with the keys for his front door. He said that despite the darkness and the nature of the weather, he happened to notice four or five men shrouded in darkness gathered near the cemetery fence. He could not make out who they were or any of their characteristics since he only saw them briefly. He told the police he was in a hurry to get inside and paid no further attention to the men. Rausch was the only person to come forward with information regarding anything unusual the night before.

Sexton Parker told the police that he had locked the churchyard gates at 4 p.m. the night before and that he returned an hour later. The Rev. Dr. J. H. Rylance, the rector of St. Mark's, performed a quiet marriage ceremony around 9:30 p.m. in the vestry of the church. The service ended at 10 p.m., and Parker locked the vestry and took one last walk through the churchyard on his way to the Stuyvesant Street main entrance. There, he locked the main gate behind him and went home. Nothing at that time had been disturbed in the churchyard. The next morning he opened the churchyard gates as usual and discovered the gruesome sight.

———— ·••··• ————

Police Commissioner Nichols commandeered a contingency of police officers and detectives, along with Judge Hilton and the city coroner, and converged on the churchyard. Every inch of the grounds was searched. Along with the bit of rope and newspaper discovered previously, the police turned up a small galvanized shovel that the robbers had used to do their dirty work and a small lantern.

The robbers had five coffins from which to choose Knowing that Stewart's coffin was the newest, the robbers went straight to it. In their haste they had stepped on one of the older coffins, crushing it and exposing its contents of bones. Since it had been Stewart's expressed wish that nothing of value be buried with him, there were no salable items inside the coffin. The handles of the casket and paneling were made of inexpensive gilded metal. The inscription plate, which was inside the casket, was made of solid silver, and it had been taken.

The police surmised that the robbers had used a large waterproof bag to transport Stewart's remains. According to the coroner, although Stewart's body was not embalmed, it would have remained in a preserved state until it was exposed to air. It then would have begun to liquefy, producing a putrid smell. The smell still permeated the vault as the police inspected it the next morning.

> The Police say that burglars are very superstitious and that not one in a thousand can be induced to enter a graveyard at night. The nerve displayed by the robbers of Mr. Stewart's grave accordingly surprises and puzzles them, but not half so much as their ability to endure the dreadful stench which they must have encountered. This was so horrible yesterday morning as to sicken strong men standing in the open air near the mouth of the vault.
>
> —*New York Times*
> November 8, 1878

The police were at a loss to explain how the robbers carried off the liquefied, putrid-smelling body of Stewart without attracting any attention. There were no footprints despite the rain-drenched grounds, and there were no clues as to where the robbers left the churchyard. Climbing over the iron spiked fence seemed doubtful. The locks on the various gates leading in and out of the churchyard showed no evidence of tampering.

If the police were stymied in determining how the robbers pulled off their dirty deed, they had their theory as to why. The robbers, they believed, hoped to get a ransom for the return of the body. According to the coroner, Stewart's remains could be hidden away anywhere for any period of time, concealed in an unobtrusive airtight box until the robbers were ready to exchange the remains for money.

Although Judge Hilton and his partner William Libbey had openly stated that they would not pay any ransom, the robbers might have been counting on Cornelia Stewart to acquiesce. Mrs. Stewart, it had been reported, was intent on building a magnificent mausoleum in Garden City where she intended to place her husband's remains. If anyone might pay a handsome ransom for the return of the Stewart bones, she would.

Despite the lack of clues, the police boasted that the investigation would be brief and that the culprits would be apprehended shortly. According to the police, it would be difficult to move the body in its condition without arousing suspicion. They intended to track down the criminals, perhaps by following the stinking trail left by Stewart's rotting corpse. Concealing the bones was one thing. Hiding the smell, even if the thieves had an "airtight" box, was another thing entirely.

As the investigation continued, tiny bits of information began to surface, propelled perhaps by the reward that Judge Hilton offered in the newspapers.

$25,000 REWARD!—Whereas, in the early morning of Nov. 7, 1878, the vault of the late Alexander T. Stewart, in St. Mark's Churchyard, in this city, was broken into, and his remains removed from there, the above reward is offered by direction of Mrs. A. T. Stewart, and will be paid for the return of the body and information which will convict the parties who were engaged in the outrage. Or a liberal reward will be paid for information which will lead to either of these results.

—Judge Henry Hilton,

—*New York Times*

November 9, 1878

An unidentified man then came forward to report seeing a covered, two-horse carriage near the church entrance that evening. The carriage was parked beneath a lighted street lamp, and the witness hadn't initially noticed anything significant about it. As the news reports began coming out, the witness decided to report it to the police.

Another witness reported to the police that he observed several men carrying a long box or trunk up Ninth Street around 2:30 a.m. the morning of the robbery. He told the police that all the men carrying the box were wearing topcoats with capes and sporting top hats or derbies. The witness merely passed off the incident as some drunken party engaged in harmless shenanigans, until he read about the robbery.

There were gas-lit street lamps on each corner of the main streets that bounded St. Mark's, which meant the area would have been fairly well-lighted, and yet no one saw anything of the robbery itself. Slowly, the police began to patch together a scenario for the grave robbery. Since none of the locks on the churchyard gates had been tampered with, the police believed that the robbers must have had a key to unlock the gates. Where they might have come by such a key was anyone's guess, but the supposition lent credence to Hilton's initial belief that it was an inside job, with one or both of the St. Mark's sextons involved. Only the sextons would have had keys to the gates. The police also surmised that the robbers must have dug down into the vault lying on their stomachs to avoid being seen. Since there were no headstones or obstructions in the churchyard—simply wide open spaces where anyone could have been seen in the light from the sidewalk gas lamps—it was the only way the robbers could have dug into the vault without being detected. Also, the small galvanized shovel that had been left behind was too small to have been used by a man standing up. It was not the typical spade used for grave digging. All together, given what the police surmised, they believed it would have taken the robbers approximately an hour or more to dig into the Stewart vault.

The first day of the investigation, Henry Hilton stayed with the police at the churchyard. As time passed, Hilton grew more impatient. He became indignant when pressed by the police and newspaper reporters about the possibility of paying a ransom for the return of the body. He was further agitated when reporters suggested that the thieves broke into Stewart's vault to steal silver, gold, or even diamonds that might have been buried with Stewart. Hilton bristled at the suggestion.

"Mr. Stewart was buried with the same simplicity that characterized his life," Hilton said.

When questioned by reporters, William Libbey expressed disbelief at the crime.

"I am at a loss to understand it, unless money was at the bottom of it," Libbey said.

He told reporters that he and Judge Hilton were prepared to spend whatever it might take to capture the robbers but "not one cent to them for the return of what they have taken."

Newspapers from the city and around the country had a field day. Page after page of front-page stories were published focusing on everything from the hard facts of the case to the rash of gossip regarding the theft of Stewart's body.

STARTLING
The Late A.T. Stewart's
Remains Stolen
An Astounding Grave Robbery—One of the Most Daring and Ghastly Deeds on Record—Ghouls in the Stewart Vault in St. Mark's Episcopal Church Yard. What the Sexton Discovered this Morning—Amazement of the Police Authorities—The Probable Motive for the Outrage.

—Brooklyn Eagle
November 8, 1878

A NEW YORK SENSATION
A.T. STEWART'S REMAINS
CARRIED OFF
The Casket Cut Open and the
Body Stolen

—Montreal Gazette
November 8, 1878

STEALING THE BODY OF A DEAD MILLIONARE
INTENSE EXCITEMENT IN NEW YORK.
Body Snatchers Invade St. Mark's Church, And Steal the Remains of A.T. Stewart. Unsuccessful Efforts of the Police to Discover Traces of the Robbers.

—Boston Globe
November 8, 1878

"It is an infamous attempt to extort money from me—one of thousands. It was my intention to have the body removed shortly to the crypt preparing for it in the Garden City Cathedral, and I had made my plans accordingly. It is a beautiful crypt, octagonal in shape, inlaid with solid marble, ornamented with statuary and stained plate glass," Hilton told newspaper reporters.

While he was living, Stewart had intended to construct a new church as the centerpiece of Garden City. Following his death, Cornelia Stewart announced plans to build the elaborate cathedral as a memorial to her late husband. Work on the project had begun in 1876 shortly after Stewart's death, and plans called for his crypt to be completed in November 1878. However, because of delays in construction, the crypt would not be completed until the spring of 1879.

According to Police Superintendent George Walling, an unnamed, semi-anarchist newspaper wrote: "There is a sort of grim justice in it, and the very irony of greed, that this cruel, avaricious, hard-hearted man, who oppressed his employees, ruined his creditors and drove his poorer competitors to bankruptcy should now have his flesh drop off and his bones rattled in a thieves' bag, while the millions he earned are enjoyed by others."

The police were able to identify where the robbers purchased the shovel they had left behind. Detectives traced the shovel's origins to

Seymour's Hardware store located at the intersection of Chatham, Broadway, Division, and Cathedral Streets, a mere stone's throw from the churchyard. The salesman at Seymour's did not know who the man was who bought the shovel and couldn't recall any distinguishing features. He did inform the police that the man returned a short time later and purchased a small lantern. It was the same lantern that the grave robbers had left at the scene of the crime.

Despite this, the investigation remained at a standstill, even with the number of police officers and detectives assigned to the case. According to the *New York Times*, the theft of Stewart's body was the first case of body snatching that had ever come to the attention of the authorities within the borders of New York City. According to a *Times* report, "It is remarked as exceedingly strange that the first case of such a nature should be not only extraordinary in its details, but should have for its subject a man among the most extraordinary that ever lived in the country."

It was no secret that Judge Hilton suspected one or both of the St. Mark's sextons, Hamill and Parker, of being involved in the crime. It seemed logical since only four people knew the location of Stewart's underground vault—he, Libbey, Hamill, and Parker. Hamill seemed the more likely culprit as far as Hilton was concerned. Hamill not only knew the location of Stewart's grave, but he had also discharged the night watchman Hilton had hired without notifying Hilton. And, if the robbers had a key to the churchyard gates, as the police suspected, then Hamill must have been the one to give it to them. Who else would? Hilton remained insistent that Hamill or Parker were somehow involved, if not directly in the gruesome act of stealing the body, then as accomplices, providing the robbers with information and keys.

The Rev. Dr. Rylance, rector of St. Mark's, stood steadfastly behind the sextons. Rylance pleaded directly to Hilton concerning Hamill's and Parker's complicity in the robbery.

"So honorable, Judge Hilton, has Mr. Hamill been in carrying out your instructions of secrecy, that when he asked me some time ago for my gate keys so that he could have them readjusted, he did not tell me why that readjustment was necessary and I did not know until this day," Rylance told Hilton.

"Doctor, you know me to be blunt and to the point," Hilton said. "You always know where to find me. It is strange. I do not believe that any person living knew how to find the entrance to that vault so accurately except the sexton and his deputy. And unless the knowledge came from them in some way I cannot imagine how it was obtained. Whether they gave it or whether it was ingeniously drawn from them you can judge for yourself. ..."

Rylance suggested that the robbers had been planning the theft for a long time and had probably marked the grave at the very beginning when Stewart was buried two years previously. They had only been waiting for the right moment to strike. Besides Rylance, the entire congregation of St. Mark's stood behind the sextons and was openly offended by Hilton's suggestion.

Seventy-five-year-old Cornelia Stewart had been ill for some time prior to the robbery of her husband's body. The news of the theft overwhelmed her with grief, and she took to her bed, where her physician and several trusted servants tended to her. Those closest to her feared that the news of the robbery would kill the frail old woman, but she hung on. The responsibility of breaking the news to her fell upon Hilton's shoulders.

Hilton was forced to inform Cornelia when reporters converged on the Stewart mansion and later newsboys hawking the latest editions carrying the story lined up in front of the Stewart home. He knew she would want to know what was going on. She was always interested in current events and stayed abreast of all the latest news. Hilton preferred that she hear it from him rather than anyone else or read it on the front page of the newspapers.

According to newspaper accounts, Mrs. Stewart "bore the shock with wonderful heroism, but it proved at length too great a strain on her weakened strength and she sank perceptibly under the blow."

Hilton assured her that he was absolutely certain of recovering the stolen remains and of having the guilty parties in custody within a short time. It was another one of Henry Hilton's empty promises.

THE BEST DETECTIVE TALENT

In which the theft of A. T. Stewart's remains causes a national media sensation and expends the resources of the entire New York City Police Department, as well as private detectives hired by Henry Hilton. While several suspects are apprehended and then released, new clues in the case are uncovered and followed but only lead to a series of dead-ends. Hilton receives hundreds of letters from unnamed sources claiming to be in possession of the body and demanding ransom payment for its return.

Given the state of A. T. Stewart's decaying corpse, reporters asked Henry Hilton if he could, beyond a shadow of a doubt, recognize the remains of his late friend if they were returned. He told reporters that it would be absolutely impossible for anyone to deceive him. According to Hilton, he had two casts of Mr. Stewart's head taken before he was buried and dental records could be used to verify the identity. The dental records Hilton spoke of were a far cry from the intricate records maintained today. What Hilton was referring to was the particular operations Stewart had done on his teeth that the dentist who had performed them could easily identify.

Michael Bruton was the night watchman hired by Hilton to watch the grave following the first theft attempt back in October. Bruton was questioned by the police and explained that he had been hired on or about October 7 or 8 that Sexton Hamill did not point out any particular place in the churchyard that he was supposed to guard, and that Hamill didn't say anything to him about the attempted grave robbery. His orders were to watch over the cemetery and to keep people out after the churchyard was closed. If he came across anyone in the yard after dark, he was ordered to throw the person out himself. Bruton explained that he inspected the cemetery at half-hour intervals and that he felt uneasy about his duties. He had no reason other than the location of the job for feeling uneasy. The idea that someone would try to rob a grave never crossed his mind, he said. He checked all the gates every time he made his rounds and never found them unlocked. He never encountered anyone in, or trying to get in, the churchyard after it was closed, and his entire employment was uneventful. He told the police he was employed for about a month and had only been recently discharged. Bruton said he was never told why he was hired or why he was let go. The police found nothing suspicious about Bruton's testimony, and he was not considered a person of interest in the case.

----·•··•·----

Police detectives reported that the bottom of Stewart's casket was covered with a foul-smelling slime, thought to be remnants of Stewart's decomposing body. The slime was also on the cover of the casket, where police surmised that the robbers had placed the body before transferring it to some type of rubber or sealed bag to transport it.

Hilton, still certain that Hamill and Parker were somehow involved, asked the police to scour all the church buildings. Since no trace of the body had been found in the churchyard, Hilton suspected that whoever stole it might be hiding the remains somewhere inside the church or its adjacent buildings. Police officers and detectives thoroughly examined the church from the cellar to the steeple, and not a single sign of the remains was discovered.

G.W. Dilks, Acting Superintendent:

Sir: Under orders received from you, we, the undersigned, proceeded to St. Mark's Church and burying grounds, corner of Stuyvesant-place and Second-avenue, for the purpose of making a thorough search of the building and grounds. We examined the grounds carefully and found no trace of their having been disturbed. We also examined two receiving vaults, one containing two and the other thirteen bodies. We then searched the entire basement, tower and several other places

in the building without obtaining any evidence of the where-
abouts of A.T. Stewart. Respectfully submitted.

    F.F. ADAMS
    GEORGE G. RADFORD
    THOMAS FERRIS
    GEORGE H. DILKS

—LETTER SUBMITTED TO SUPERINTENDENT OF POLICE ON NOVEMBER 8, 1878

Police Captain Henry McCullagh stumbled on what he thought was a break in the Stewart case when he interviewed twenty-two-year-old George Brown. Brown worked at a saloon on Third Avenue and claimed that he had been returning home around 2:15 a.m. the morning of the grave robbery when he ran into a group of six men carrying a wooden box on their shoulders. The men were dressed in long dark coats and tall silk top hats. According to Brown, the men were joking and laughing among themselves and when they saw him, they asked if he wanted to give them a hand. McCullagh discounted the absurd story. Those involved in such a ghastly deed would have taken great pains to conceal their activity and would not have broadcast it by hauling around what appeared to be a wooden casket on their shoulders and marching down the street. Brown's information was disregarded as the police continued their search for the culprits and the missing corpse.

The question of how the grave robbers were able to locate Stewart's vault in the dark during a rainstorm without any distinguishing marker remained a mystery to the police. Some, like Hilton, continued to believe it was an inside job with either Hamill or Parker or both providing the robbers with the information and a set of keys to unlock the churchyard gate. Although the police initially considered the idea, it was ultimately dismissed. There was no hard evidence to link either of the sextons to the crime, and the nature of their characters had been wholly supported by the Rev. Dr. Rylance, rector of St. Mark's, and nearly all the members of the church.

Besides that, the police slowly began to uncover evidence that supported another theory, thanks in no small part to the reporting of the *New York Times*. An unnamed enterprising *New York Times* reporter pointed out to the police and readers alike that "an examination of the fence shows that at the extreme western end there is a spot which can be scaled with the greatest ease."

According to a front-page article in the November 9 *Times*, "Outside there are two low railings, either extremely convenient for stepping on, and the iron balcony of the adjoining house and the large latticed iron end-post of the fence afford just what is needed in the way of support in getting in or out."

The next day, police investigators began a further examination of the western end of the churchyard and soon enough uncovered evidence showing the way the grave robbers had entered and fled the crime scene.

The detectives say that on Thursday morning they found a blue penciled letter 'B' on one of the iron fence posts on the Second-avenue side and two posters bearing the name 'Augustus Sebell' crossed on a post on the Eleventh-street side. These have since been removed, but the detectives say that by drawing imaginary lines from the two marked posts to two opposite trees the spot where the lines cross would be directly over the hole that was dug.

—*New York Times*
November 9, 1878

The police soon discounted the theory that the robbers must have had a set of keys to unlock the churchyard gates. Based on the *New York Times* story the previous day, an examination of the iron fence on the western end of the churchyard confirmed the theory that there were several places along the far western end where the iron fence surrounding the yard could have been easily scaled. Outside the spots were two low railings that could have been used to climb on and a conveniently located iron balcony nearby that could have helped the robbers enter and exit.

Although the police had scoured the churchyard looking for clues, finding nothing, upon reexamination they discovered two large, greasy, dark stains near the western gate that emitted a nauseating smell—the same odor that permeated the Stewart vault. Similar greasy, foul-smelling stains were discovered on the sidewalk and street outside the gate leading from the churchyard. The police surmised that the liquefying body of Stewart caused the stains as it was being carried away. Bloodhounds were brought in to follow the stench. The trail led past the church to the western gate and out onto the street. Mud was found caked on several of the iron fence braces and on several spikes at the top of the fence, leading the police to believe that the robbers had hauled Stewart's body up and over the fence at that exact spot. They followed the trail of stains up East Tenth Street to the courtyard of a nearby boardinghouse. There in the courtyard the stains disappeared. The police believed that in this courtyard the body of A. T. Stewart was loaded into the back of a wagon or carriage and spirited away under the cloak of darkness.

———

The boardinghouse stood back from the sidewalk. The iron fence surrounding the churchyard ran back toward it. At one particular point along the fence, there was a tree with low-hanging limbs. One limb forked out over the fence and into the street, making it a convenient stepping stone for the robbers to scale the fence in and out. More importantly, the police discovered an iron balcony that ran along the length of the boardinghouse at 129 East Tenth Street. According to the police, the low iron fence at the western side of the churchyard along Tenth Street, the forked tree limb leading over the fence, and the adjacent iron balcony on the boardinghouse gave the grave robbers perfect access in and out of St. Mark's.

The courtyard of the boardinghouse was hidden from the road, giving the robbers concealment from prying eyes to carry out their ghoulish business. And there was more. The police also discovered several small patches of clay caked on the fork of the tree, indicating that someone had climbed onto it. Further examination revealed that the balcony on the boardinghouse was also caked with similar mud, showing a distinct mark of a boot heel in it. Several iron spikes on top of the fence had a greasy, foul-smelling substance stuck to them. It became evident to the police that the robbers had entered the church-yard using the western side of the fence, done their business, and exited with Stewart's remains using the same location. The existence of the stains led the police to discount the theory that the robbers had placed Stewart's remains in a rubber or airtight bag since neither would have allowed the substance to leak or leave behind such a foul-smelling trail. The police began to surmise that the robbers carried the remains out in a blanket or cloth and that they had a box or casket waiting for them in the wagon or carriage parked in the boardinghouse courtyard. There the robbers transferred the body to some airtight con-tainer for transportation and subsequent storage.

No one could have been more ecstatic over the new developments than Sexton George Hamill, who maintained that the new evidence cleared him of any complicity in the case.

THE GRAVE DESECRATORS
TRACING THE ROBBERS OF MR. STEWART'S GRAVE
The Manner Of Their Entrance To And Exit From The Yard—Route Taken In Removing The Body—The Police Working On Several Clues— The Suspicions Against The Sexton

Late on Friday afternoon Capt. McCullagh, of the Seventeenth Precinct, strolled over to St. Mark's church-yard and began another careful examination of the premises. ... The Captain noticed on the flags directly behind the two screens large stains, looking at first glance like dried tobacco spittle, but proving on closer examination to be of a greasy nature. He knelt down and smelled them. They gave out a sickening odor. He took out his penknife and scraped the spot, and then smelled the scrapings.

He immediately became sick to the stomach. ... The officials all bent down and smelled of these spots. The odor was horrible and satisfied them that the stains had been caused by oozings from the body through some kind of cloth. On the side of the western screen above the two blotches were many clayey marks, as though someone had wiped his soiled fingers on it in a downward direction. ... In yesterday's TIMES it was pointed out that at the extreme westerly corner of the cemetery the fence might be readily scaled with the assistance of a forked tree, the balcony of the adjacent house and the top of the courtyard railing. The Police officials went there and saw in an instant that the TIMES' suggestion was a correct one. The house, which is No. 129 East tenth-street, and is a boarding house kept by a Miss Newton, stands back several feet from the sidewalk and the cemetery fence runs back toward it being joined to its side wall at the top by a strip of iron let in to the bricks.

—*New York Times*
November 10, 1878

When news of the police findings hit the front pages of New York City's newspapers, numerous stories about wagons being seen in the vicinity of the churchyard on the night of the robbery began to flood into police headquarters. One witness reported seeing a rickety open wagon along Eleventh Street near the cemetery fence around 11 p.m. According to the witness, the single horse drawing the wagon appeared to be in a heated condition, steaming with sweat. He told the police that he saw no one around the horse and wagon but that it stayed parked at the rear of the church unattended for the entire time it took him to walk home that evening.

Another unidentified man reported to the police that he saw a black painted wagon parked along Eleventh Street near the rear of the church around 3 a.m. on Thursday, the morning after the grave robbery reportedly took place. He too reported seeing no one in the immediate vicinity of the dark wagon but made no mention of the condition of the single horse that was attached to it.

A third report stated that a covered wagon, with side gates similar to those on delivery wagons, was seen parked on Stuyvesant Street near the front of the church. Although the reported wagon sightings tied into the theory of how Stewart's body had been spirited away, the police were no closer to identifying the robbers than they had been before.

Other curious incidents were also reported to the police. A well-dressed gentleman asked for a meeting with Police Superintendent George Walling claiming that foreign phrenologists had stolen the body so that they could dissect Stewart's brain for the purpose of obtaining information about how Stewart became such a wealthy man. The secrets to his success, the gentleman maintained, were hidden deep within Stewart's brain. He said that the body had been shipped overseas on a cargo ship and told Walling that if he wanted to locate it, he should wire overseas to several ports to have the cargoes of ships searched on arrival. Walling found the man's claim absurd and politely refused the meeting request. When the gentleman became angry at Walling's refusal, the superintendent had him escorted from police headquarters.

Captain Thomas Byrnes of the Fifteenth Precinct brought a boy into police headquarters for questioning, claiming that the boy had evidence that would break the case wide open. Byrnes, who had a penchant for generating publicity for himself, also told newspaper reporters that the boy's testimony would prove to be important in solving the case. When asked by the press what the boy had to say, Byrnes refused to divulge the information, claiming that revealing the boy's testimony might jeopardize the ongoing investigation.

Walling and Commissioner Nichols told reporters that the entire police department was working on the case and that they hoped to be able to apprehend the criminals shortly. They were both noncommittal on what evidence they had gathered that would prompt them to make their claim. Like Captain Byrnes, they suggested that divulging any information might harm the investigation.

What was clear was that the police had begun to focus their investigation on the boardinghouse courtyard at 129 East Tenth

Street. Detectives questioned Erasmus Garnsey and his wif at the boardinghouse. They occupied the bedroom clos courtyard. Garnsey reported that sometime between 1 and Thursday morning, he and his wife were both awakened by a loud thud that sounded as if a heavy body had fallen against their window shutters. According to Garnsey, immediately after they heard the noise, they heard a man's voice say, "Come. It's about time for us to be out of here."

Garnsey said he paid no attention to it thinking it was simply some young lovers in a secret early morning rendezvous.

The police questioned Mary Newton, the owner of the boardinghouse, who reported that her sister and brother-in-law, who lived at the house, came home around 10:30 on Wednesday night and didn't report seeing anything unusual about the church, churchyard, or along the street.

The greasy, foul-smelling droplets that had been left behind at the crime scene were analyzed and were identified as decomposing flesh. The stains clearly marked the trail. The grave robbers carried Stewart's rotting remains from St. Mark's Churchyard over the iron fence on the far western end of the cemetery, across East Tenth Street and into the boardinghouse courtyard, where they placed it in a waiting wagon to transport it.

The New York Herald was quick to dispute the police theory about the stains. According to a Herald reporter, the stains more likely came from the chemical Allekton, a liquid used to preserve decomposing bodies. The chemical, which had previously been written about in the Herald, was a new discovery being sold to undertakers by the company of Middleton and Warner, located on Bond Street. Detectives, following up on the Herald's lead, questioned C. N. Middleton, one of the business's owners, who told the police that in October 1878, around the time of the first attempted grave robbery at St. Mark's, an unidentified man came to his Bond Street address asking to buy a supply of Allekton and all the apparatus needed to inject it into a

body. Since he only sold the new chemical to professional undertakers and since the man could not produce any professional credentials,
he refused to sell him the body preservative. According to Middleton,
the man left and never returned to his business again.

After reading about the grave robbery, Middleton immediately
contacted Judge Hilton and William Libbey, informing them of
the incident and suggesting that the man who had tried to buy the
Allekton might somehow be mixed up in the robbery. Middleton
agreed to go to police headquarters and look at the police department's "rogue's gallery"—a collection of photographs of known
criminals—to see if he could identify the man who came in to buy
the chemical. Middleton carefully went through all the photographs
and finally identified twenty-two-year-old Thomas McCarty, a petty
criminal known for being a pickpocket. More damning than that,
when the police showed the photograph of McCarty to the clerk
at Seymour's Hardware, where the police had traced the shovel
and lantern found at the crime scene, the store clerk also identified
McCarty as the man who purchased both items. McCarty was picked
up for questioning, and after a lengthy interrogation, the police concluded that he knew nothing about the case and that Middleton and
the hardware store clerk had been mistaken in their identification.
McCarty, as far as the police were concerned, was a simple-minded
petty thief and nothing more.

Perhaps angered by the police department's refusal to pursue the
two sextons or with their lack of success in uncovering any leads,
Hilton hired his own Pinkerton private detectives to conduct an investigation. He didn't bother to consult with the police about the Pinkertons' findings. Hilton had his private detectives follow up on every
lead, no matter how absurd. They too remained stymied.

Letters began to pour into Hilton's office ranging from missives penned
by spiritualists who claimed to have been in touch with the ghost of A.
T. Stewart and knew the whereabouts of the missing remains, to angry
letters saying that Stewart got what he deserved. Some claimed the

"Jews" had committed the crime as retribution for Hilton's prejudice against them.

An anonymous letter sent from Rutland, Vermont, on November 13, 1878, to police headquarters stated: "In one hour I will be in Canada with A.T. Stewart's body. A woman has his remains."

The letter was composed from letters and words cut from newspapers.

Another message sent directly to Judge Hilton on November 9, 1878, stated:

Proper and honorable negotiations will be made with yourself and the widow of the late A.T. Stewart, Esq., and in the meantime, let me assure you that the remains of this gentleman are safe beyond the possibility of detection and have been for some time. We will require the most substantial reward before you can hope to obtain the return of the body. ... To be brief, when a reward of $1,000,000 shall be paid and perfect immunity from prosecution be most thoroughly guaranteed, then, and not till then, shall we for the instant entertain any idea of opening negotiations with yourself or any of the friends of the deceased.

The letter was signed by "Oswald Baxter."

Another letter dated November 8, 1878, written decidedly in the handwriting of a woman, was sent directly to Mrs. Stewart (although intercepted by Hilton).

Mrs. Cornelia Stewart:

Dear Madam: Your terms are unsatisfactory. Whenever you wish to make the sum $100,000, you will place a personal in the Herald *as follows:*

Agreed to —S.H.H.C.

Until then you will not hear again from us.

The letter was unsigned.

Another letter complete with a hand-drawn skull and crossbones and the words DEATH written in huge letters was addressed to Mrs. A. T. Stewart, Judge Hilton, and Mr. Libbey. The letter stated: "If this reward is not given in 5 days it shall be lost" and was signed SAM, Pres., WILL, Vice-Pres., MICH, Tres. And CONNERS, Sec.

Yet another among the glut of missives sent to Hilton stated: "Dear Sir: If you will promise not to lock me up, and give me $10,000, I will tell you where the body and robbers of the late A.T. Stewart is." It was signed: ONE OF THE ROBBERS. At the end of the letter, the author wrote: "This is private."

A letter sent to the *New York Herald* from a source identifying itself as "A Company" advised: "If the executors of the late A. T. Stewart will donate $500,000 for some needed public charity in the city of New York the whereabouts of his remains will be immediately divulged and not one penny will be asked for the expense we have incurred."

A brief, small, enigmatic ad appearing in the *Herald* stated: "NICHOLS & HILTON.—CALL OFF BLOODHOUNDS and discipline the Police. P. X. Y-$100,000.00."

In yet another unsigned letter sent to Judge Hilton, the author advised: "Privately offer the Roman Catholic Bishop from $1,000 to $5,000 for the return of A.T. Stewart's body and I think it will be returned without the thieves being rewarded for their labors."

The police and Hilton considered none of the letters to be reliable, or, in fact, the true ransom note for which they had been waiting. Still, the correspondences flooded into the hands of the authorities, Hilton, and newspapers from places as far away as Canada and London, England.

Anything more depraved in the way of journalism than the behavior of the press during the past few days on the subject of the Stewart grave-robbery it would be difficult to conceive. The facts which have been published do not concern the public in any way. The thieves, having made away with the body, appear to have opened negotiations, as everybody knew they would do, with the Stewart family, through 'counsel,' and, the family having refused their terms, the matter was dropped. Is this any reason why we should now have column after column of the body-snatchers' letters, the replies of their 'counsel' through the Herald *'Personal' column, accompanied by details as to the condition of the corpse, followed by an acrimonious controversy as to whether Judge Hilton did or did not deceive Mrs. Stewart about the return of her husband's body, and persuade her that it had been returned while it had not? Some of the newspapers, while publishing all the details of the negotiations, dwell feelingly on the agony that the whole affair must have caused Mrs. Stewart, and the consequent heartless brutality of the thieves. What sort of work is this.*

—Nation, July–December, 1879

It appeared to most that the Stewart case was at a standstill, but then suddenly, five days after the grave robbery and despite an endless stream of dead-ends, the *New York Times* erroneously reported on November 12, 1878, that the hiding place of Stewart's remains had been discovered. Where the body was, how it arrived there, and who stole it remained a mystery, and neither the police nor Judge Hilton would provide any answers.

Superintendent Walling released no new information to reporters. With the news of Stewart's body being located, police officials maintained that the culprits would now be in a race to turn state's evidence to avoid prosecution.

Hilton said, "I have nothing to say," when asked by reporters if indeed Stewart's body had been located.

The unfounded and sensational rumors abounded. According to the police, they had followed up on more than 150 leads, all of them leading nowhere. It had been rumored that Stewart's body had been found in Newark, New Jersey, in the home of a man named J. B. Hayes. An investigation by Newark police turned up nothing.

SEEKING FOR THE GHOULS.
MR. STEWART'S BODY LIKELY TO BE RECOVERED
Indications That The Robbers Have Been Traced—Extreme Reticence On The Part Of The Police—A Promising Trail Struck—An Explanation By The Sexton

Yesterday was a day of mysteries in the Stewart body-snatching case. The surface indications were all corroborative of the information drawn from Judge Hilton's manner and language on Sunday night that the hiding place of the body had been discovered. The Police were busier than ever and went briskly about with countenances aglow with suppressed exultation. Judge Hilton was in unusually good spirits all day.

—*New York Times*
November 12, 1878

In a development that may or may not have been a ploy to get the robbers to tip their hand to authorities, it was reported that Cornelia Stewart had become bedridden because of the shocking news of the theft of her husband's body and that her health was failing rapidly. According to the *New York Times*, "Should she die, the probabilities are, it is said, that Judge Hilton will immediately withdraw his offered reward, and refuse to entertain any propositions for the return of the body except in connection with the arrest and conviction of the perpetrators."

It was clear to most that the twenty-five thousand-dollar reward initially offered by Hilton had been done to appease Mrs. Stewart and was not a reflection of his own sentiments. In the five days since the robbery, no credible ransom note had been sent to either Hilton or the police.

The reports on November 12, 1878, that the police had located Stewart's body were short-lived. In the next day's edition of the *New*

York Times, Captain McCullagh said that, despite all the investigative work done on the case, the police "had not succeeded in tracing the body beyond the curbstone of 129 East Tenth-street."

Without any resolution in the case, the New York City Police Department came under fire from publications inside and outside the city. An editorial in the New York *Evening Telegram* called the police good at locating crimes but not criminals. It referred to the police as "dogberries" and hailed the force as a collection of poorly educated incompetents. The *New York Evening Express* wrote: "That the body of the merchant millionaire should have been carried away from a teeming center in this populous city set every soul agog." It urged the police to solve the case quickly to put the city's mind at ease. The *Herald* berated the authorities for moving too slowly on the case. An editorial in the *Chicago Tribune* called the police investigation incompetent and the work of the grave robbers a radical political trend aimed at striking back at the wealthy with its roots in the principles of Communism. The *Tribune* editorial called on citizens to resort to vigilantism if the police were unable to protect them from these radicalized grave robbers.

Despite the criticism from the papers, in public Judge Hilton steadfastly maintained his faith in the police investigation.

I have the best detective talent of all kinds that I could find engaged to assist me, but I am really depending largely on the regular Police force. I have every reason for the greatest faith and confidence in the earnestness and zeal of their efforts. They could not possibly do more than they have done and I am entirely satisfied with them.

—Judge Henry Hilton,
—*New York Times*
November 14, 1878

THE SEARCH CONTINUES

In which the motive for the theft continues to elude the police while clues suggest it is the handiwork of professional grave robbers, most notably George Christian, a notorious "resurrectionist" who steals bodies for medical research. Yet, neither Christian nor the flood of mysterious letters claiming to know the location of Stewart's body lead the police to the culprits. Stewart's body remains missing.

Despite the endless number of dead-ends, the New York police continued their investigation into the A. T. Stewart grave robbery, pursuing every possible lead. They questioned hundreds of people, traveling across the city from one end to the other and beyond. The usual known suspects—criminals of every ilk—were rounded up, brought to police headquarters on Mulberry Street, questioned, and released. Despite their dedication, the police remained stymied by the theft.

The grave robbery took precedent over every case on the police dockets, and hundreds of officers and detectives were assigned to it. No stone would be left unturned according to Police Superintendent George Walling. Henry Hilton's twenty-five-thousand-dollar reward had produced nothing except one outlandish lead after another.

———◆·•·◆———

"You will have to excuse me. I have made a solemn vow to Inspector William Murray not to open my mouth to representatives of the press until this case is concluded," Hilton told reporters in late December.

The reporters put to him in detail various points of fresh information they had gleaned and asked him whether they were true.

"Do you know what you are asking me?" Judge Hilton queried. "You say that all the hounds are on the scent, and ask whether they will catch the fox? You cannot expect me to answer?"

"But suppose they fail to catch the fox?" one reporter suggested.

"What!" Hilton exclaimed. "With the hounds on the scent and the fox in sight, and they near him, and not catch him? There is no such word as fail in this case."

It was, by all accounts, the single biggest police investigation in the city's history. Law enforcement watched all the ferries and railroad stations, stopping and questioning every suspicious-looking character. Police officers and newspaper reporters staked out St. Mark's Churchyard. Throngs of curiosity seekers riveted with macabre fascination flooded to the robbery site. The police tried as best they could to keep the gawkers at bay, fearing they might disturb some evidence or worse, stumble on some clue the police had overlooked.

Hilton increased the number of Pinkerton agents he hired and spent much of his time in and out of police headquarters. He relied heavily on the advice of his son-in-law, Horace Russell, who was a New York City assistant district attorney. Together, they kept a constant vigil at police headquarters, and evenings were spent with trusted advisors and Pinkerton detectives, sometimes police detectives, going over the investigation in an attempt to pinpoint any minute detail they might have missed.

Without any real information to go on, newspaper reporters resorted to publishing speculation and innuendos. Neither the police department nor Henry Hilton would divulge any details about the investigation, determined not to leak anything to the press that would hinder their apprehension of the ghouls. Superintendent Walling grew especially impatient with newspaper reporters hounding his officers and even more so with papers publishing stories that had no basis in reality. He firmly believed that the entire investigation would benefit if his department was able to work without the press looking over its shoulders.

When reporters were unable to get any information from the police department—Walling had given strict orders to his men to maintain a code of silence—they sought out Judge Hilton, who had been known in the past as a good source of candid information, but they were frustrated too by Hilton's reluctance to talk.

Because of the sensitive nature of the case and because of A. T. Stewart's prominence, the police department relied on direction from Hilton. The department did not want to overstep its bounds or undercut Hilton's desires in the case. Walling's general silence to reporters stemmed from his well-founded belief that even if the police were able to find those responsible, proving that the suspects did it would be difficult. On one occasion, Walling told reporters, "How could you prove that they went into that graveyard and took the body? Nobody saw them and no jury would convict them without some evidence of their guilt." He was right.

————

Without a verifiable ransom note, a motive for the Stewart grave robbery remained elusive. The police developed several theories, including the idea that the robbery was the ghoulish handiwork of the Washington, D.C., "resurrectionist," Dr. George A. Christian. Christian, who was not a medical doctor, was a government clerk employed in the Surgeon General's Office in Washington.

Newspapers in Washington described Christian as a short man, well under six feet tall, weighing approximately 120 pounds. He had high cheekbones, long, dark hair, and a sallow complexion. His face was highly recognizable to anyone. According to the newspapers, Christian had an annoying habit of rolling his large, dark eyes, and he also had a disfigured mouth; his lips twisted down on the right side, and he spoke out of the left side of his mouth, which gave him the appearance of someone who might have suffered a stroke and whose face had been immobilized on one side. Because of this anomaly, his face was unforgettable.

According to newspaper accounts, he was always stylishly dressed, especially for a government employee. How could he afford such fashionable attire? Reports said that his abundant supply of clothing was stolen from corpses in his other, more lucrative line of business—grave robbing. Christian had been a medical student at Georgetown College, although he never finished. He had shown great promise and was especially adept at dissection. He had been questioned on several occasions while in school about his involvement in robbing graves from

Potter's Field in the District of Columbia and selling the cadavers to the medical school for research. He, of course, denied any involvement in such undertakings. But in point of fact, Christian and four partners, two men and two women, ran a grave-robbing operation out of a small shack where they kept bodies and valuables taken from graveyards. Christian and his colleagues stole bodies to sell to hospitals and doctors across the country for the study of anatomy and research. The bodies were injected with a variety of preservatives, including whiskey; packed into wooden barrels, soaked in whiskey; taken to the Army Medical Museum; and from there shipped to various medical schools and doctors. Christian and his gang made forty to one hundred dollars per body depending on the demand.

Christian's downfall came in 1873, in no small part due to his fondness for the whiskey he used to preserve the stolen bodies. Driving back from one of their grisly deeds, the gang's wagon was stopped by an alert Washington, D.C., police officer, who noticed the vehicle veering from one side of the road to the other. When the officer pulled the wagon over, he found a highly intoxicated Christian at the reins. After charging him with being drunk and disorderly, the officer searched the wagon and found the newly exhumed body of a man concealed in a sack, along with chemicals used to preserve bodies. More damaging was a diary found in Christian's possession in which he had detailed much of the skullduggery he and his gang had undertaken. They were all charged with grave robbing and selling bodies. Christian was dishonorably discharged from his government position, and he was sentenced to one year in jail and a thousand-dollar fine. Because of Christian's diary, excerpts of which were published in the Washington *Evening Star* newspaper, Christian became known as the country's leading "resurrectionist."

January 3d 1873 B. and C. went out and got two cadavers tonight.
April 4th Dr. C. and I went to the Washington Asylum Cemetery
tonight and confiscated two sets of extremities and one head.
—EXCERPTS FROM GEORGE CHRISTIAN'S DIARY, *Evening Star,* WASHINGTON,
D.C., DECEMBER 15, 1873

Body snatching was big business in America during the nineteenth century, and resurrectionists, people engaged in robbing graves for medical research, were kept busy meeting the needs of medical schools throughout the country. According to Suzanne M. Shultz in her book *Body Snatching: The Robbing of Graves for the Education of Physicians in Early Nineteenth Century America,* the term *resurrectionist* came from the belief that a burial ground was a sacred place and that the removal of a body from it was "interference with the plan of Providence and the great Resurrection. Thus resurrectionists and body snatchers became synonymous terms."

> *And my Prentices now will surely come*
> *And carve me bone from bone,*
> *And I who have rifled the dead man's grave*
> *Shall never have rest in my own.*
> *Bury me in lead when I am dead,*
> *My brethren I intreat,*
> *And see the coffin weigh'd I beg*
> *Lest the Plumber should be a cheat.*
> *And let it be solder'd closely down*
> *Strong as strong can be I implore,*
> *And put it in a patent coffin,*
> *That I may rise no more.*
> —"SURGEON'S WARNING," POEM BY ROBERT SOUTHEY, 1799

How George Christian came to be a suspect in the Stewart case was merely a matter of conjecture. There was no real proof he had been involved at all. The Washington, D.C., police surmised that the Stewart grave robbery had to be the handiwork of professional grave robbers because it appeared to be so well planned. Christian had acquired the dubious distinction of being the most professional of all grave robbers. For years the police had tried to connect Christian with the infamous failed attempt to steal President Abraham Lincoln's body in 1876. However, there was never any substantial proof linking him to the deed.

———•◦•◦•———

On the night of November 7, 1876, a gang of counterfeiters, led by "Big Jim" Kinealy, attempted to steal the body of Abraham Lincoln from his tomb at the Oak Ridge Cemetery in Springfield, Illinois. The grave robbers were able to dismantle Lincoln's sarcophagus and pull out the unopened coffin before Secret Service agents surrounded the tomb and scared the ghouls off. Subsequently, a Springfield grand jury indicted Terrance Mullen and Jack Hughes, charging them with the attempted theft. "Big Jim" Kinealy and Chicago teamster Herbert Nelson were arrested as accomplices, but both men were never formally charged. Mullen and Hughes were found guilty and sentenced to a year in Joliet Penitentiary. At no time was George A. Christian ever linked to the case, but since he had been highly successful in this endeavor—that is, until he was arrested—Christian's name was forever associated with high-profile grave-robbing attempts.

According to the Washington, D.C., police, if New York City detectives could locate Christian, they would find Stewart's body. It seemed as likely as any story detectives had heard.

———•◦•◦•———

Since getting out of prison in September 1874, Christian actually had been involved in a series of grave robberies. Just two months after his release, he was arrested for stealing two bodies and trying to ship them to a medical school in Ohio. Christian jumped bail on the charge and did not resurface again until May 1876, when he was arrested on a train heading from Baltimore to Washington, D.C. Although his bail had been revoked, Christian somehow managed to escape from the police again and disappeared.

When news about Stewart's grave robbery hit the newspapers, the police in Washington were certain that Christian was back at work.

GRAVE-ROBBER CHRISTIAN.
HE TURNS UP IN THE STEWART CASE.
Dr. Douglass Of East Fourteenth Street, Positively Identified As The Notorious Washington Resurrectionist— The Body Said To Have Been Found Five Days Ago—A Sketch Of Mr. John J. Clare Of Orange.

The mysterious "Doctor" alluded to in yesterday's TIMES as the alleged chief conspirator and organizer of the robbery of Mr. Stewart's grave was yesterday positively identified as George A. Christian, the notorious Washington resurrection-ist, who was arrested on suspicion of being one of the parties who attempted to break into ex-President Lincoln's tomb. The Boarding house spoken of as his abode previous to the robbery is No. 306 East Fourteenth street and the landlady's name is Campbell. Christian's alias was Dr. George Douglass.

—New York Times
November 21, 1878

According to newspaper accounts, Christian had been positively identified by several guests at Campbell's boardinghouse at 306 East Fourteenth Street in New York City. A dentist, Dr. George Evans, was one of those who reported to the police that Dr. Douglass and George Christian were one and the same. Evans told authorities that, after reading a newspaper description of Christian, he decided that Dr. Douglass fit the description perfectly.

It is a fashionable boarding house in the vicinity of St. Mark's grave-yard. ... A few days previous to Oct. 7, the date of the first attempt on the vault, the man in question, who may be designated as Dr. A—, applied for board, and asked to be shown a comfortable room. He selected a hall bedroom on the fourth floor, fronting southward, and giving a good view of the graveyard. He was decently but not extravagantly attired in a blue flannel suit and had one valise with him. He bargained before engaging the room for the privilege of advertising himself as a physician. He promised that he would do none but legitimate advertising, whereupon the landlady said she had no objection. He paid his board in advance ... the landlady describes Dr. A. as a middle-aged man with a round face, brown curly hair, bright blue eyes, brown silken mustache, white smooth forehead, fine complexion, and a disagreeable looking mouth, the lower jaw being twisted to one side by an accident from a gun the Doctor said. ... He appeared to be very familiar with drugs and chemicals and was continually engaged in arguments with three medical students who were also boarders in the same house about the various known processes for annihilating the odor of decomposed matter and about the embalming of dead bodies and often boasted of his ability to deodorize a human carcass, no matter how long it might have been buried.

—*New York Times*
November 20, 1878

A few days after the robbery, and while Douglass' curious and coincidental disappearance was still fresh in his mind, Dr. Evans came across a printed description of Christian in one of the newspapers. It struck him at once as a perfect pen-picture of Douglass. There were the same rolling eyes, the same peculiar twitch of the left corner of the mouth and the same general appearance all over. The only thing different was in regard to the beard. When Douglass first went to Mrs. Campbell's he wore a full beard. This he afterward had shaved off, except two little whiskers just alongside the ears, and a few days before the robbery these too, disappeared, leaving only the long, silken mustache.

—*New York Times*
November 21, 1878

The dentist, Dr. Evans, became even more convinced that Douglass and Christian were the same person when he learned that Christian had once been a medical student, which explained how Douglass obtained much of the medical knowledge he espoused.

Evans took his information directly to Judge Hilton and not to the police. Hilton informed the dentist that Douglass/Christian was already a suspect in the case and that Hilton was having the notorious resurrectionist followed in the hope he might lead authorities to Stewart's body. Hilton had his Pinkerton detectives bring Evans a photograph of George Christian, which Evans immediately identified as Dr. Douglass. Other boarders at Campbell's identified Christian as well. The elusive George Christian was now a prime suspect in the case, but like every promising lead, this one led nowhere. Despite the authorities' best efforts to shadow him, Christian once again managed to avoid capture. He was gone and with him any chance the police had to question him about his involvement in the Stewart body snatching.

———

From George Christian to the flood of mysterious letters claiming to know where Stewart's body was and who had taken it, the police worked day and night tracking down every lead they could, but the clues always led to the exact same place—a dead-end. Since the theft, so many letters and notes had been sent to the police that it became impossible for authorities to distinguish what was real information and what was not. If the grave robbers even *had* wanted to demand a ransom, there was no way of knowing which of the hundreds of missives came from the real culprits. The ability of the police to identify an authentic lead became a dilemma.

There was one letter that did attract police attention. It came from an enigmatic group calling itself "A Company," no doubt mocking Stewart's own company. The intriguing letter was sent directly to the editors at the *New York Herald*. In it the unnamed authors stated: "If the executors of the late A. T. Stewart will donate $500,000 for some needed public charity in the city of New York the whereabouts of his remains will be immediately divulged and not one penny will be asked for the expense we have incurred."

The authorities reacted to it with some concern. It was well known that Stewart had not been known as a philanthropist and that his will left very little of his massive fortune to charity. A second letter signed by "A Company" was sent to the *Herald* shortly after the first. In this one, the authors again implored Mrs. Stewart to donate the requested $500,000 to some public charity. This time, however, the letter to the *Herald* demanded that the donation be made soon since they were unable to conceal the body much longer. A deadline of noon on Wednesday, November 13, was set for the charitable donation to be made. If it wasn't made, then "A Company" threatened to destroy Stewart's remains "in order to avoid detection."

Judge Hilton refused to respond to the demand, and the deadline came and went. After the deadline passed, a third and final letter was sent to the *Herald* from "A Company." In it the authors alluded to Stewart's fate being tied to his past desecration of the old Amity Street Baptist Church cemetery and informed readers that, since the deadline for the $500,000 charitable donation had not been met, Stewart's remains had been carved up into "small particles," then "wrapped separately in comparatively small bundles" and sent to "different towns in different countries." They would, according to "A Company," never be found.

It would not be the last time that the issue of the desecration of the old Amity Street Baptist Church cemetery had come up. In January 1887, an anonymous letter writer to the *New York Herald* blamed Stewart for his own comeuppance, claiming that the grave robbery was retribution for Stewart's act of desecrating the bodies buried in the old Baptist Church cemetery. Stewart had bought the church building in 1864 and converted it into a stable. The stable housed Stewart's fleet of wagons and horses used to deliver merchandise to customers. It was considered a very important part of Stewart's business.

When the church moved its congregation farther uptown, Stewart bought the property on Amity Street, near Broadway, to accommodate his department store. The stable was considered one of the best in the city and housed thirty-one variously sized horse-drawn wagons to deliver a variety of goods both large and small.

The anonymous writer of the letter claimed Stewart had excavated the cemetery to build his stable and hauled away wagons full of old bones and skulls. Stewart put a fence up around the excavation, but it did little to stop angry crowds from gathering there to protest the callous disposal of the bodies. A riot nearly broke out, and the police had to be called to disperse the angry crowd and guard the site. Stewart, it was said, never responded to the entreaties of relatives who wished to have the remains of their loved ones taken away and buried elsewhere. According to the anonymous writer, a curse was on Stewart for the desecration and he would never be allowed to rest in peace.

Henry Hilton was quick to dismiss the letter as hogwash. According to Hilton, all the bodies buried at the church had been removed before Stewart's excavation, and although a few random bones and skulls had been uncovered during the digging, they had all been rightfully turned over to the city morgue. Hilton had no time to waste on supposed curses and retribution from beyond the grave. He had real matters to contend with.

"I do not wish to conceal from the public the fact that I have the best detective talent in the country covering every possible point," Hilton told the press.

Another potential lead surfaced in the village of Tuckahoe, Westchester County, New York. The luxurious Stewart mansion on Fifth Avenue was built with stone from the Tuckahoe quarry. The costs associated with the construction of the mansion had caused the building contractor, Alexander Maxwell, as well as the stone quarry's owners, to go bankrupt. Maxwell and the owners underestimated the expenses they would incur, and it was rumored that Stewart refused to release either business from their original contracts. Maxwell had died before the mansion was completed. Rumormongers contended that the dispute gave the Maxwell family a motive for stealing Stewart's body. Nothing ever came of the rumor, however, and no one in Maxwell's immediate family was investigated. It was more of the same—grasping for straws.

Another angle that the police entertained was the involvement of a former employee of Stewart's who had embezzled fourteen thousand dollars. Although the man offered to repay the money, Stewart refused and the thief was prosecuted to the fullest extent of the law. The embezzler vowed revenge, and the police began a search for the former employee in case the theft of Stewart's body was his handiwork. The police were never able to locate the man, and so another rumored motive turned to dust.

Authorities turned some of their attention to locating a man identified as William H. May. A man of English descent who spoke with a thick northern English accent, May worked at 30 Chambers Street as a soda maker. Known as a big drinker, he had been reported to the police as being obsessed with the Stewart grave robbery, often telling his drinking mates how a man could get rich pulling off such a caper. May reportedly told one drinking companion that any stolen cadaver could be easily preserved and hidden away in a sealed container filled with soda water. Most barroom patrons shrugged off May's ramblings as alcohol-induced. Still, when informed of his ramblings about Stewart, the police became interested in questioning him.

There was another reason. May, a tall, pot-bellied, gregarious man with bushy muttonchop sideburns and a reddish handlebar mustache, readily recognizable by anyone who met him, was reported to have been a visitor to the East Fourteenth Street boardinghouse where the mysterious Dr. Douglass, later identified as the infamous resurrectionist George Christian, had been staying. It was reported that May had actually been seen in the company of Douglass/Christian. And there was more. A report out of Chicago linked May to the 1876 attempt to rob Lincoln's tomb. Two unidentified men reported to the *Chicago Tribune* that May had tried to recruit them to help steal Stewart's body, promising a share of the ransom. The men reportedly refused but took their information, not to the police, but directly to the newspaper.

New York police became even more interested in finding May when friends revealed that he was an avid reader of the magazine *Scientific American* and was especially interested in studying chemical composition. He bragged to drinking buddies that he knew all there was to know about how to preserve dead bodies. Although all of the evidence was purely circumstantial, it led the police to an all-out search for the Englishman, one that proved futile. During the investigation it was learned that May had left the city in a hurry, packing up a few belongings and selling all his known possessions, including his soda-water-making business, to his landlord. Coincidently, May had fled the city on or about November 8, the day after the theft of Stewart's body had been discovered. The police had no leads as to where he had gone, and he was never again linked as a suspect in the case.

HOW GRAVE-ROBBERS WORK
CONFESSION OF A DETECTED THIEF— A COUNTRY PHYSICIAN'S ASSISTANCE.
Special Dispatch to the New York Times.

CLEVELAND, Ohio, Nov. 12—Important developments giving some inkling of the plan pursued by grave-robbers in despoiling graves have just been made here. Joiner, one of the villains who robbed Mr. French's grave in Willoughby about a month ago, confessed to Mr. French's son that his gang went to Bedford, a suburb of this city, about the middle of August, to get the body of a young woman whose name was Cutchlow, who had died of consumption. They did not know where the cemetery was, nor where the grave was in the cemetery and so they decided to find a doctor first. Joiner pretended to be very sick, stopped at a store and called a physician. One was called, and by giving him a sign the thieves induced him to retire with them. The latter made their business known. The doctor told them that he did not know where the body was, but his daughter did and if they would be at a certain place within an hour he would have the required information. They did so and were directed to the spot but warned to be very careful as the grave was very near to that of Thomas Patterson, father of W.D. Patterson, Superintendent of the Workhouse of this city and as he had been buried for a year his corpse would be of no use. The robbers proceeded to the grave and digging down applied their usual test—that of trying the ear; if this pulls off, the body is too far decomposed to be of any use. The ear came off and a horrible stench arose, which made all sick and they decided to retire and get something to drink. When they returned it was thought to be so late that it was not practicable to open another grave and so the Patterson's grave was refilled and the party returned to the city.

Superintendent Patterson has just been investigating this whole case, and upon opening his father's grave he found the ear missing from his father's corpse as described, and the coffin broken open. The suburban doctor who assisted in the case has since died. He was a leading church member, and died very much respected.

—*New York Times*
November 13, 1878

On November 15, 1878, the *New York Times* ran a story claiming the ghouls had been identified and would be in police custody soon. The story was based on reports given by unnamed sources, and much of it was predicated purely on speculation. The *Times* reported that not only had the body been found but that the grave robbers, all of them unnamed, had been identified.

The *Times* story maintained that all the sufficient evidence against the robbers had been secured and that all of the culprits were under surveillance and would be arrested shortly. This, the *Times* stated, was based on information provided to them from "the highest authorities connected with the Stewart body-snatching case."

According to the *Times*, the case had been solved through the concerted efforts of both the New York City Police Department and the private detectives hired by Judge Hilton, working in unison. The *Times* contended that the authorities had learned that there were two distinct bands of villains in the case: those who had actually stolen the body and those who had hired them and had the Stewart remains in their possession. Although the *Times* reporter wrote that he was not at liberty to divulge the names of the robbers, he claimed that according to one of his unnamed high-ranking sources, their identities "will raise the hair on the heads of the people of New York."

The culprits were, according to the *Times*, people of unquestionable respectability, including one very prominent attorney. The arrests had not been made because Stewart's body had still not been recovered. When the body was safely in the possession of the authorities, then and only then would the robbers be taken into custody. According to the *Times*, "The entire 'gang' has been known for two days past, but the evidence against all was not considered complete until last evening. Hence the delay in making the arrest. Judge Hilton does not want to let a single man escape by any possibility. It is believed that the guilty parties know that they are shadowed for they all exhibit considerable nervousness."

Despite the *Times* headline of November 15, purporting the arrests of the grave robbers as imminent, anonymous letters claiming to know the whereabouts of Stewart's body continued to pour in.

The police received the following:

DEAR SIR: One week last night Mr. Stewart's body was taken. Your detectives have been within a block of it within 48 hours, and they may hunt until doomsday, they cannot find it, but *for $200,000 and no questions asked it will be delivered. A personal in the Herald saying you will pay this amount with guaranty, will be answered. Yours, XERXES.*

Judge Hilton received the following unsigned letter on the same day:

DEAR SIR: My opinion is that the Jews have something to do with the affair. It would do no harm to search the large safes in and around Broad-street. In one particular office the smell is far from pleasant. Excuse pencil."

Regardless of the unsubstantiated news story in the *New York Times,* the headlines the next day seemed to confirm the initial report: Two of the grave robbers had been apprehended, and this time the *Times* named them—Henry Vreeland and William Burke.

THE CEMETERY ROBBERY
TWO OF THE GHOULS ARRESTED.
The Whole Gang Said To Be In
The Power Of The Police—
Name Of The Leader Engaged In
The Robbery—How The Body Was
Stolen And Where It Was Taken To.

—*New York Times*
November 16, 1878

8
VREELAND AND BURKE

In which the noted investigator, New York City Police Captain Thomas Byrnes, makes a breakthrough in the sensational case and arrests two men, Henry Vreeland and William Burke, charging them with the heinous crime. The two men lead the police on a merry chase through parts of New Jersey where they claim the body is buried.

At 1 A.M. on Thursday morning Capt. Byrnes arrested a man and took him manacled to the Fifteenth Precinct Police Station. He was described on the police records as Henry Vreeland, aged 25, of No. 38 Chauncey-street, Brooklyn, suspicious person. He was kept entirely secluded until yesterday morning. He was not put into a cell, and the place of his confinement is not known even now except to the authorities.

—*New York Times*
November 16, 1878

Henry Vreeland was taken to the Jefferson Market Police Court under a shroud of secrecy. Judge B. T. Morgan held a private hearing with Vreeland, Captain Thomas Byrnes, and four police detectives. The hearing lasted a matter of minutes. After the hearing, the details of which were kept secret, Vreeland was taken from the courthouse to police headquarters under heavy guard. Later that same day, Byrnes along with Inspector William Murray arrested a second man whose identity and charges against him were kept from the press. He was described in newspaper accounts as "of medium height, of athletic build, but slim, has regular features, sallow complexion, close shaven face and dark hair. He walked as though lame and had a handkerchief around his head."

The police refused to divulge any information about either man, but the rumor circulating through the New York City press corps was that Byrnes had finally captured two of the grave robbers. The district attorney's office let it slip that four arrests had been made in the Stewart case but that only these first two suspects, Vreeland and the unnamed young man, had been physically brought to police headquarters.

According once again to unnamed police sources, authorities now knew the exact time the grave robbers entered St. Mark's Cemetery, when they left, and where they went. The *Times* reported that the ghouls entered the cemetery at 3:17 a.m. and had Stewart's body outside the cemetery fence within an hour. According to the *Times,* a man named Mahoney, who had previously worked at one of the city cemeteries, did the principal work on securing Stewart's body from the tomb. Mahoney, it was reported, fled the city the next day but was under police surveillance and would be apprehended shortly.

Stewart's body had been placed inside a canvas bag and carried out of the cemetery to the sidewalk, where it was put in the back of a wagon and taken to a notorious "fence" (someone who dealt in stolen goods) named Murphy. Stewart's body was kept at Murphy's office on Forty-second Street near the ferry landing and had since been moved to another unnamed location. None of the published reports were substantiated by anyone in authority. Yet it was clear that one Henry Vreeland of Brooklyn and another man, who was later revealed to be William Burke of 402 East Twelfth Street in New York City, had been arrested and were being held in connection with the case.

CLOSING ON THE GHOULS
SUCCESSFUL EFFORTS TO CATCH THEM
A Telegram Announcing The Recovery Of The Body Expected Every Moment —The Police Starting Out To Make Wholesale Arrests Last Night—The Two Captured Ghouls In Court— Their Antecedents.

Late last night the TIMES reporter learned that a grand movement was taking place to capture the robbers of Mr. Stewart's grave, and that the body was on its way to New York. ...

Shortly before midnight, Inspector Dilks, who was on duty at the Central office, was visited and told that the reporter had positive information that Chief of Detectives Kealy had gone to Weehawken to take possession of the body in the name of Judge Hilton. The Inspector was a little staggered at first and said that Mr. Kealy had been on the track of the body four days. On the story being repeated to him, however, he acknowledged that he was expecting a telegram every moment from Mr. Kealy announcing that the body had been found.

—*New York Times*
November 17, 1878

When the Jefferson Market Police Court convened at 2 p.m. on November 16, Vreeland and Burke sat in the prisoners' dock. Seated in the first row of the courtroom were two women. One was a tall, gray-haired woman wearing a dark dress, a bonnet, and a shawl. Seated next to her was a younger woman: tall, slim with hazel eyes and dark hair, dressed in a black silk dress and black velvet bonnet. They were Burke's mother and sister. Burke was described as being about thirty-eight years old, about five-foot-ten or five-foot-eleven in height, well shaped, and "decidedly handsome." He was bald and had a flaxen-colored mustache.

Vreeland was described as being approximately ten years older. According to the *New York Times*, "His head was covered with a thick, strong growth of dark hair, plentifully sprinkled with gray. He wore full close-cropped whiskers and mustache of the same color. He looked like a well-to-do business man."

The courtroom was filled with uniformed police officers and detectives. Police Captain Thomas Byrnes first met with Judge B. T. Morgan in his private chambers where he outlined the evidence against the two men. When the door to Judge Morgan's chambers opened ten minutes later, Burke and Vreeland were escorted into the chambers under heavy police guard. Court-appointed attorney Joseph Stiner was allowed to accompany the two men into Morgan's chambers, and again the door to the private chamber was closed. Nearly a half hour later, the door to the chamber opened and Captain Byrnes stepped into the courtroom and beckoned the two women, Burke's mother and sister, into the judge's chamber, once again closing the door behind them. Byrnes informed the court that he would be filing a formal complaint against the two men, charging them with being two of the robbers of Stewart's grave. Byrnes asked the court to hold the two men without bail until then, to allow him to secure additional evidence. The judge granted his request. The two prisoners were escorted from the court, under heavy police guard, out the rear of the courthouse to the Mercer Street Police Station, where they were confined to cells to await a further hearing. Attorney Stiner accompanied Burke's mother and sister to the station, where Stiner was allowed to meet privately with his two clients.

POLICE COURT — SECOND DISTRICT
State of New York, City and County of New York.

Thomas Byrnes, Captain of the Fifteenth Precinct Police, being duly sworn, says that on or about the 6th day of November, 1878, at the City of New York, in the County of New York, Henry Vreeland and William Burke (both now here) did, then and there acting in concert together, feloniously remove the dead body of a human being from the place of its interment, for the purpose of selling the same, and for the purpose of dissection, and with mere wantonness did remove the dead body of the late Alexander T. Stewart from the vault in the church-yard of St. Mark's Church, situated on the Second-avenue, between Ninth and Tenth streets, being a grave-yard in the said City, from the fact that the said Henry Vreeland and William Burke did acknowledge and confess to this deponent, in the presence of witnesses, that they had possession of the aforesaid dead body of the said Alexander T. Stewart, as more fully appears from the sworn statement of deponent hereto attached, and forming part of this complaint.

THOMAS BYRNES

Sworn to before me this 19th day of November 1878, B. T. Morgan, Police Justice.

Captain Byrnes had arrested Burke at his home at 402 East Twelfth Street. Byrnes, who had made a reputation for himself as a relentless law enforcement officer, would later go on to become the chief of New York City's detective bureau and then superintendent of the force. Byrnes had expected to also apprehend Vreeland, who reportedly lived at the same address, but Vreeland was not there. Byrnes and several police officers laid a trap for Vreeland, once Burke was in custody, and finally two days after the arrest of Burke, Vreeland showed up at 402 East Twelfth Street where he was placed in custody.

Burke was no stranger to the authorities. In 1872 he was convicted of burglary and sentenced to prison for five years. Vreeland, who had gone under the alias of Frank Whelan, had served three years in Sing Sing prison on pickpocket charges. According to the police, no sooner had Vreeland been released from prison than he was arrested again, this time for stealing a pair of shoes. He was ordered held for six months and had only been released from the Crow Hill Penitentiary in late October. The police all agreed that Burke and Vreeland did not have the capacity to plan such a bold and daring grave robbery and that they must have been hired by the real masterminds of the gruesome theft. That left the real thieves still at large.

CAPT. BYRNES CORROBORATES THE TIMES' STATEMENT
Where The Hitch Is In Clearing Up The Mystery—Further Details Of The Conspiracy—A Sensational Court Scene—A Search For The Body Described—A Day Of Extraordinary Developments.

The TIMES reporter ascertained yesterday what the hitch in the Stewart matter is. The robbery was the result of a con-

spiracy in which five men were engaged. These men are neither thieves nor crooked men of any kind. They are, on the
contrary, men occupying respectable social positions. More
than that, they are no "ordinary men" of their class. These
men had nothing to do with the practical side of the outrage.
They hired other men, like Burke and Vreeland, to do the work
of despoiling the grave and concealing the remains, paying
them large sums for their services and promising them continued percentages in case everything turned out well. These
five men were to have been arrested on Saturday night. Three
of them either were arrested or are in such a position that
they cannot escape. ... Two succeeded in bribing private detectives employed to shadow them and were permitted to escape.
The country is now being searched for them and they cannot
remain long concealed. As soon as their whereabouts are discovered they will be immediately apprehended and the body
of Mr. Stewart will be produced and the entire story of the
conspiracy and the chase will be given to the public.

—*New York Times*
November 19, 1878

During the second Burke and Vreeland hearing, held before Judge
B. T. Morgan at the Jefferson Market Police Court on November 18,
Captain Byrnes testified that an unidentified man had approached
him with information that Burke had come to him and said, "I can put
you in something where you can make some money." According to
Byrnes, this unidentified man accepted the offer. Judge Morgan asked
Byrnes if he would provide the court with the name of the man.

"If the court thinks right, I would rather, for the present, not,"
Byrnes said.

Byrnes told the court that the unidentified man asked Burke what
the job was.

"Well, I can't tell you about it now, but it is a job where there is
going to be a good deal of money," Burke reportedly told him.

"It ain't the bursting of another bank?" the man asked.

"Bank! Why a bank ain't a circumstance in this. This matter will astonish the whole country," Burke said.

Following the discovery of the Stewart grave robbery, the unidentified man concluded that Burke must have been talking about the robbery. Based on this scant bit of evidence, Burke was arrested on suspicion of being involved in the Stewart grave robbery.

Byrnes told the court that at first Burke denied being involved in the case, but that later at police headquarters, following further questioning, he admitted to knowing something about the robbery. According to Byrnes, Burke confessed to being a party to the theft, "after the body was stolen."

"I was to get a percentage for what I did. The man who was with me when I was arrested was the man who put up the money and did the whole job. His name is Hank Vreeland," Burke reportedly told Byrnes.

According to Burke, Vreeland had stolen the body, taken it to a hiding place in New Jersey, and buried it. According to Burke, Vreeland had subsequently rented a horse and wagon in New Jersey and had gone back to the spot where he initially buried Stewart's body and removed it to another hiding place. If the police went to Orange, New Jersey, and found the place where Vreeland had rented the horse and wagon, he was sure, they would be able to find where Vreeland had buried Stewart's body the second time.

Byrnes told the court that he, Burke, and another police officer went to Orange, New Jersey, where they interviewed a livery stable owner named Harrison, who immediately identified Vreeland as the man who had rented a horse and wagon from him the weekend before. According to Harrison, Vreeland had hired the wagon only for a short time but kept it out all night. He returned it the following morning.

Then, according to Byrnes's testimony to the judge, Burke offered to help locate the spot where Vreeland had buried the body. Although Burke showed them several places where he thought Vreeland had taken the body, Byrnes could not find any location that looked as though it had been freshly dug. After several futile attempts led by Burke, Byrnes halted the search.

"You don't know where that body was buried," Byrnes said to Burke. "And there is only one that does. That is Hank Vreeland. We have got to get him."

According to Byrnes, with Burke and Vreeland now in custody, both men talked freely about the grave robbery.

Vreeland agreed to take the police to the site in New Jersey where he had hidden the body. On the way there, Vreeland told the authorities, "The stiff stunk so that I had to get out and run behind the wagon." He also told Byrnes that once they had dug Stewart's body up, they would have to put it on top of the coach for the long ride back to New York because the smell would sicken them all.

Vreeland led the police to Chatham, New Jersey, eight miles out of Orange, to a deserted mill in a secluded spot just off the main road. There, he claimed, was where he buried the body.

"Where the body is planted we will have to do some digging and we can't do it with our hands," Vreeland told the police.

The police entourage, with Vreeland in the lead, walked past the old mill, up along a dam, and across an open field. They traipsed through the woods for nearly an hour without Vreeland stopping. Finally, when they reached a large stone sitting by itself in the middle of an open field, Vreeland stopped.

"Is this the place?" Byrnes asked him.

Vreeland said no and then turned to Burke.

"What will they give a man for this job?" Vreeland asked his friend Burke.

"One stretcher [meaning one year] and a $250 fine," Burke told him.

Vreeland turned to Byrnes.

"I don't know anything about this thing. I don't know where any body is buried," he blurted out.

Byrnes could barely contain his anger. He had been led on a wild-goose chase, and Vreeland and Burke had made a fool out of him and the entire police force.

From the moment Vreeland knew he could get only one year he wouldn't open his mouth. I asked him what he meant by taking us there. He said it was all a put up job; that he fell into it supposing that Billy was in trouble and he could help him out. The result was that we returned to New York.

—New York Times NOVEMBER 19, 1878

According to trial transcripts, the following testimony transpired:

JUSTICE MORGAN: Did Vreeland confess that he was one of the parties to the removal of the body from St. Mark's graveyard?

CAPT. BYRNES: No.

JUSTICE MORGAN: That he was one of the parties to the robbery after it left the cemetery?

CAPT. BYRNES: Yes. He said that he went there for the purpose of selecting that place. One thing that I omitted was this: Burke said to Hank two or three times "Why don't you find the place? We have got to get away from here quick." Hank retorted: "Why don't you find it? You know it as well as I."

JUSTICE MORGAN: Have Burke and Vreeland confessed that they had the body in their possession?

CAPT. BYRNES: Yes; in Burke's room in Twelfth-street. They told me they would show me where it was if I would give them the reward. I told them they could have the reward; I didn't want any of it. They both told me that they had a nigger in the job. They couldn't stomach the carrying of the body or the other dirty work and they got the nigger to do it.

JUSTICE MORGAN: That's all your statement?

CAPT. BYRNES: Yes, except that Burke told me on Saturday or Sunday—three or four times after the search—that the body had been removed and that he thought the others wanted to beat him out of his share. He told this to two or three other parties besides myself.

COUNSEL: Didn't they make a statement subsequently that it was all a hoax; that they were getting you on a string?

CAPT. BYRNES: No, Sir.

—HEARING TESTIMONY, JEFFERSON MARKET POLICE COURT,
JUDGE B. T. MORGAN PRESIDING, NOVEMBER 18, 1878

Attorney Joseph Stiner told the court, "Your Honor, we don't dispute the removal of the body. We simply deny that our clients did the removing."

Stiner made a motion to dismiss the charges against his two clients based on Byrnes's hearsay evidence, but Judge Morgan would have nothing to do with it. The two men had made a mockery of Byrnes's investigation and wasted the court's time. That alone would garner the two men some jail time. Judge Morgan ordered Vreeland and Burke held on the charges issued in Byrnes's complaint. Morgan set bail at five thousand dollars each and remanded them to the Jefferson Market Prison.

Burke continued to taunt the police captain by telling reporters that the whole incident was a charade to embarrass the mighty Thomas Byrnes. According to Burke, they wanted to give Captain Byrnes, using the vernacular of the times, "the kid to his heart's content."

Byrnes was considered one of the most brilliant up-and-coming officers in the New York City Police Department. He had risen quickly through the ranks by solving several sensational crimes, including the murder of the flamboyant Wall Street speculator Jubilee Jim Fisk by one of his partners, Edward Stokes, who shot and killed Fisk in a New York City hotel on January 6, 1872. Byrnes was instrumental in apprehending Stokes. Byrnes had also developed a reputation as an innovator in crime detection and in his free and frequent use of the "third degree" (physical abuse) to coerce confessions out of criminals. The very public humiliation caused by Burke and Vreeland drew Byrnes's ire. Guilty or not, Byrnes decided to prosecute the two jokers regardless of their lack of involvement in the Stewart case.

THE BODY SAID TO BE UNDER GUARD

Information was received in Jersey City last evening which strongly corroborates the statement that the New-York Police, or some other of Judge Hilton's agents have succeeded in fixing the location of the body of the late Mr. Stewart. The story, as detailed to the reporter, was as follows: Last Saturday night at a somewhat late hour a New-York detective, whose name was not given, went into one of the telegraph offices in Jersey City and sent a dispatch to Inspector Walling, at New York Police Headquarters, stating that the body had been found, and advising that the detectives who were elsewhere engaged in hunting it be called off. ... The detective allowed it to be understood that the body was under Police guard, but vouchsafed no reason why immediate possession was not taken of it.

—*New York Times*
November 19, 1878

Unnamed police sources declared that the case was over. Although Vreeland and Burke, who had intimated the body of Stewart was buried there, had recanted their story, claiming it was all a hoax, no one took them seriously and the search went on for several days.

"Have you got the body?" a reporter asked police officials.

"Why of course we have the body, but there are two men still to be arrested," the reporter was informed.

Judge Hilton maintained his vow of silence on the case and told reporters nothing. The only thing Hilton would talk about, of course, was money. He informed reporters that he had given Police Inspector Murray a check to defray the costs of the investigation but that Murray refused to accept the check. Hilton said he offered one thousand dollars to Captain Byrnes to cover his personal expenses during the investigation but Byrnes too refused to accept any money. Hilton praised the work of the police department and told reporters he would be "grateful to them as long as he lived."

The residents of Chatham, New Jersey, were in a tizzy over the possibility that the body of A. T. Stewart was buried somewhere there. Police and Pinkerton detectives converged on the sleepy hamlet with shovels and wagons and began the long and laborious task of trying to find the burial spot. Any number of New York City and New Jersey reporters also converged on the small town. Detectives, police, reporters, and Chatham townsfolk searched relentlessly along the banks of the Passaic River, where it was reported that Stewart's remains were buried. The prime hunting grounds for eager grave hunters hoping to win a portion of the reward was a small strip of land along the border of Union County and the river. It was about three hundred yards long and fifty to one hundred feet wide, situated along the sloping bank leading to the river. The searchers found nothing.

Vreeland and Burke were back before Judge Morgan on November 19, and according to the *New York Times*, the prisoners were on hand early under their usual strong escort of detectives. They looked haggard and nervous, according to the *Times,* "particularly Burke, whose natural sneaking cur-like expression of countenance would seem difficult to improve upon. He is one of the meanest looking thieves. How any person could trust him with a secret seems as much a puzzle as to explain how the sharp, pretty woman who calls him husband can possibly live with such a wretch."

Byrnes had filed his formal affidavit, bail was set at five thousand dollars each, and both men were charged with grave robbing. Judge Morgan ordered the paperwork in the case turned over to the district attorney's office. The complaint only contained Byrnes's affidavit and the testimony that Byrnes gave to the court previously. It was not much to bring to a grand jury. In fact, after reviewing the case, the opinion in the district attorney's office was that there wasn't enough evidence to connect either Burke or Vreeland to the Stewart case. But even if Burke and Vreeland were not guilty of that crime, at the urging of Captain Byrnes, whose reputation as a hard-nosed crime fighter had been publicly tarnished by the two men, they would be found guilty of something, one way or another. That much was certain.

Holding Burke in custody was no problem for the authorities. He was a repeat offender and well known to the police as a burglar. Byrnes filed additional charges against Burke for forgery. If found guilty, Burke would face five years in prison—a stiff sentence for pulling a practical joke on the illustrious police captain Thomas Byrnes. And just to ensure that Burke would pay for the embarrassment he caused Byrnes and the entire police department, Byrnes filed charges of grand larceny against him as well. If found guilty on both charges, Burke could face ten years in prison.

No effort has been made to send the case of Baker (aka Burke) and Vreeland for alleged complicity in the grave-robbing before the Grand Jury, nor is it probable that any steps in that direction will be taken. No evidence connecting them with that transaction, beyond their own statements, is in possession of the District Attorney, and it is not believed that either of them have had anything to do with the robbery.

—*New York Times*
November 22, 1878

Byrnes might not have arrested the *right* criminals, but he had at least arrested *some* criminals, and as the case dragged on—nearly two weeks had passed without a break in the case—it appeared to appease the public's frustration and condemnation of the police department. This grace period didn't last very long, however, and things just went from bad to worse.

Without enough evidence to link Burke and Vreeland to the Stewart grave robbery, the grand jury instead indicted Burke on charges of forgery, stemming from an unrelated incident in which he forged a four hundred-dollar check drawn on the West Side Bank. There was nothing to charge Vreeland with, and he was held until December 3, 1878, when he was finally released from jail.

HENRY VREELAND DISCHARGED

Two weeks ago Capt. Byrnes, of the Fifteenth Precinct, had Henry Vreeland, of Brooklyn, and William Burke, of No. 402 East Twelfth-street, the two men who pretended to know the whereabouts of Mr. Stewart's remains in New Jersey, committed to await the action of the Grand Jury, on suspicion of their implication in the stealing of the body. No evidence connecting them with the offense was produced, however, and the Grand Jury did not inquire into the case. Burke, however, was identified as a man who had uttered a forged check on the West Side

Bank, and an indictment for forgery was found against him. Yesterday, Vreeland was taken before Judge Gildersleeve, in the General Sessions, and discharged, Assistant District Attorney Horace Russell stating in his endorsement of the papers that there was no evidence to connect him with the offense charged. Burke still remains in the Tombs, awaiting trial on forgery charges.

—*New York Times*
December 4, 1878

Reports in the *New York Times* following the release of Vreeland claimed that Captain Byrnes's actions were "fully approved by his superiors, one of whom said yesterday that he would have deserved dismissal from the force if he had neglected to follow up the information given by Burke, which, however, proved utterly valueless."

By November 26, nearly three weeks after the A. T. Stewart grave robbery, the vast number of police officers and detectives previously assigned to the case had been withdrawn. The search for the grave robbers was assigned to Inspector William Murray and Captain James Kealy. Captain Byrnes, after his public humiliation at the hands of Burke and Vreeland, had moved on to another sensational unsolved case, the robbery of the Manhattan Savings Institution, in which thieves broke into the fortresslike bank and stole approximately three million dollars in cash and securities. Although the robbery had occurred on October 27, 1878, prior to the Stewart grave robbery, Byrnes's superiors had immediately reassigned him to the bank-robbery case, following the Burke and Vreeland debacle.

Despite extensive searches in New York and New Jersey, the body of A. T. Stewart had not been located, as the *New York Times* and other newspapers had previously reported. Burke and Vreeland could not be linked to the robbery. The notorious Washington, D.C., "resurrectionist," Dr. George A. Christian, could not be located, and even if he was, there was nothing linking him to Stewart's grave robbery. The mysterious letters claiming to know where the body of Stewart was and who had taken it continued to flood into police headquarters and to Judge Hilton, but they led nowhere. And the police were unable to uncover the whereabouts of William May, the New York City soda maker rumored to be somehow connected to the robbery. The search for the A. T. Stewart grave robbers and Stewart's remains came to a dead stop.

THE STEWART GRAVE-ROBBERY
A Number Of Detectives Withdrawn From The Case—What The Police Found At Paterson.

There was nothing new developed yesterday in the search for the robbers of the Stewart vault, and the detectives who have been assiduously working up the multitude of clues furnished from all sources have made no further progress in clearing up the mystery. A number of the Central office detectives who have been devoting themselves to this case have been withdrawn for the present, and are attending to their usual duties.

—*New York Times*
November 26, 1878

KEEPING UP WITH THE JONESES

In which, by early 1879, it appears that all leads in the A. T. Stewart grave robbery have been exhausted and the story fades from the front pages until Patrick Jones, a lawyer and former New York postmaster, reports to the press that he has been in contact with Stewart's grave robbers, who demand more than two hundred thousand dollars for the return of the body. Despite New York City police officials verifying the authenticity of the demand, Henry Hilton refuses to negotiate with the unnamed criminals and dismisses Jones's evidence as another elaborate ploy to squeeze money from the Stewart estate.

Only a year and a half had passed since Judge Henry Hilton had excluded New York City banker Joseph Seligman from the Grand Union Hotel in Saratoga, causing a backlash against Hilton and the Stewart retail empire. At the end of 1878, Hilton, perhaps in an overt effort to make amends, sent a letter to three of the principal Jewish charitable organizations in New York, announcing a financial contribution to be made on behalf of the Stewart family. Hilton contacted Mount Sinai Hospital, the Jewish Orphan Asylum, and the Home for Infirm and Aged Hebrews. The hospital and orphanage were given $500 each while the home was given $250.

Although the contributions were needed, there were mixed feelings among the city's Jewish community. Many prominent members of the Jewish community were strongly opposed to accepting any contributions from Hilton. Still others argued that the donations came directly from Cornelia Stewart, not Henry Hilton, and therefore should be accepted.

DEAR SIR: Mrs. Alexander T. Stewart is desirous to donate $500 to the Mount Sinai Hospital. Your Treasurer can get the money by calling with this letter any afternoon after 2 o'clock. Yours respectfully, HENRY HILTON.
—JUDGE HENRY HILTON, DECEMBER 12, 1878

THE HEBREWS EXCITED
Donations By Mrs. Stewart To Jewish Charitable Institutions—Will They Be Rejected?

A wide difference of opinion prevails among the Jewish people as to what is best to be done in the matter, on account of the ill-feeling engendered by Judge Hilton's action in excluding Mr. Joseph Seligman and his family from the Grand Union Hotel, at Saratoga, in the Summer of 1877, an act which caused no little excitement at the time, and the memory of which is revived by Judge Hilton's letters to the three institutions. ... The question of the acceptance or rejection of Mrs. Stewart's liberal donations will probably be left undecided until the Trustees of the different institutions have discussed it in the regular board meetings.

—New York Times
December 17, 1878

Hilton became livid after reading the December 17, 1878, *New York Times* article on the charitable donations. He insisted to the papers that charity was a private matter and should not be dragged into a public forum such as the newspaper.

Hilton refused to speak to reporters about the matter and conveyed his distaste for the article through his private secretary, who told reporters, "It has been the custom of Mrs. Stewart and Judge Hilton every year about this time, to select a list of charitable institutions deserving of help and send them gifts."

The private secretary went on to inform newspaper reporters that Mrs. Stewart had made a list of some fifty organizations to which she intended to make substantial donations and Judge Hilton had added thirty more institutions. According to the secretary, the list included almost all the religious denominations. The donations were made to Mount Sinai Hospital, the Jewish Orphan Asylum, and the Home for

Infirm and Aged Hebrews because those organizations were deserving, not because they belonged to or were managed by people of the Hebrew faith. The explanation provided by Hilton's private secretary didn't quell any of the Jewish community's objections. If anything, it only inflamed the outwardly hostile reception of the charitable gifts.

Mrs. Joseph Stiner, vice president of the Home for Infirm and Aged Hebrews, told reporters that the problem wasn't with Mrs. Stewart's gift, but with Hilton being associated with it. "Our people will not be under any obligations to him. We will not take gifts from him. We will rather contribute the amounts among ourselves," Stiner said.

She went on to scold Hilton, saying that if the donations were bids to try to get Jewish shoppers back in his store, it was "very poor, very shabby, and very impolitic."

Less than a week after Mrs. Stewart and Hilton offered their donations, the Jewish Orphan Asylum declined. Two days before Christmas, the Board of Directors of Mount Sinai Hospital voted to decline the donation. In turn, the board members voted to make up the five-hundred-dollar contribution out of their own pockets. The Home for Infirm and Aged Hebrews also declined to accept its donation. If the donations had indeed been a covert method of attempting to lure the Jewish trade back to the now-Hilton-run department store, it failed miserably.

At the end of 1878 and into the next year, it appeared that Hilton was failing on all fronts. He was not able to lure Jewish shoppers back into his stores, and he wasn't able to negotiate for the return of Stewart's missing body.

The year 1878 ended without any further developments in the Stewart case. As the new year began, a scaled-back investigation continued. Even though the case remained unsolved—no one had been indicted and Stewart's bones were still missing— the public's interest in the case appeared to be fully satiated. Public attention turned toward the construction of the massive, expensive Cathedral of the Incarnation in Garden City on Long Island. It was there that the remains of A. T.

Stewart, if and when they were recovered, and those of his widow, Cornelia, would be buried. In early 1879, a noticeable change had come over Cornelia Stewart, as if her heavy burden had been lifted. She appeared more frequently in public, and she seemed healthier and in better spirits than she had been since the theft of her husband's bones. Whether she was preoccupied with the building of the cathedral or whether her husband's remains had been secretly recovered, no one knew for sure, and no one—neither Cornelia nor Judge Hilton—was saying.

Hundreds of curiosity seekers turned their attention from the site of the grave robbery, St. Mark's, to the construction site of the new cathedral. Crowds of people converged on Garden City to catch a glimpse of the building of the ornate church. Many people, including members of the New York City press, speculated that Stewart's remains had somehow been miraculously returned and were now in safe keeping in the newly constructed burial vault in the cathedral. It was all purely speculation but fueled in part by Hilton's placing around-the-clock guards at the white marble vault beneath the huge church. The approximately twenty-foot-tall vault was substantial and sumptuous and included nine windows and two staircases that connected it to the sanctuary of the cathedral. When finally completed, the cathedral would be a magnificent structure, befitting a "Merchant Prince."

From January 1879 until July, New York's newspapers weren't able to provide readers with any further tantalizing stories about the still unsolved case. The police too remained thwarted in their investigation. And the public, thinking it had been cheated out of some portion of the ongoing mystery, continued to maintain its opinion that Stewart's remains had been recovered in secret and lay at rest in Garden City. It was New York City Police Superintendent George Walling who finally put that speculation to rest when he publicly stated that A. T. Stewart's remains had not been found. To reinforce Walling's announcement, reporters from the *New York Tribune* went to Garden City and inspected the Stewart vault themselves. They reported that after inspecting the mausoleum they were certain it was empty. On August 14, however, the Stewart case broke open with sensational news.

A former New York postmaster, Patrick Jones, reported to the press that he had repeatedly been in contact with Stewart's grave robbers, beginning on January 26, 1879. Jones revealed to reporters that he had received a letter and a mysterious package on that date at his offices on Nassau Street. Jones was then a practicing attorney in the city. Why Jones had been contacted remained a matter of great speculation, but it was readily assumed he had been chosen as the go-between in the case because the robbers might have worked for him during his tenure as postmaster. The letter, Jones told reporters, had been sent from Montreal, Canada. The author of the letter stated that Stewart's body had been spirited to a hiding place in Canada where the robbers still had it under safe keeping. The letter was signed: "Henry G. Romaine." According to Jones, a one hundred-dollar bill was enclosed with the letter. The mystery only deepened. Studying the letter, Jones concluded that whoever "Romaine" was, he had gone to great lengths to conceal his handwriting. Although the letter was written in the most formal business format—leading Jones to believe that whoever wrote it was well-educated —the author had taken great pains to intentionally misspell certain words and use a curious combination of capital and lowercase letters. Jones was certain the author was trying to disguise his handwriting in case either Jones or the authorities attempted to trace the letter using handwriting analysis.

In the mysterious letter, Romaine directed Jones to inspect the package sent along with the letter. In it, Romaine claimed, were certain items that had been stolen from the Stewart crypt during the November 7 robbery. According to the letter, the robbers were now ready to negotiate for the return of Stewart's remains. The one hundred-dollar bill enclosed with the letter was a retainer for Jones to act in his legal capacity as the negotiator for the transaction. If Jones accepted the role and the retainer, he was instructed to contact Judge Hilton to begin talks. The letter said Jones would be paid more as the negotiations progressed.

Romaine indicated that he had great faith in Jones's ability to act honestly on behalf of the robbers and that he would bargain in good faith. Romaine explained that the robbers had decided the time was right to open up discussions with Hilton for the return of Stewart's body because at this point every possible avenue of investigation had seemingly been exhausted and neither Hilton nor the authorities were any closer to solving the case. Romaine was certain that at this point Hilton would be more than willing to negotiate for the safe return of Stewart's bones. According to Romaine, the authorities had never come close to solving the crime and they never would unless they agreed to the demands.

The letter stated that Stewart's body was stolen from St. Mark's Cemetery before midnight on November 6 and not in the early morning of November 7 as the police and newspapers had speculated. And, according to Romaine, the body was not transported from the cemetery in a carriage but had been carefully concealed in a grocery wagon that had gone completely undetected by the authorities. The body was never taken to a nearby house but instead was taken by the grocery wagon to a house near 116th Street.

They were enclosed in a zinc-lined trunk, previously prepared and left on the early morning train. They went to Plattsburg, and from there to the Dominion; there they were buried. Except that the eyes have disappeared, the flesh is as firm and the features as natural as the day of internment, and can, therefore, be instantly identified."

—LETTER SENT FROM HENRY G. ROMAINE TO PATRICK JONES,
JANUARY 26, 1879

Romaine ended his letter by urging Jones to meet immediately with the Rev. Dr. Joseph Rylance, Judge Henry Hilton, and Mrs. Stewart to begin the discussions for the return of the remains. The letter and all its information, boasts, and demands could have been brushed aside by Jones had it not been for the one hundred-dollar bill inside— who would spend that much money on a practical joke? And then there was the package.

Inside the package Jones found several screws that he assumed had been taken from Stewart's coffin. There was no way to know if they were authentic or not. Also in the package was a piece of velvet cloth that had been cut from the casket lining on the night of the robbery. If all of the enclosed materials were not enough to convince Jones that Romaine was being truthful about his boast of having Stewart's body, Jones was instructed to place a small personal ad in the *New York Herald* and the nameplate from Stewart's coffin would be sent directly to him. Jones was convinced he was onto something but wasn't exactly sure what. He consulted with several other attorneys before he went to New York City Police Superintendent George Walling with the letter and the contents of the package several days later.

"A man who formerly served under me in the army claims to know something about the Stewart body. I believe that with proper encouragement I can get information that will lead to its recovery," Jones told Walling.

Walling was skeptical. Still, Jones was no crackpot and had an admirable reputation, so Walling, against his better judgment, went to Hilton with the news. Walling advised Jones to proceed apace with his end of the negotiations and to pursue the matter as best he could.

Walling, who was at best doubtful of the Jones entreaty, had little luck in convincing Hilton of the authenticity of the letter. Even if he had, Hilton still refused to negotiate with anyone for the return of his mentor's remains. "I felt and expressed my serious doubts about the correctness of the information, but Jones was persistent and wanted to work up the case and make arrangements for buying the body. He brought a letter or two, which he asserted had come from the thieves," Walling wrote in his memoir.

According to Walling's memoir, *Recollections of a New York City Chief of Police,* Hilton said, "We must never compound a felony. It isn't, of course, the money, but the principle. If we were to pay these infamous scoundrels, what rich man's or woman's dead body would hereafter be safe? We will never pay a cent except for the conviction of the criminals."

But the next revelation was difficult to ignore. Jones had followed the instructions and contacted Romaine by running a small personal ad in the *New York Herald.* Shortly after the ad was placed, Jones received a package in the mail that was sent to him by express from Boston. In it was the original coffin plate stolen with Stewart's remains. Jones brought the plate to Walling, who sent for the engraver of the plate to examine it. After careful examination he informed Walling and Jones that the plate was indeed authentic.

"That's the very one," he told them.

Walling immediately dispatched detectives to the Boston express office and was able to learn that an unidentified woman had mailed the package. According to express office personnel, the woman had come into the office with her face covered up to her eyes with a scarf. There was no way anyone in the office could identify her. But even with the new information—the authenticated coffin plate—Hilton remained inflexible. He refused to get involved in any negotiations regardless of the evidence, unless the talks included the apprehension and conviction of the robbers. He wouldn't budge from his stance.

All the evidence presented so far to Jones seemed legitimate. Even Superintendent Walling was convinced that whoever Romaine was, he had Stewart's body. In all the volumes of anonymous crank letters the police, the newspapers, and Judge Hilton had received right after the theft, there had been one that lent some credence to the Romaine missive. The letter in question, filed away among all the other messages in the police files, had been written using words cut out from a newspaper and pasted to the page. "In one hour I will be in Canada with A. T. Stewart's body. A woman has the remains," the message said. And there was yet another. This one, sent directly to Superintendent Walling, stating, "Farewell and tell Judge Hilton that the body will never be found unless he pays princely." It was signed, "Canada."

Now that Walling was convinced he was dealing with the real grave robbers, rather than enter into negotiations with them as they requested, he decided to concoct a plan to capture the thieves and put the A. T. Stewart grave robbery to rest at long last.

POLICE DEPARTMENT OF THE CITY OF NEW YORK,
No. 300 MULBERRY STREET, NEW YORK, Feb. 1, 1879,
Received of Gen. Patrick H. Jones, a package containing plate supposed to be taken from the coffin of the late Alexander T. Stewart, and marked as follows: *"Alexander T. Stewart, born Oct. 12, 1803, died April 10, 1876.*

—RECEIPT GIVEN TO PATRICK JONES FROM

NEW YORK CITY POLICE SUPERINTENDENT GEORGE WALLING,

FEBRUARY 1879

Regardless of all the work Walling and Jones had done, the ultimate decision would be made by Hilton. Walling arranged a meeting between Jones and Hilton in the hopes that Jones could persuade the judge to open up negotiations with the thieves. But this proved futile, as well. Jones had a brief meeting with Hilton but felt that Hilton had made a fool out of him. Jones left the meeting angry and frustrated. Instead of viewing Jones's information as a breakthrough in the case, Hilton only railed at the unknown robbers and dismissed Jones's evidence as another elaborate ploy to squeeze money from the Stewart estate. He wouldn't be a party to any of it. Hilton dismissed any idea of negotiating with Romaine or anyone else outright. Hilton didn't even thank Jones for his involvement in the case.

Despite Hilton's rigid stance, Jones decided to negotiate with Romaine on his own. As instructed, he posted an ad in the *Herald* again, this time acknowledging the receipt of the evidence he had been sent thus far and declaring that Hilton was ready to negotiate for the return of the body.

Romaine responded to Jones in a February 11, 1879, letter that was sent from Boston. In it, Romaine wrote that the price for the safe return of Stewart's body was two hundred thousand dollars. After payment of the ransom by Hilton, Stewart's remains would be released to Jones and Hilton at an as yet unnamed location near Montreal. No one except Jones and Hilton would take part in the exchange. Romaine wrote that Jones could hold the two hundred thousand-dollar ransom until such time as Hilton was satisfied that the remains were indeed those of A. T. Stewart. Once Hilton made this confirmation, Jones would deliver the money to Romaine's designated go-between. Finally Romaine demanded that the entire exchange and every detail of it must be kept secret before, during, and ever-after the transfer. Romaine required that Jones deal directly with Hilton in the negotiations. If Hilton accepted the terms of Romaine's arrangement, Jones was told to place yet another ad in the *Herald.* In it, Jones was instructed to write: "Canada terms accepted. Counsel."

Jones was hesitant to respond immediately to the mysterious Romaine. He had made no headway with Hilton, and Walling had abdicated his role in the matter, instructing Jones to deal directly with Hilton since he was in charge of the case.

When Jones didn't contact Romaine again, another letter from Boston arrived at Jones's offices. The letter contained $250 in cash, as payment to Jones for his efforts. Jones made another appointment to meet with Hilton to discuss what had transpired. Regardless of the news, Hilton remained steadfast in his refusal to deal with anyone for the return of Stewart's body.

"If these scoundrels imagine that they are to get any money from me to compromise their crime they will get tired of the business too. I will hunt them down if it costs a fortune!" Hilton said.

Hilton then gave Jones the message he wanted published in the *Herald.* The message read: "Canada-Terms not accepted. Counsel."

"Judge, I think the best thing I can do is to close this whole business. I am getting tired of it," Jones said.

The ad Hilton had given Jones ran in the *Herald* the next day. Jones broke off all communications with Hilton following the publication of the ad. He had become apprehensive, fearing that Hilton might begin to suspect him of being part of the conspiracy. He wasn't far off the mark. Hilton had several Pinkerton detectives follow Jones for several months after, and detectives staked out Jones's Nassau Street office, but their investigation into Jones's affairs turned up nothing.

Romaine continued to write to Jones, even after the ad appeared in the newspaper. On February 19, 1879, Jones received a letter postmarked from Montreal. In it Romaine called the unmoving Hilton "the vilest of human reptiles."

Jones responded in a return letter that "I do not care to have much more to do with this business," and he expressed his opinion that Hilton did not appear to want the remains returned.

Romaine wrote back, again from the Montreal post office. This time his letter sounded more cordial. He was, at least based on Jones's interpretation, willing to listen to any proposal Hilton might come up with regarding the exchange of the body for some unnamed ransom amount. This sudden change in Romaine's previously unwavering stance—two hundred thousand dollars or nothing—was enough to prompt Jones to make another attempt at persuading Hilton to negotiate with the robbers. He took the new letter from Romaine to Hilton, but the judge once again was unwilling to entertain the arrangement proposed by Romaine. However, Hilton did begin to bend his stance slightly. He told Jones that he might be willing to negotiate for the return of Stewart's remains if the ransom was reduced to five thousand dollars. He had other demands. Hilton refused to go to Canada to identify and retrieve the body, if indeed it was the body of Stewart, which he was still skeptical of. Instead, he proposed that the robbers return the body to New York.

When Jones wrote to Romaine of Hilton's new demands, the robber told Jones in a letter dated February 28 to end all his negotiations with the stubborn, tightwad Hilton and instead take the ransom deal directly to the attention of Cornelia Stewart. According to the letter, Romaine promised that if his demands were met, Mrs. Stewart would have her husband's body back within two days. She, unlike Judge Hilton, was sure to agree to the ransom arrangement.

Cornelia Stewart had wandered around in a dreamlike state, floating in and out of reality, grieving to the point of near physical exhaustion, since the theft of her husband's body. Surely she would pay whatever price for her husband's return. Although Jones could not make direct contact with Mrs. Stewart, whom Hilton kept under close surveillance, he did manage to contact Mrs. Stewart's personal physician, Dr. Sidney Carney. The doctor informed Jones that he, working under the sanction of Judge Hilton, was authorized to pay twenty-five thousand dollars, the initial amount Hilton offered in his reward to anyone aiding in the capture of the grave robbers and for the safe return of Stewart's body. Again Jones wrote to Romaine with the new offer. Romaine refused to negotiate with Carney, but he had a new stipulation to offer to Hilton. If Hilton himself would not travel to Canada to view and retrieve the body, then he could send his son-in-law, the attorney Horace Russell. But the measly twenty-five thousand-dollar ransom was out of the question.

Jones was determined. He insisted that Romaine reconsider the twenty-five thousand-dollar offer and agree to allow Dr. Carney to make the trip to Canada to pick up the body. Romaine replied to Jones's entreaty on April 5, agreeing this time that he didn't care who came to pick up the body. However, he made no mention of what he had previously viewed as a paltry ransom amount. Jones's plan to become the hero of the A. T. Stewart grave robbery was over. Whoever Henry G. Romaine might have been, he thereafter discontinued his correspondence with Jones.

THE BODY OF A.T. STEWART
NEW STORIES CONCERNING THE GRAVE YARD ROBBERY
How Gen. P.H. Jones Acted As Counsel For The Thieves—The Coffin Plate Sent To Him Through The Mails—An Italian Stone-Cutter's Remarkable Yard

It is asserted that the body has not yet been recovered, although Judge Hilton knew of its whereabouts, and the haunts of the thieves as long ago as January last. The thieves, according to the story, tried to enter into negotiations with Judge Hilton, with a view to a compromise, through the agency of ex-

Postmaster P.H. Jones. So far from denying his connection with the matter, Gen. Jones told a TIMES reporter yesterday a story of a brief but most remarkable experience as the counsel of the grave-robbers, how he received the missing coffin plate and some other articles, and what conversations he had on the subject with Police Superintendent Walling and Judge Hilton. For many months past it has been pretty generally believed that the body has been recovered and placed in the unfinished crypt at Garden City, which is now guarded by four watchmen. ... Moreover, Mrs. Stewart had recovered her former cheerfulness and mingled once more with her friends, and from this it was argued that the great source of her grief had been removed. But it is now asserted that Mrs. Stewart had simply been deceived. And that Judge Hilton's composure and the engagement of extra watchmen at Garden City were in accordance with a plan designed to produce precisely the impression it was so successful in producing: that no compromise has been effected with the thieves and that they are still beyond the reach of the law.

—*New York Times*
August 14, 1879

WHAT GEN. JONES SAYS
His Mysterious Correspondence With "Romaine"—The Coffin Plate, The Scrap Of Paper, And The Screw Tops

The body of Alexander T. Stewart, it is asserted, is concealed somewhere in Canada, although it is admitted that its precise whereabouts is known only to the men who took it away. The story was made known to Judge Hilton last Winter. ... [According to Jones] "The letter was postmarked Montreal and addressed in a scrawling hand, with which I was perfectly unfamiliar. Upon opening it a one hundred dollar bill dropped to the floor. The writing inside was even more peculiar than on the envelope. It was the most perfect attempt at a disguise that I have ever remember to have seen. ... I have been receiving letters from Romaine ever since last January, until within a few month's past. Lately I have heard nothing from the robbers. They may be in prison by this time, or they may be dead. If they are dead their secret has died with them, and the body of Mr. Stewart will never be recovered."

—*New York Times*
August 14, 1879

The controversy regarding the return of A. T. Stewart's body swirled out of control in an ongoing tornado of misinformation and wishful thinking, with each New York City newspaper periodically heralding a scoop on the case. In January 1879, the *New York Sun* reported that Stewart's body had been recovered, delivered to Judge Hilton, and placed in a guarded and secure vault awaiting the completion of the crypt at the cathedral in Garden City where it would be entombed. According to the *Sun,* Judge Hilton had been approached by a representative of an unnamed law firm serving as an intermediary for the grave robbers. Negotiations were begun with the robbers and concluded with the return of the body in payment of fifty thousand dollars in ransom. When reporters from other newspapers tried to verify the story, they were met by one denial after another.

New York City Police Superintendent George Washington Walling told reporters: "If Stewart's body has been recovered, I have no knowledge of it."

Responding to the *Sun* story, Captain Kealy, the chief of detectives, told reporters: "Another ghost story, I see. I have no knowledge of any new features in the Stewart case and certainly cannot know that the body has been recovered."

Not even Henry Hilton would confirm (or deny) the story.

"Having no information I desire to communicate, I prefer at present not speaking on the subject further," Hilton said.

A.T. STEWART
THE REPORTED RECOVERY
OF HIS BODY
Judge Hilton Declines To Say Anything
And The Police Authorities Say That
They Know Nothing

It is stated upon authority so trustworthy as to leave but little
if any doubt of the entire correctness of the report, that Mrs.
A.T. Stewart has said to at least two persons ... that the body
of her husband has been recovered.

—Brooklyn Eagle
January 16, 1879

The credentials of Patrick Jones were impeccable. He was a lawyer, a former postmaster of New York City, and a decorated Union
army veteran. There was no reason for the authorities, Mrs. Stewart,
or anyone else, including Henry Hilton, to mistrust his intentions. Hilton, however, was suspicious of anyone who came to him with information that might lead to the return of A. T. Stewart's remains.

Born in Ireland, Jones immigrated to America in 1840. He became
a lawyer in 1856 and established himself as one of the most prominent lawyers in western New York. At the outbreak of the Civil War
in 1861, he enlisted in the Union army. He rose quickly through the
ranks, displaying what was reported as "gallant conduct." In 1862,
he was promoted to the rank of colonel and later led his troops
in the Battle of Chancellorsville. Jones was wounded during this
battle and captured by Confederate forces. He was a prisoner of war
before being released in a prisoner exchange in 1863. He took part
in General William Tecumseh Sherman's March to the Sea and was
commissioned as a brigadier general. In 1869, President Ulysses S.
Grant appointed him postmaster of New York City, a position he
held until 1872. He then returned to private practice. Jones's role
in the Stewart case was not one he sought or desired, and it became

an albatross around his good name chiefly because of the actions of Henry Hilton.

According to George Washington Walling's 1887 account, published in *Recollections of a New York City Chief of Police,* "No trace of the body or thieves was found until January of the following year, when General Patrick H. Jones, of No. 150 Nassau Street, called upon me at police headquarters. He brought with him a parcel and showed me the contents. They were the silver knobs and several of the handles belonging to the coffin in which the body had been buried. He also showed me some letters which he had received. They purported to have been written in Canada, and were signed by 'Henry G. Romaine.' With the first letter a hundred-dollar bill was enclosed as a retainer for him to act as attorney for the return of the body, upon the payment of the ransom.

Walling recalled how this initial act of goodwill by Jones led to little more than contempt from Hilton. "Judge Hilton refused to agree to the terms proposed, and, further, declined to negotiate through the medium of 'personals,'" Walling wrote.

Besides refusing to negotiate with the thieves, Hilton, in his usual brash manner, impugned the reputation of Jones. Jones had supplied Hilton and the authorities with all the various correspondence he'd received from the mysterious "Romaine."

"I took that letter to Judge Hilton and he was even more offensive than on my first visit," Jones told reporters.

"I see that he has not been giving me a very enviable character ... but during our intercourse in this business he never said anything to me that could be construed as an insult, or evincing any want of faith in my honor," Jones told *Times* reporters.

"I suppose from what I read this morning that he was under the impression all the time that I was simply an agent for the robbers. ... I find that I have been abused and misrepresented in this business throughout," he said.

"If Judge Hilton attempts to impugn my motives I will make public the entire correspondence, from last January until now, and leave my friends to judge whether I have done right or wrong in the course I have taken."

SENSATIONAL
THE GHASTLY STORY OF A NEGOTIATION WITH GHOULS
The Recovery Of The Body Of A.T. Stewart
Denied—A Strange Account Of An Attempt To Make A Big Stake

Not long ago a certain Nassau street lawyer received a letter from Montreal signed "Romaine." The writer wanted to know if he would take charge of negotiations for the return of the body of Mr. Stewart and the securing of the sum demanded for its delivery—namely $250,000. ... The package contained the silver knobs and part of a handle of Stewart's coffin. ... The lawyer took his letters and ghastly proofs and had a personal interview with Superintendent Walling. ... Judge Hilton was next sought. He declared the payment of $250,000 for the remains as preposterous. He would not pay one red cent. He wanted not the body but the robbers and would have nothing to do with the lawyer. The twain parted angrily and Judge Hilton had the lawyer "shadowed" by detectives. ... At last communication with Judge Hilton was closed entirely and transcripts of the letters were laid before Mrs. Stewart. It was ascertained that she believed the remains had been recovered and that they were reposing them in Hempstead Cathedral.

—*Brooklyn Eagle*
August 15, 1879

Hilton told reporters that Jones was under surveillance by the police. He then told both Jones and reporters that he would not hesitate to prosecute *any* man suspected of having the least connection with the grave robbers or their associates, no matter who he might be, implying even the highly decorated Union army veteran and former New York City postmaster.

Reports that Stewart's body had indeed been recovered through negotiations with the robbers were disputed in various newspaper accounts and even caused a round of finger pointing and finger wagging. The *World* claimed that the ransom had been paid, and Stewart's remains had been recovered. This account was disputed immediately by the *New York Herald*, which claimed that not only had Stewart's remains not been recovered, but the thieves had entered into negotiations with an unnamed New York City lawyer (Jones) for the return of the body and were asking $250,000. In response to the *Herald* story, Hilton acknowledged that Stewart's body had not been recovered.

The *New York Times* reported on Jones's correspondence with the mysterious "Romaine" and his futile attempts at negotiating the return of the remains through Judge Hilton. But the *Brooklyn Eagle* was quick to place the blame for the ongoing controversy regarding Stewart's remains squarely on the shoulders of the New York City Police Department. Regarding the erroneous reports in the *World* that Stewart's body had been recovered, the *Brooklyn Eagle* proclaimed, "Let it be very cautious about stating as fact what is in reality only the conjecture of a posse of uniformed and uninformed blockheads and numbskulls, to wit: the police of New York."

When a *New York Times* reporter asked Jones if he had been in contact with Mrs. Stewart, Jones said, "I never saw Mrs. Stewart in my life." But Jones went on to tell the reporter that he had the correspondence between himself and the mysterious Romaine copied into a book and sent to Mrs. Stewart.

"I thought she was entitled to know the exact truth about her husband's remains, and believed that it was cruel in Judge Hilton to deceive her by pretending that they were recovered; besides, if she saw fit to compromise with the desecrators of Mr. Stewart's grave, it was none of my business, and, I think, none of Judge Hilton's business," Jones told reporters.

NEW YORK PUBLIC LIBRARY

Alexander Turney Stewart, hailed as the father of the American department store, was one of the richest men in America when he died in 1876, leaving behind an estimated fortune of forty million dollars. His fortune was derived from his massive retail and wholesale dry goods business.

LIBRARY OF CONGRESS

A. T. Stewart's cast-iron front department store, built in 1862, occupied an entire city block at Broadway and Tenth Street. It was considered the first "true" department store with nineteen departments and employing upwards of two thousand people.

NEW YORK PUBLIC LIBRARY

Along with his retail business, Stewart ran a successful wholesale business out of the massive store located on Broadway, Chambers, and Reade Streets.
FROM *THE SUCCESSFUL BUSINESS HOUSES OF NEW YORK* (1872)

A. T. Stewart & Co.

Are constantly offering a large and varied assortment of

Dry Goods,

REPRESENTING the choicest fabrics of this class of manufactures throughout the world, and adapted to the wants of buyers from all parts of the country. Selected with special reference to the assortment required in each of the various departments of their business.

EMBRACING

Silks,   Velvets,   Shawls,
   Satins,   Ribbons,   Suits,
      Laces,   Embroideries,   Sacques.

DRESS FABRICS,
In all Textures.

White Goods,   Hosiery,
   Linens,   Gloves,
      Domestic Cottons,   Underwear.

FURNISHING AND UPHOLSTERING GOODS
In every variety.

Oil Cloths,   Blankets,   Furs,
   Carpets,   Mattings,   Flannels,
Yankee Notions,
      Foreign Fancy Goods,
            Millinery Goods.

—◦❀◦—

Retail Department,

BROADWAY, FOURTH AVENUE, NINTH & TENTH STS.

An advertisement for A. T. Stewart & Company's retail goods demonstrated the vast and varied dry goods made available to New York shoppers, especially women.
FROM *THE SUCCESSFUL BUSINESS HOUSES OF NEW YORK* (1872)

Nothing ever escaped the eye of A. T. Stewart, and he made sure that his clerks didn't misrepresent his products or display his goods in a gaudy fashion.
FROM *FRANK LESLIE'S ILLUSTRATED*

Stewart often reminded his clerks, "You must be wise, but not too wise. You must never actually cheat the customer, even if you can. If she pays the full figure, present her a hank of dress-braid, a card of buttons, a pair of shoestrings. You must make her happy and satisfied, so she will come back."
FROM *FRANK LESLIE'S ILLUSTRATED*

A. T. Stewart & Company's "Marble Palace" employed more than 150 women in its sewing room, where seamstresses were kept constantly busy making alterations to goods and merchandise.
FROM *Frank Leslie's Illustrated*

The Working Women's Hotel, located on Fourth Avenue between Thirty-second and Thirty-third Streets, was built by A. T. Stewart to provide New York City working women with safe and reasonably priced accommodations. The hotel had 502 private rooms.
FROM *Frank Leslie's Illustrated*

Stewart's home, a huge Italian marble mansion, was on the corner of Fifth Avenue and Thirty-fourth Street. It was considered one of them most ornate and elaborate private homes in America.
LIBRARY OF CONGRESS

It was built in 1864–1869 at a cost estimated at two million dollars. The designer of Stewart's marble mansion was John Kellum, who designed all of Stewart's buildings, including the cast iron retail store, the women's hotel, and the buildings and homes at Garden City.
NEW YORK PUBLIC LIBRARY

When all of Fifth Avenue's stately homes were magnificent brownstones, Stewart's was the only one with a white marble façade. There is little doubt that Stewart's marble mansion was calculated to impress and outdo his wealthy, illustrious neighbors.
NEW YORK PUBLIC LIBRARY

Stewart's funeral was an elaborate and lavish affair befitting a man of his wealth and stature. The pomp and circumstance surrounding it equaled that of the death of an American statesman. His widow, Cornelia, and his legal advisor, Judge Henry Hilton, paid their last respects.
FROM *FRANK LESLIE'S ILLUSTRATED*

An hour before dawn, on the morning of Wednesday, November 7, 1878, ghouls broke into A. T. Stewart's family vault in St. Mark's Church cemetery and stole the body of the great retail magnate and held it for ransom.
W. P. SNYDER/*HARPER'S WEEKLY*

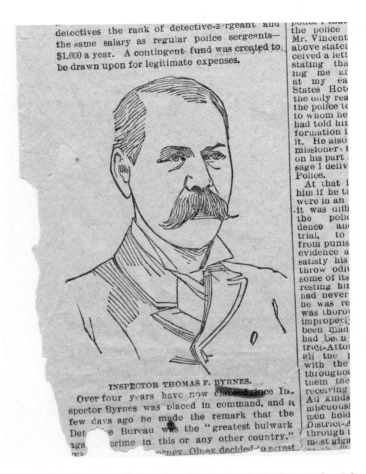

detectives the rank of detective-sergeant and the same salary as regular police sergeants— $1,600 a year. A contingent fund was created to be drawn upon for legitimate expenses.

the police
Mr. Vincent
above stated
ceived a lett
stating tha
ing me at
at my ea
States Hot
the only rea
the police t
to whom he
had told hir
formation i
it. He also
missioners t
on his part
sage I deliv
Police.
At that i
him if he tl
were in an
it was diffi
the polic
dence au
trial, to
from punis
evidence a
satisy his
throw odi
some of its
resting hir
had never
he was re
was thoro
improperl
been mad
had been
trict-Atto
all the
with the
throughou
them the
receiving
All kinds
miscuous
men hold
District-A
through t
most sign

INSPECTOR THOMAS F. BYRNES.

Over four years have now passed since Inspector Byrnes was placed in command, and a few days ago he made the remark that the Detective Bureau was the "greatest bulwark against crime in this or any other country."

orney Olney decided to arrest

Captain Thomas Byrnes of the Fifteenth Precinct, who had a penchant for gaining publicity, told reporters that he was sure his investigation would lead to an immediate arrest in the case, along with the recovery of Stewart's body.

PRINT COLLECTION, MIRIAM AND IRA D. WALLACH DIVISION OF ART, PRINTS AND PHOTOGRAPHS, THE NEW YORK PUBLIC LIBRARY, ASTOR, LENOX, AND TILDEN FOUNDATIONS

In 1879, Attorney Patrick Jones, a former New York postmaster and Civil War veteran, reported that he had been contacted by A. T. Stewart's grave robbers, who asked that he act as an intermediary in negotiations for the return of the body.

In June 1877, New York City banker Joseph Seligman was refused accommodations at the Grand Union Hotel in Saratoga by its owner, Judge Henry Hilton. A firestorm of protest followed, and the New York City Jewish community boycotted the A. T. Stewart stores in retaliation for Hilton's behavior.

Stewart's closest friend and confidant, Judge Henry Hilton, became the executor of Stewart's will and overseer of his forty-million-dollar fortune. Hilton's lack of business savvy, his imperious management style, and a series of egregious public relations blunders all ultimately led to the liquidation of the once successful retail company and the depletion of the Stewart family fortune.

FROM *HISTORY OF THE COURT OF COMMON PLEAS OF THE CITY AND COUNTY OF NEW YORK* (1896)

Cornelia Stewart commissioned the building of the elaborate Gothic-style Cathedral of the Incarnation in Garden City, New York, as a monument to her husband's memory. Her husband's remains were interred in the crypt at the Cathedral. (Or, were they?)

Judge Hilton's efforts to conceal Jones's negotiations with the mysterious Romaine ended when Jones sent a copy of the correspondence to Cornelia Stewart's private attorneys at the New York law firm Evarts, Southmayd, and Choatt. The firm, whose reputation was impeccable, examined the letters and decided to turn them all over to Mrs. Stewart. Despite what she read, Mrs. Stewart remained steadfast in her support of Hilton and, at least outwardly, appeared to believe or want to believe what Hilton had told her—that her husband's body had been recovered and was now resting in the crypt in Garden City.

When Cornelia Stewart's private attorneys gave her the Romaine letters, she confronted Hilton, who vehemently maintained that the body had been recovered and was in safekeeping until it could be transported to the crypt in Garden City. Hilton went on to debunk the Jones and Romaine correspondence, arguing that Romaine was merely another con artist looking for a big payday. Further feathering his own cap, Hilton assured Cornelia Stewart that he had worked diligently to protect her from scams that men or women like Romaine tried to perpetrate on the grieving widow. Mrs. Stewart, who had grown to treat Hilton as a son, much like her husband, chose to believe Hilton over the obvious facts presented to her. With Mrs. Stewart's renewed faith in him, Hilton went on the offensive against Jones, who had damaged the judge's credibility, not only with Mrs. Stewart but also in the public's eyes.

According to a *New York Sun* account published in early 1879, Hilton had assured Mrs. Stewart that her husband's remains had been recovered from the grave robbers after paying a ransom of fifty thousand dollars. Although the robbers were not identified, the *Sun* claimed that an unnamed law firm had conducted negotiations for the return of the body. The robbers had first demanded one hundred thousand dollars for the return of Stewart's remains but settled on fifty thousand dollars. Hilton allegedly told the widow that the remains were identified beyond a doubt and that they were immediately placed in a secret vault that was guarded around the clock until they could be interned in the crypt at the cathedral in Garden City. Despite the many rumors to the contrary, Mrs. Stewart seemed willing to believe that Hilton had indeed recovered her husband's remains and all was right with the world again.

Hitting back at Jones's claim that he had deliberately misled Mrs. Stewart, Hilton told reporters that he believed Jones was in fact one of the robbers and not the go-between, as he claimed to be. According to Hilton, the Romaine letters were fraudulent and did not originate in Canada as Jones claimed but were composed in New York City and made to appear to have been sent from a Canadian address. Hilton provided no proof to back up his claims. According to Hilton, he knew who the grave robbers were and where they were located and said that authorities were closing in on them. Also, again, Hilton offered no substantial proof to back up this claim.

Jones threatened to sue Hilton for slander for implicating him in the grave robbery. The New York City press was divided on the ongoing mystery. The *New York Times* was content to support Jones in his story about the mysterious Romaine hiding in Canada, and so too was the *New York Herald*. The *World,* another New York newspaper, called Jones a "politician" and discredited his entire story. According to the *World,* Jones's story was riddled with flaws, including the fact that as a former postmaster, Jones hadn't contacted the authorities at the Montreal post office from which Romaine's letters were supposedly mailed. And the newspaper questioned why Jones didn't ask to have the police stationed at the post office where the mysterious Romaine dropped off and picked up his mail in order to identify the culprit. Given the severity of the crime and its sensational nature, there would be no reason not to apprehend Romaine in Montreal and hold him for questioning. But Jones never made any attempt to do this. The *World* questioned his motives and called him a fraud. At the least, according to the *World,* Jones was after some notoriety to further his political career, and at the worst, he was trying to make some easy money off Hilton and the grieving Mrs. Stewart.

"I have told you now all that I know about the business."
—PATRICK JONES, AUGUST 1879

THE MYSTERIOUS PACKAGE

In which Italian sculptor Giuseppe F. Sala makes a startling claim that he was involved with men who stole Stewart's body. Sala had previously been mixed up in the infamous Cardiff Giant hoax, in which a giant was reportedly discovered on a farm in upstate New York. The "giant" turns out to be a body carved out of gypsum by Sala. His claim regarding the body of A. T. Stewart turns out to be merely another hoax. In August 1881, new leads come to light when New York City private detective J. M. Fuller reports he has received a mysterious package that includes a painting showing where Stewart's body is buried in Cypress Hills Cemetery.

No sooner had the Jones involvement in the case of A. T. Stewart's remains ended than another controversy arose, this time involving Giuseppe Sala, an Italian sculptor. Sala took his story to the authorities and directly to Judge Hilton. Sala claimed that he met several people in 1876 who were planning to steal Stewart's body from St. Mark's. He claimed that one of the conspirators was a beautiful young woman who bankrolled the robbery and served as the leader of the gang of thieves. The gang had three other members, all men.

Sala was known to the gang because of his role in several hoaxes, including arguably the most famous hoax in American history, that of the Cardiff Giant. Sala alleged that his participation in the Cardiff scam began when New York tobacconist George Hull hired him to sculpt a ten-foot-tall giant out of gypsum. Hull had the giant buried and then dug up on October 16, 1869, by workers preparing a well behind the barn of William Newell in Cardiff, New York. The "giant" was hailed as a petrified man, and a tent was erected over it. People came from all over to pay fifty cents each to see the famous Cardiff Giant. Hull later sold the giant for thirty-seven thousand dollars to a group of investors, who moved it to Syracuse, New York, to put on display. P. T. Barnum even had an imitation made.

According to Sala, the gang of thieves who stole Stewart's body knew all about the illicit Cardiff Giant affair, as well as other shady ventures he had participated in. He further claimed that the gang wanted Sala to petrify the bones of A. T. Stewart. Sala told the police that besides his uncanny ability to carve humanlike statues, he was adept at the process of preserving the remains of the dead. Sala said he agreed to join the gang, demanding that his share be paid in advance and that all his expenses be paid for. He said that they had struck a deal and that the gang reportedly first planned to steal the body of Benedict Arnold (1741–1801), the infamous Revolutionary War traitor, who was buried in a cemetery in London.

Sala and his colleagues abandoned their scheme when they discovered that the English police were far more vigilant in protecting the dead than the police were in America. They then discussed several other options, including an attempt at replicating the infamous Cardiff Giant with a sculpted figure they would bury near the Giant's Causeway in Ireland. It would be unearthed and hailed as the petrified remains of Finn McCool, the giant of the causeway.

The Giant's Causeway, on the northeast coast of Northern Ireland, is a mesmerizing mass of tightly packed stone columns. According to the Northern Ireland Tourist Board, "The tops of the columns form stepping stones that lead from the cliff foot and disappear under the sea. Altogether there are 40,000 of these stone columns." Irish legend has it that Finn McCool was a giant who built the stone causeway as a path to take to Scotland to battle his Scottish counterpart and archenemy, the giant Benandonner.

The gang decided to proceed with the Irish endeavor, and Sala reportedly sculpted their giant Finn McCool. This time, however, when the giant stone hoax was unearthed and rumors swirled that it was the petrified remains of Finn McCool, the Irish press and scientists immediately uncovered the attempted deception, and the gang fled back to America to hatch another plot.

Still under the leadership of the unknown beautiful woman, the gang discussed stealing Stewart's body and holding it for ransom. According to Sala, he had a falling out with the woman and parted ways with the schemers. Shortly after that, Sala told authorities, he read the newspaper accounts of the theft of Stewart's remains. He knew immediately it was the work of his former colleagues.

Sala agreed to take the police to Troy, New York, where he claimed he would be able to identify the woman and her accomplices. He told the police that one of the gang members was named Ford and that the beautiful unnamed woman was Ford's wife or mistress. Sala and several New York City detectives went to Troy, but upon arrival, Sala had a change of heart, claiming that he feared for his life and wanting assurances from Hilton that he would pay for his personal protection. Hearing this, Judge Hilton was reported to have said, "Let the matter rest." And rest it did. Sala was not heard from afterward.

SALA'S REMARKABLE STORY
AN ITALIAN STONE-CUTTER'S QUEER EXPERIENCES—
One Series Of Clues Given To The Police

Shortly after the robbery in St. Mark's Church-yard, Judge Hilton was visited by Giuseppe F. Sala, an Italian sculptor, who now has a studio at No. 141 West Thirty-fourth-street, on the site of the old Gospel tent. Sala speaks English poorly, and when he visited Judge Hilton he tried his patience by his inability to talk as quickly and distinctly as the Judge, who is at times impatient, desired. Sala, however, told part of his story to Judge Hilton, and the rest to a person in his confidence. It was an extraordinary one, and its entire verification involved the expenditure of a large sum. It was, however, considered of sufficient importance to warrant an outlay of about $75, to enable Sala to go to Troy and point out some persons, who, according to him, were implicated in the grave robbery. Sala went to Troy, but failed to do what he promised.

—*New York Times*
August 14, 1879

"There were giants in the earth in those days; and also after that, when the sons of God came in unto the daughters of men, and they bear children to them, the same became mighty men which were of old, men of renown."

—GENESIS 6:4, King James Bible

MORE FACTS ABOUT SALA
The Man Who Thought He Knew Who Stole Stewart's Body—His Friends In Troy

Troy, Aug. 14—Sala, who was mentioned in THE TIMES to-day as the exposer of a band of resurrectionists, lived in Troy about 10 years ago. He was born in Italy, and is a man of ability, but was a slave to liquor during his residence here. He went to Ireland a few years ago with E.J. Ford and a stone-cutter named Dye. They took with them a stone image, which they subsequently endeavored to pass upon the Irish people as the petrified body of Finn McCool. They returned about three years ago and Ford, whose father had meantime been elected Superintendent of the Poor of this county, made him his clerk. Last year a committee of the Supervisors reported that grave frauds marked the administration of the Poor Department, in consequence of which the senior Ford resigned, and he and his son and others were charged. They are now out on bail awaiting trial. While Ford is tricky and unprincipled, it is not believed by his acquaintances that he would dare to embark in so great an undertaking as the stealing of Stewart's body. It is thought here that Sala has told the truth on non-essential and falsehoods on essential points.

—*New York Times*
August 15, 1879

As the case of Stewart's missing corpse dragged on and on, it was becoming increasingly obvious that the New York City Police Department was simply not competent. The entire matter became the subject of ridicule and parody. *Puck,* an irreverent New York City–based humor magazine, ran a series of unflattering cartoons depicting Henry Hilton as a self-indulgent puppet master with the missing remains of A. T. Stewart as the puppet, pulling the strings in the ongoing investigation fiasco. The cartoons leveled the harshest criticism upon Hilton's arrogant behavior in his dealings with the city's Jewish community and his handling of the Jones affair. Many felt privately what the cartoons expressed publicly—that Hilton was manipulating the case to feather his own financial nest, while at the same time, running A. T. Stewart's once prosperous retail empire into the ground.

As if *Puck*'s indictment of him wasn't enough, none other than America's premiere humorist, Mark Twain, decided to get in on the act. His parody of the Stewart affair, written in 1879 and called "The Stolen White Elephant," was published in 1882. The story features an Indian elephant that disappears in New Jersey just before it is to be shipped to Britain as a gift from the King of Siam to the Queen of England. In Twain's story, the local police and the case of the missing elephant are headed by Chief Inspector Blunt. Twain reportedly modeled Blunt after Allan Pinkerton, the director of the famous Chicago-based Pinkerton National Detective Agency, and gave Blunt an assistant named Burns, reportedly modeled after New York City's top cop, Captain Thomas Byrnes.

The story is replete with satirical headlines from various New York City newspapers, similar to the real headlines that appeared during the coverage of the Stewart case, and absurd letters similar to the ones sent by Romaine and others claiming to know where the body was hidden. In the tale, the police undertake a massive investigation, but the mystery ends badly for everyone involved. The story was originally to appear in Twain's book *A Tramp Abroad,* published in 1880, but was left out of that work. In a preface to the short story, Twain wrote that he left it out of *A Tramp Abroad* because it was feared that some of the particulars had been exaggerated and that others were not true. Before these suspicions had proven groundless, the book had gone to press.

In the story, the overconfident Inspector Blunt orders his men to search for the missing white elephant throughout New York and in other neighboring states. The bungling police are unable to locate the elephant despite paying out a sizable ransom to the elephant thieves. Ultimately the missing elephant is found right beneath the very noses of the police, in a hidden vault—a vault in which police officers played cards and slept—but the poor animal is dead. Still, the incompetent Blunt is hailed as a hero. The story was a scathing indictment of the entire Stewart disaster, the police, the Pinkertons, and Henry Hilton.

"Now, what does the elephant eat, and how much?"
"Well, as to what he eats,—he will eat anything. He will eat a man, he will eat a Bible,—he will eat anything between a man and a Bible."
"Good,—very good indeed, but too general. Details are nec-essary.—details are the only valuable things in our trade. ... How many Bibles would he eat at a meal?"
"He would eat an entire edition."
"It is hardly succinct enough. Do you mean the ordinary octavo, or the family illustrated?"
—MARK TWAIN, "THE STOLEN WHITE ELEPHANT," 1879

For two long years, the A. T. Stewart case languished. If indeed there was any investigation, neither Hilton nor the police spoke of it, and the city's newspapers had little to publish. Cornelia Stewart appeared to be at peace, although no one knew why. Speculation was that Hilton had convinced her of a miraculous recovery of her husband's stolen body, which he told her lay at rest in the crypt at the cathedral being built for him in Garden City. Meanwhile, Hilton brushed away any questions regarding the case as arrogantly as he brushed aside the ongoing dispute with the Jewish community. By then, the police were on to more press-ing matters, including the apprehension of the thieves who broke into the Manhattan Savings Institution in October 1878 and stole close to three million dollars in cash and securities.

For all its sensationalism, the case slipped into obscurity following the Romaine incident, and the last news of any merit for two years
appeared in late August 1879.

Yet, the public and the newspapers' fascination remained in the
background, and despite the two-year hiatus in media attention, the
Stewart case again came to the forefront of the city's attention in
August 1881. Reports surfaced that private detectives were working
on a large excavation project at Cypress Hills Cemetery on Long Island
in search of what they hoped were the remains of A. T. Stewart.

A.T. STEWART'S REMAINS
THE NEWLY AROUSED INTEREST
IN CYPRESS HILLS CEMETERY.
A Large Number Of People Visit The
Place Yesterday—The Search To Be
Resumed To-Day

The story of the recent moves made by the Fuller Detective
Bureau ... was on every lip, and argumentative visitors discuss the case in every aspect, few agreeing upon any essential
point. There were those present who energetically scoffed at
the idea of any importance attaching to the newly declared
clues, many maintaining that the dead millionaire's remains
were safely sealed in the crypt at Garden City. Others as earnestly contended that Detective Fuller's clues were worthy of
the most thorough investigation. ... He [J.M. Fuller] summarized the story ... beginning with the receipt on the evening
of the 13th of the oil sketch of the landscape in Cypress Hills
from the mysterious woman who disappeared and could not
be found. ... Upon the picture was plainly written within a
grave shaped diagram: Cypress Hills: Stewart is buried here.
... Fuller spoke of his having entered into a correspondence
with Judge Hilton, who seemed to have exhibited much inter-

est in the matter, and had dispatched from Saratoga a representative specially to act in his stead.

—*New York Times*
August 22, 1881

"Judge Hilton does not bear a single penny of the expenses. Mr. E.D. Harris accompanied me to the cemetery on Saturday and our investigations were begun under his supervision and with his endorsement, but every move of importance that has been made in the case has been my own. Do I believe that Mr. Stewart's body is really buried here? Of course, there is a strong doubt in my mind as to that, but to me it seems that everything favors the idea that the grave is located here, and that our clues will turn out to be no hoax."

—J. M. FULLER, FULLER'S NEW YORK DETECTIVE BUREAU, AUGUST 1881

Despite the revived widespread attention to the search for A. T. Stewart, it played second fiddle to an even more dastardly crime and one with more far-reaching effect—the assassination of President James A. Garfield, who was shot and seriously wounded on Saturday, July 2, 1881. Garfield was fired upon as he walked through the waiting room of the Baltimore & Potomac Railroad in Washington, D.C. He was on his way to deliver a speech at his alma mater, Williams College.

Garfield, the twentieth president of the United States, died on September 19, 1881, eleven weeks after the shooting. While bedridden at the White House, he suffered from fever, hallucinations, and extreme pain. On September 6, 1881, he was transported to Long Branch, New Jersey, to escape the sweltering heat of Washington. By then, blood poisoning had set in. Although doctors had probed the wound and extracted the bullet near his spine, he became increasingly weak and sick. He died of a massive heart attack on the morning of September 19.

His assassin, Charles J. Guiteau, was an emotionally disturbed man who had failed to gain an appointment in Garfield's administration. Guiteau fired two bullets at Garfield. One bullet grazed his arm, but the other lodged in his back. Garfield had no bodyguards with him at the time.

During his trial, Guiteau claimed that Garfield's murder was "an act of God" and that he was only serving as an instrument of God's will. His trial became a media sensation, largely because of Guiteau's increasingly bizarre behavior: He recited poems he had written to the jury, sang a rendition of "John Brown's Body," and sent notes to spectators imploring them to help him with his defense.

His trial was one of the first high-profile cases in the American judicial system during which the defense entered an insanity plea on behalf of its client. Guiteau vehemently disputed his lawyers' claims. The jury found him guilty on January 25, 1882, and he was hanged on June 30, 1882, in the District of Columbia. Standing on the scaffold, Guiteau asked to recite a poem he had written called "I Am Going to the Lordy."

A GREAT NATION IN GRIEF
PRESIDENT GARFIELD SHOT BY AN ASSASSIN.
Though Seriously Wounded He Still Survives
The Would Be Murderer Lodged In Prison.
The President Of The United States
Attacked And Terribly Wounded By
A Fanatical Office-Seeker On The Eve Of
Independence Day—The Nation Horrified
And The Whole Civilized World Shocked—
The President Still Alive And His Recovery
Possible.

The appalling intelligence came from Washington yesterday morning that President Garfield had been assassinated and was dead. Later dispatches, however, modified this startling

news by the announcement that the President, while danger-
ously wounded, was still living, and that there was a slight
hope of his recovery.

—*New York Times*
July 3, 1881

THE TRAGEDY IN THE DEPOT
Guiteau Fires His Cruel Shots From Behind The President—The Wounded Man's Removal To The White House— Amazement And Horror Of The Populace

—*New York Times*
July 3, 1881

While the country was absorbed in news concerning Garfield's hoped-for recovery and subsequent death, New York City kept an eye on the A. T. Stewart mystery. J. M. Fuller's investigation into Stewart's missing remains began when a mysterious package was delivered to his offices at 841 Broadway on Saturday, August 13, 1881.

A small, unidentified boy delivered the package, expertly wrapped in white paper, directly to Fuller. According to the boy, he was acting on instructions given to him by a shadowy woman. In his small hand, the boy was holding a silver coin the woman had given to him as payment for making the delivery. Although detectives grilled him about the identity of his employer, he was unable to describe her. Detectives took the boy with them as they scoured Broadway and several other blocks looking for the woman and trying to have the boy pick her out of the crowd. It was useless. The young messenger knew nothing about the woman. It was another dead-end, except for the package.

The package included an enigmatic note, not unlike the host of other messages that had surfaced during the early days of the Stewart investigation. The message read: "The violet bed was removed the middle of April, 1881. Do not make inquiries of the man about the grounds or allow the painting to be seen. You will be followed if you are seen making special observations." It was signed with the letters: COR.

The package also contained a twelve-inch-by-twelve-inch, ornately framed oil painting on stretched canvas. The painting, which was by all accounts done by a skilled practitioner of the arts, was of a cemetery with various roads and trees. In its center was a large oak tree and below it two flat stones resembling grave markers. Next to the stones was what looked like a mound of freshly dug soil. On the mound were painted the words: "Cypress Hills. Stewart is buried here."

A cautious and conservative man by nature and profession, Fuller still came to the conclusion that the painting indicated the burial site of A. T. Stewart. It was not a conclusion Fuller came to readily or without great pains. Why Fuller was chosen to receive the mysterious package remained a mystery, although it was assumed that whoever sent the package knew that Fuller's detective agency had worked for Judge Hilton during the earliest investigation into the disappearance of Stewart's body. The sender must have assumed that Fuller had access to Hilton and hence would be able to negotiate if need be for the return of the body. Perhaps the most substantial reason for choosing Fuller was that he was not the type of man or detective to be easily fooled or to engage in a snap judgment merely to arouse sensational speculation and headlines. By all accounts he was an excellent choice. With J. M. Fuller in the lead, the A. T. Stewart case again made headlines.

STEWART'S BODY SOUGHT
AN IMPORATNT EXCAVATION BEGUN AT CYPRESS HILLS.
The Clue On Which Mr. Fuller And His Detectives Are Working—Ex-Judge Hilton's Interest—A Singular Chapter In A Story Of Crime

Detectives from this City have during the past week been slowly and patiently working on a clue which they believe may lead to the recovery of the remains of the late Alexander Turney Stewart, the stealing of which from St. Mark's Church graveyard excited such intense public interest and horror nearly three years ago. Under the direction of these detectives, workmen yesterday began to dig up a part of the ground in Cypress Hills Cemetery in a plot belonging to Mr. John T. Runice, and the work will be continued until the success or failure of the effort is made apparent.

—New York Times
August 21, 1881

Fuller's Detective Bureau
New-York. Aug 16, 1881
The Hon. Henry Hilton, Woodlawn, Saratoga, NY.:
DEAR SIR: On last Saturday evening a small boy brought to this office a package which contained a note and an oil sketch. In one portion of the sketch is a white ground in the form of a grave and written in pencil are the words, Stewart is buried here, and immediately above the location is given. The note reads: Don't make inquiries of the men about the grounds or allow the painting to be seen; you will be followed if you are seen making special observations, Signed Cor. The moment we discovered the contents of the package the boy was questioned and he stated that a lady had given it to him with instructions to hand it to me personally. He readily accompanied our young men and they began a search in the immediate vicinity for the lady but she had disappeared. To be frank with you, I don't take much stock in the thing and thought I would like your views on the matter before taking any steps. Hoping to hear from you soon, I remain yours respectfully, J.M. FULLER

—LETTER SENT TO JUDGE HILTON, AUGUST 1881

THE CYPRESS HILLS CEMETERY INCIDENT

In which J. M. Fuller begins excavation of a section of Cypress Hills Cemetery in his quest to locate the remains of A. T. Stewart. As word leaks out of Fuller's search, hundreds of curiosity seekers converge on the excavation site, hampering the investigation. Despite digging up a huge section of the cemetery, Fuller and his men uncover nothing. The excavation is abandoned.

Although J. M. Fuller remained skeptical, he was determined to see the case through to the end. Not known as a frivolous man or as a gold digger, Fuller wasn't looking to make a fast buck from Mrs. Stewart or Judge Hilton. He also knew that in order to pursue the matter to its fullest, he needed Hilton's approval. On August 16, 1881, he sent Hilton a letter explaining the details of the case, knowing full well that it would be an uphill battle. Hilton maintained publicly and to Cornelia Stewart that the body had been recovered long ago and was safely interred in the vault at Garden City. Agreeing to take part in Fuller's investigation would require Hilton to admit the body had not been recovered. If Hilton didn't respond to his letter, Fuller knew the note and letter would be considered just another hoax. However, if Hilton did reply, Fuller would be safe to proceed with the investigation. He did not have to wait long. A day after he sent the letter, Hilton responded. Although he was not able to join Fuller, Hilton agreed to send Edward Harris to represent his interests.

> *Superintendent J.M. Fuller, New-York:*
>
> *Telegram received. Edward D. Harris leaves here this afternoon and will be at my store tomorrow morning. You may confer with him on the subject and he will act as I would.*
>
> *HENRY HILTON*
>
> —TELEGRAM SENT AUGUST 19, 1881

On August 20, Fuller and five other people, including Hilton's surrogate, Edward Harris, descended on Cypress Hills Cemetery. Their goal was to find the various locations depicted in the painting sent to Fuller's offices. Along with Fuller and Harris came a *Times* reporter, two detectives from Fuller's staff, and a young woman. To throw off any suspicion and to keep crowds of curiosity seekers off guard, the group strolled casually through the cemetery, acting nonchalant and giving no impression to the outside world that indeed they were on a mission.

Established in 1849, Cypress Hills Cemetery was located along the Brooklyn and Queens border. Cypress Hills offered inexpensive burial plots. Serene and charming, it looked more like a park than a cemetery, and people often went there to stroll aimlessly around, admiring the stone markers and trying to ascertain the names and dates on the gravestones. Some settled onto the rolling hills to sit peacefully and contemplate, while still others brought pads and pens to sketch one or another of the idyllic landscape scenes. Fuller and his group were positive that they could blend into this everyday scene without raising suspicion.

The attractive young woman in the group, who was clothed in a colorful dress, caught the eye of many of the cemetery workers on the grounds that day. They nodded and tipped their work caps at her as the group walked leisurely along the winding walkways. The young woman was all part of Fuller's planned diversion. No one would suspect that such a beautiful young woman, dressed in her finest, was doing anything other than wandering the peaceful grounds in the company of family and friends—a typical and accepted custom.

Following a well-thought-out plan, Fuller and his group traipsed along the winding roads, stopping here and there to chat and pretend to examine a gravestone or sculpture. If anyone was watching, they would not have been the least suspicious as the team made its way through the main part of the cemetery and then turned up Lake Road, following along an old, whitewashed picket fence.

Fuller was following the exact route depicted in the oil painting. Finally the group came to Section 18 of the cemetery, the precise location the artist had indicated. In front of them stood the old stable and a crumbling stone building that Fuller identified as the conservatory illustrated in the painting. Both structures were situated as they had been portrayed, right beside the picket fence. Halfway between the two structures was a large weeping willow growing out of a double-tiered trunk, and nearby stood an old oak tree with a stack of flat stones aligned along its trunk. They had found the spot. Upon further investigation of the area, they discovered a secluded roadway that entered into the cemetery. Neither the roadway nor the spot were in public view. Fuller was certain this was the place where the culprits had done their dirty work. A coach or a wagon could have been hidden from public view along the roadway, and Stewart's bones, if hidden inside a coffin, could have been easily transported into the cemetery and the coffin buried without anyone ever knowing. The spot was overgrown with brush, and several mounds of dirt had been dumped there. It was a perfect site for the crime.

"A body would be safer here than in a Garden City crypt," Fuller told his colleagues.

Although Fuller proclaimed he was a man who only dealt in facts, he did have an affinity to one superstition regarding the number thirteen—the same number that had aroused fearful superstition in A. T. Stewart.

During the investigation into Cypress Hills Cemetery, Fuller admitted to reporters that the number thirteen had always been lucky for him, and he was sure the number, with its odd connection to the investigation, would prove lucky again.

Fuller was born on the thirteenth of the month. His detective agency was begun on February 13, 1876. The digits in his office building address, 841 Broadway, totaled the number thirteen when added together. The mysterious package containing the note and the painting arrived at his offices on the thirteenth of the month on a day when thirteen of his officers were in the office. There was more, especially as it related to the Cypress Hills investigation. The number on the train car that he and his cohorts had occupied en route was thirteen, and the conductor on that train had the number sewn onto his uniform. Based on the maps of Cypress Hills Cemetery, the section of the graveyard depicted in the mysterious oil painting fell within cemetery lot number 175—once again, individual numbers that added up to thirteen. Was Fuller's notion of success heightened by these numeric coincidences? Absolutely, he claimed, but it would only be the cold, hard facts—the discovery of Stewart's remains—that would actually provide a successful conclusion to the case.

SOME CURIOUS FACTS
FOR SUPERSTITIOUS PEOPLE

"In contrast with Detective Fuller's faith in the virtue of 13 was the superstition of Mr. Stewart as to the ill-fortune attending the same number. He would break up a dinner party rather than make one of a company of 13; the prominence of the number in a business transaction he never construed favorably, and more than one instance is remembered by his friends wherein he chose to be made the subject of ridicule rather than to suppress his convictions in this one matter."

—*New York Times*
August 22, 1881

As Fuller and his party made their way along the picket fence by the hidden roadway, they were being watched. A cemetery worker had taken notice of the group, and as the man busied himself raking, he kept an eye on Fuller's contingency. For all intents and purposes, the cemetery worker looked like every other worker they had passed while perusing the Cypress Hills grounds. He wore a wide-brim straw hat that shaded much of his face, a denim frock coat, and work gloves. Yet when the man was brought to Fuller's attention—Fuller was a stickler for details—Fuller noticed something unusual. The groundskeeper was wearing a pair of expensive shoes, not the kind any worker going about his duties would wear. The other workers they had passed, although dressed in similar attire, all wore "Wellies"—high, green Wellington garden boots, but not this man. The finely polished dress shoes were a dead giveaway.

Fuller approached the man casually enough. Although he tried to engage him in small talk about the weather and the beauty of the grounds, the man was reticent. Fuller even offered the man a cigar, which he refused. The man offered to show Fuller and the others another area of the grounds that they might find interesting, trying his best to lure the group away from the spot. Fuller pretended to fall for the man's entreaty and urged his companions to follow the man. They did, but only until they were satisfied that the worker with the expensive shoes thought they were gone from the area for good. Finally, the worker, seemingly convinced he had led them off the track, wandered away, leaving Fuller and his group to their own devices.

———•·•·•———

Fuller was certain that whoever had stolen Stewart's body had chosen this particular spot at Cypress Hills Cemetery to hide the body because it was so secluded. Who stole the body remained a mystery, but Fuller was sure that whoever had sent him the painting knew the whereabouts of it. Certain that he was onto something, Fuller immediately wired Hilton after he and his party returned from the cemetery. He told Hilton that they had found the exact spot depicted in the mysterious painting and that he was sure that excavation of the area would prove successful. He asked Hilton to join him, but Hilton still refused. Fuller wired Hilton back that he was prepared to begin digging up the area. Hilton, again without completely lending his approval to the operation, advised Fuller to keep Harris, his envoy, informed and to proceed apace as he planned.

Fuller next contacted John Runice, the seventy-year-old controller of the Cypress Hills grounds and asked for permission to excavate a portion of the cemetery. Fuller did not mention that the request had anything to do with the prospect of A. T. Stewart's body being buried there, for fear of another media circus erupting. Instead, he told Runice that he was investigating a case and that several valuable clues to the undisclosed crime were buried in that section of the cemetery. In the ensuing release of misinformation, the *New York Herald* reported that Fuller had apprised Runice of all the details surrounding the case, explaining that he was looking "for the body of A. T. Stewart." Fuller denied having ever told Runice anything of the sort. Regardless of who leaked the information about Fuller's extraordinary undertaking, word of it spread quickly to the press, the public, and the New York City Police Department. The search was on again for the missing body of A. T. Stewart.

A PERMIT FOR AN EXCAVATION
The Controller Of The Cypress Hills Cemetery Astonished.

FULLER: We have called to ask a favor. We desire that you will give us your support in a matter of more than ordinary moment. The Cypress Hills Cemetery has been imposed upon. A crime has been committed, and the proof of it, we believe, lies buried beneath a certain part of your cemetery's surface, a part we are able to locate.

RUNICE: You can't mean it. A Crime committed; Cypress Hills in it. Well, well, this is strange. Now gentlemen I will do anything in the world that I can do. Of course I will. Ask whatever you want, gentlemen.

FULLER: We want a permit to make an excavation.

RUNICE: But can you tell me in what part of the cemetery, in public or private ground?

FULLER: In ground that has not been graded: in ground that probably has not been sold into lots.

RUNICE: In what part of the cemetery?

FULLER: I am willing to treat with you in confidence; the spot to which we refer I can readily point out upon a map of the cemetery. We want to make our excavations in section 18, near the conjunction of West Dolorosa with the Lake Road.

RUNICE: Section 18. Well, now, that is strange. Why, do you know, I myself own that part of the section where the avenues cross? Somebody buried there, eh? Well, that is news. You see, section 18 at that point has not been improved; in fact the men have used it for a place to dump their extra dirt ... you're right, anything buried in that ground could be depended upon to stay buried.

FULLER: Then can we have the permit?

RUNICE: Have the permit? Well, I should say you could. When do you want to begin your operations?

FULLER: To-morrow afternoon at 1 o'clock.

RUNICE: All right gentlemen, I will meet you then and you shall have any number of my men necessary to do the work you desire.

—*New York Times*
August 21, 1881

The next day, Fuller and his staff, as well as Harris and Runice, began the operation. Runice ordered all his cemetery workers to concentrate their day's workload on the far end of the cemetery, out of view of the secluded area where the excavation was to begin. Runice brought with him three men he trusted. Using a long, pointed iron rod, Runice poked at the ground. The deep punctures—soundings—were made to determine if the soil below the surface had been recently disturbed or if something might have been recently buried there. Soundings were made throughout the area, but the depth of the soundings was limited because the ground was too rocky. What had been an operation planned in deep secrecy was suddenly laid bare when curiosity seekers—about a dozen people: men, women, several newspaper reporters, and even several New York City police officers—converged on the scene.

Edward Harris, Judge Hilton's representative at the excavation site, was aghast. Under orders from Hilton, the excavation was supposed to be a secret undertaking and in no way linked to either his approval or the case of Stewart's missing body. If word got out, as it surely had, Hilton would be made to look the fool, since he had publicly announced that Stewart's body had been recovered and was safe and sound in a Garden City crypt. Harris demanded that the digging stop. Fuller agreed. Yet, Runice remained adamant about continuing the operation. It was, after all, his cemetery, and Fuller realized that with or without him, Runice could continue the excavation. If Runice alone made the discovery of Stewart's remains, then all the fame, not to mention any reward, would go to him, regardless of any legwork Fuller had done. In no uncertain terms, Fuller made it clear to the crowd of onlookers who had descended on the scene, and especially to members of the police department, that the excavation was being conducted under his direct auspices and that any discovery made would be his and his alone. In other words, the crowd could stay but would not share in any of the fame, glory, or proceeds connected with the operation.

As the day wore on, more and more people gathered to watch. Fuller's secret was now out in the open, and there was nothing he could do to stop it. It then spread like wildfire across the city.

The soundings went on for several hours, and finally Runice, on Fuller's orders, began digging. Workers dug a trench several feet long and about six feet deep near the entrance of the secluded roadway. All they discovered was a pile of buried cobblestones, most likely put there for drainage. The digging continued for much of the day and by twilight, despite its best efforts, the team had turned up nothing. As word spread about the excavation, more and more people began to arrive at the scene until a crowd of about one hundred people had gathered, requiring Fuller's men to set up a barricade to keep the onlookers at a comfortable distance. Although the day ended without any satisfactory discovery, Fuller remained upbeat, determined to continue the excavation the next day. He had some of his detectives guard the site overnight. By the next day, the city was abuzz again with speculation about the A. T. Stewart case, and even more people came to watch the undertaking at Cypress Hills Cemetery.

THE SEARCH BEGUN
Unexpected Parties Appear On The Scene, But The Work Goes On

Promptly at 1 o'clock yesterday afternoon Controller Runice was at the cemetery grounds, and he found there Detective Fuller, surrounded by members of his staff, and with them Mr. Edward D. Harris, representing Judge Hilton. ... The men who were ordered to obey Mr. Fuller were kept busy for several hours. The digging for the most part was confined to one special locality, no effort being made to cover all of the territory which the clues in hand embrace. ... Hundreds of people walking and driving through the cemetery during the afternoon looked on in wonderment upon the strange work in progress, but the innumerable questions propounded received anything but thoroughly satisfactory replies. When Detective Fuller left the cemetery last night he placed Section No. 18 under guard. ... Superintendent Fuller declared that he was not discouraged, and proposed to prosecute his investigations much more fully than he had yet attempted. The digging will be resumed at an early hour to-morrow morning.

—*New York Times*
August 21, 1881

Not everyone was enamored of Fuller's work. The *Brooklyn Eagle* mocked the private detective.

Detective Fuller, who is in energetic search of the remains of A.T. Stewart at Cypress Hills Cemetery, yesterday succeeded in digging a trench nearly one hundred feet long by four feet deep and three feet wide. This was a noble day's work, but the industrious detective has mistaken his true field of labor. Nothing could prevent a man of his phenomenal powers with the spade and pickax from making a fortune in the mining regions.

Still, the news of Fuller's excavation at Cypress Hills had rejuvenated the public's interest in the Stewart grave robbery. The *New York Times,* the *Herald,* and almost every other New York City newspaper ran front-page stories. As fast as the news spread, people from Brooklyn, New York, and other points of interest flocked to the cemetery to watch. Whole families turned out, bringing picnic baskets with them. Wandering around the cemetery in wide-eyed astonishment, many of them engaged in conjecture over the exact location of Stewart's body. Some set up camps on the outskirts of the Section 18 excavation, laying down blankets, popping open bottles of beer, and uncorking wine, settling in comfortably to watch and often provide running commentary on the proceedings. Some wandered the grounds, women sporting parasols, men in derbies, smoking cigars, children toddling along behind them carrying balloons. The whole enterprise took on a macabre gaiety that did little to assist the excavation or endear itself to the single-mindedness of Fuller.

A. T. STEWART'S REMAINS
THE NEWLY AROUSED INTEREST IN CYPRESS HILLS CEMETERY
A Large Number Of People Visit The Place Yesterday—The Search To Be Resumed To-Day—

The passenger railway lines from New-York and Brooklyn to the Cypress Hills Cemetery received an unusually large patronage yesterday. Hundreds of people went in quest of the alleged site of the burial place of the body of A.T. Stewart and the trench dug in section 18 of the cemetery was closely scanned by the crowds. The story of the recent moves made by the Fuller Detective Bureau, as told yesterday in THE TIMES was on every lip, and argumentative visitors discussed the case in every aspect, few agreeing upon any essential point. There were those present who energetically scoffed at the idea of any importance attaching to the newly declared clues, many maintaining that the dead millionaire's remains were safely sealed in the crypt at Garden City. Others as earnestly contended that Detective Fuller's clues were worthy of the most thorough investigation.

—*New York Times*
August 22, 1881

Fuller had brought with him a tintype (a metal photograph) of the mysterious painting that had been sent to him. It was plainly discernable in the tintype copy that Section 18, where the excavation was being undertaken, was indeed the place depicted in the painting. The low picket fence near the deserted road, the ramshackle buildings, the double trunk willow tree were all clearly visible. The words written on the painting were still legible in the copy Fuller brought with him—"Cypress Hills. Stewart is buried here." There could be no doubt about it, Fuller had located the exact spot even though they were unable to turn up anything, not even the slightest clue to the whereabouts of Stewart's remains.

Now that word was out about Fuller's endeavor, he was repeatedly asked about Judge Hilton's involvement. Fuller tried to dispel such notions.

"I am conducting this investigation, though, on my own account purely. Judge Hilton does not bear a single penny of the expenses. Every move of importance in this case has been my own," Fuller told reporters.

The New York City Police Department stationed three men at the excavation site in case Fuller did find Stewart's remains. Having been soundly ridiculed for its ineptness in the case, the police weren't about to be shut out of an opportunity, no matter how far-fetched, to regain some modicum of respectability. No one in the police department was optimistic about the potential outcome, but still, their presence was deemed necessary should Fuller's work be successful.

Fuller was brimming with confidence. He would excavate every foot of ground in Section 18 if that's what it took. Fuller's detectives and Cypress Hills Cemetery workers were enthusiastically engaged in the digging. Off and on there could be heard the excited shouts of these men claiming to have struck something of importance, but further digging only turned up more rock and dirt. The original trench was dug deeper and wider, extending in all directions. The mysterious man that Fuller had run into on his first excursion to the cemetery— the man wearing expertly polished shoes along with cemetery worker's garb—was ultimately identified. James Dagner lived in a house not far from the deserted road leading out of the cemetery. He turned out to be just a well-soled cemetery employee and was solicited to help with the digging. Fuller remained dubious of him and went so far as to question Runice about the possibility that Dagner might have been involved in the case. Runice dispelled such theories, explaining that Dagner had only tried to lead Fuller's group away from Section 18 because it was private property, belonging to Runice, and supposedly not accessible to the general public. Still, Fuller kept a watchful eye on Dagner, just in case.

After two days of digging, on August 20 and 21, not a single clue or anything of any consequence was found. By the end of the second day, Section 18, once bustling with spectators and a cadre of enthusiastic and relentless diggers, was reduced to a paltry three workers and only a dozen or so onlookers. Every shovelful of dirt brought Fuller's excavation closer to an end. Fuller himself abandoned the site on the 23rd. The next day, he officially abandoned the search for A. T. Stewart's body, faced the newspaper reporters, and admitted he had been fooled. The painting had been, after all, a hoax. Fuller made a public apology.

"I do not hesitate to say that I believe I have been fooled," Fuller said.

Still, the question remained: "Why try to fool this particular detective?"

Fuller concluded that the hoax had been designed by culprits intent on embarrassing Hilton and Mrs. Stewart and creating some sensational journalism at his expense.

THE CYPRESS HILLS SEARCH ABANDONED

Detective J. M. Fuller announced yesterday afternoon, at an early hour, that he was satisfied that no good results would follow a further prosecution of his excavation work in the Cypress Hills Cemetery, and the digging was thereupon abandoned, the workmen receiving orders to refill the long, deep trenches which had been made.

—*New York Times*
August 24, 1881

GOING OUT OF BUSINESS

In which, in early April 1882, it is announced that A. T. Stewart & Co., the once prosperous retail empire, is going out of business. Although surprising to the general public, it comes as no surprise to New York City's mercantile community and bankers, or even to Wall Street. Many agree that Henry Hilton's lack of business savvy, his imperious management style, and a series of egregious public relations blunders ultimately led to the liquidation of the company. Hilton refuses to accept any blame for the company's demise.

No news regarding A. T. Stewart could have been more startling to the general public than the front-page headlines that appeared across the city on April 15, 1882—the once vast and profitable firm of A. T. Stewart & Co. was going out of business. The recovery of Stewart's remains and the apprehension of his grave robbers wouldn't have caused as many gasps. Yet, while the news shocked the public, it did not surprise New York City's mercantile community and bankers, or even Wall Street. They knew the end was coming, and many knew why. They just didn't know when.

RETIRING FROM BUSINESS
THE FIRM OF A.T. STEWART & CO.
WINDING UP AFFAIRS
Merchandise And Mill Properties
Offered For Sale—What Judge Hilton
Says Is The Cause For Discontinuing
Business—Views Of The Trade

The advertisement in the morning newspapers of yesterday that A.T. Stewart & Co. had determined to discontinue their dry goods and manufacturing business and offered their stock of merchandise and mill properties for sale, excited general interest, but the fact that the firm had thus given notice of their intention to retire from the business created little excitement in the mercantile community. Merchants declared they were not astonished and seemed to have determined long ago that the closing of the firm's business was merely a question of a very short time. ... When these advertisements first appeared Judge Henry Hilton was appealed to for information. He then said he had nothing to communicate to the public. ... Rumors obtained good headway that the business of the house was rapidly declining. ... Bankers yesterday admitted that the firm had been forced to borrow money, but said that that fact did not indicate they would be unable to meet their liabilities. ... Wall street was not at all disturbed over the announcement that the firm is to withdraw from business and it seemed to be the general opinion that extraordinary opposition had forced the firm to surrender, leaving the field to their competitors. The placard "For Sale" was displayed on the windows of the uptown establishments ... and were viewed with surprise by persons who daily pass those buildings.

—*New York Times*
April 16, 1882

Six years after Henry Hilton had gained control of A. T. Stewart & Co., liquidation of the once prosperous retail empire was announced. While Hilton refused to accept any blame for the company's demise, refused to acknowledge that the closing was predicated by a series of his business and public blunders, it is quite clear that the fall of the A. T. Stewart empire can be placed squarely at the feet of Hilton, based on five distinct and interlocking catastrophic mistakes.

The first of Hilton's mistakes was opening a Chicago-based wholesale branch in 1876, following Stewart's death. It was one of his first acts as the head of the Stewart empire, and it proved fatal. During his lifetime, A. T. Stewart had eyed the Chicago market with caution. Although the city was blossoming into a leading dry-goods market, it already had a predominant dry-goods impresario in Marshall Field as well as other up-and-coming dry-goods merchants. Stewart would be an interloper in the Chicago market and would face stiff if not insurmountable competition. Although Stewart established a small sales office in Chicago, merely carrying samples and not fully stocked, he did not open a full-scale branch in the bustling city. Hilton went full steam ahead. He leased three large buildings on the corner of Washington Street and Wabash Avenue in 1876 and opened a fully stocked wholesale outlet. A price war ensued, and Hilton got the worst of it. Although the Chicago branch managed to stay afloat until the liquidation in 1882, its overall income declined year after year, and its impact in the Chicago marketplace all but vanished.

According to Robert Twyman in *The History of Marshall Field and Company* (1954), "From the spring of 1877 on the competition of Stewart's was to perturb Field, Leiter & Co. and the other Western Firms but little."

"There was no clearer recognition of the decline of the once-great firm of A.T. Stewart & Co., and the rise in the world esteem of Field's," Twyman wrote.

———————

Hilton's Chicago blunder was followed in 1877 by the catastrophic public relations gaffe in Saratoga when Hilton refused to allow New York City banker Joseph Seligman and his family admittance to the Grand Union Hotel. His actions were viewed as racially prejudiced and personally malicious. Seligman predicted the company's demise, writing to Hilton, "I regret you are making no headway in your wholesale departments in New York and Chicago, and that the Ninth Street retail store, so popular and prosperous under the management of the late Mr. Stewart, has lost its best patrons."

Seligman went on to advise Hilton to sell off the dry-goods business and hotels if he ever wished to save what was left of the Stewart estate. Hilton, however, never admitted his mistake nor did he ever apologize for his actions. Hilton denied that the company had suffered any significant loss.

When asked by a *Times* reporter whether there was any truth to the rumor that the Stewart company lost a large amount of Hebrew trade after the Seligman incident, Hilton responded curtly, "The firm lost some Jewish customers, but our business was never injured in the slightest degree."

———•••••———

A third factor contributing to the demise of the Stewart business was Hilton's downsizing of Stewart's once grand and far-reaching empire and the move of the wholesale business uptown to Astor Place. According to Hilton, "The down-town wholesale store was given up solely as a matter of business policy. The trade was moving away from there, the tendency being up town, and we thought it best to have our stock where it would best suit the convenience of our customers."

By 1882, only three of the twelve manufacturing mills established and owned by A. T. Stewart before his death were still in operation, Hilton having sold most of them off. Only one foreign mill was still run by the Stewart Company, and all the plants manufacturing apparel and household goods had been closed. The retail store, which during Stewart's reign had employed more than two thousand people, had a mere eight hundred employees at the time of the liquidation sale.

———•••••———

The fourth move by Hilton that damaged Stewart's empire was his sabotaging of the Working Women's Hotel in New York City. Even following Stewart's death in 1876, women kept faith in the project and were overjoyed when Hilton announced that plans for establishing the Working Women's Hotel would go forward under his leadership. They never did, and it was a slap in the face to women throughout New York City, who, in retribution, singled out Stewart's business for an ongoing boycott.

On May 26, 1878, Hilton announced that the project had not attracted enough renters, making it a failure as a charitable enterprise. He immediately announced that it would reopen as the Park Avenue Hotel, a fully commercial operation. In response, thousands of women from all walks of life, feminist and non-feminist alike, from New York City and beyond, boycotted A. T. Stewart's retail operations. The women's boycott, estimated to have lasted some five years, cost the Stewart retail business dearly, cutting off its supply of oxygen. According to the article "The Decline and Fall of the Commercial Empire of A. T. Stewart," by Harry Resseguie, "In conjunction with the earlier boycott it made it necessary for Hilton and Libbey to liquidate the firm four years later."

Lastly, but perhaps more so than anything else, it was Hilton's handling of the theft of A. T. Stewart's body from St. Mark's Cemetery that caused the downfall of the Stewart empire. Thousands upon thousands of people read and watched as Hilton played out his role as a greedy, self-important, soulless tyrant.

As reported in the *New York Tribune* and attributed to one of Cornelia Stewart's relatives, "One day she was rich, the next day she was poor; while one day Hilton was poor, and the next day he was rich." While a slight misperception (Mrs. Stewart remained wealthy even though she was stripped of all cash assets and all of her personal expenses were obtained through Hilton, at an interest-bearing rate), the idea that Hilton seemed to get rich on the back of the widow Stewart only made his behavior during the search for Stewart's remains and their thieves all the more suspicious.

Hilton recklessly charged people with the crime, including the church sextons Hamill and Parker. He refused to offer an effective reward for the return of the body. He spread false rumors that the body had been recovered. He kept the widow Stewart in the dark regarding the ongoing investigations and negotiations associated with the return of her husband's remains. In 1879, when what appeared to be a bona fide offer from the culprits to return the body for two hundred thousand dollars (a mere pittance compared to what Hilton had inherited as the executor of the Stewart estate), Hilton not only refused to negotiate but once again lashed out rashly. He accused the one person chosen as the go-between, Patrick Jones, a well-known lawyer with an impeccable record of public service, of being in cahoots with the criminals.

*"Hilton's failure to ransom the body at any cost, and the hyp-
ocritical attitude which many felt he had taken during the
period of active search for the criminals, widened the circle
of those who resented or despised him, and hastened the
liquidation."*

—HARRY RESSEGUIE, "THE DECLINE AND FALL OF THE COMMERCIAL EMPIRE OF
A.T. STEWART," *The Business History Review,* 1962

All of Hilton's actions regarding the return of his former friend
and patron's remains became a public display of his selfish, callous
persona. And further, they showed Hilton to be insensitive to the
heartache and angst felt by Mrs. Stewart during this trying period.

———————

When asked by reporters if his policies had in any way led to the liquidation of the business, Hilton responded: "It has been also said that
I made radical changes in the method of conducting the business. That
too is false. I was in Mr. Stewart's confidence for many years previous
to his death, and we were in perfect accord in all business matters,
therefore it is not likely that I should have been included to make any
radical changes in the system so thoroughly perfected by him."

Then why exactly was the Stewart company closing? According
to Hilton: "I am tired. I have worked hard all of these years and I feel
that I am entitled to rest."

"I am well aware that all sorts of idle stories have been afloat concerning both this business and myself, but few of such stories have the
slightest foundation in fact. What has been said about me personally
has not disturbed me at all, however. No matter what people may say
about the dissolution of this business, I tell you the reason of it is simply I am tired," he said.

"A.T. Stewart & Company is a very extensive one and to prop-
erly attend to all of its details requires a great deal of care, labor and
energy. Its exactions upon myself are greater than I can afford to comply with at my time of life and I want to relieve myself honorably and
creditably while I have the health and ability to do so."

The business and financial community in New York City was of a different opinion.

"Judge Hilton was not a practical business man and there was no one to take the place of the late Mr. Stewart."
—SUPERINTENDENT HENRY WHITE, BRADSTREET'S COMMERCIAL AGENCY,
New York Times, APRIL 16, 1882

"Their trade had declined for various reasons. One was Judge Hilton's inability to conduct it as Mr. Stewart would have done."
—R.G. DUN & CO.'s COMMERCIAL AGENCY, UNIDENTIFIED SPOKESMAN,
New York Times, APRIL 16, 1882

"The action is no surprise and it can have no effect. The business of the City is too large to have the retirement of any one house, however large, produce, other than a ripple. ... The saying was among merchants that with Mr. Stewart's death the brains of the firm also died. ... The methods of the firm's management was faulty in the extreme."
—MR. BLISS, BLISS, FABIAN & CO., *New York Times,* APRIL 16, 1882

"Stewart died at an opportune time so far as the fortunes of the house of which he was the founder were concerned. The house had already attained the zenith of its prosperity when Stewart passed away and would probably never have risen to higher repute in the commercial world."
—MR. JAMES M. CONSTABLE, ARNOLD CONSTABLE & CO.,
New York Times, APRIL 16, 1882

"It was the most natural thing in the world that Judge Hilton should find mercantile life irksome and unsuited to his taste. He was not trained for business and no man could take up in detail and manage such vast interests as Stewart controlled

*who was not bred to business affairs and had not passed his
life from boyhood up in the dry goods business."*
—MR. SAMUEL LORD, LORD & TAYLOR, *New York Times,* APRIL 16, 1882

THE CHICAGO TRADE BRANCH

*CHICAGO, April 15—The manager of A.T. Stewart's estab-
lishment here said this morning that all he knew of the New
York firm's determination to wind up affairs was that he had
received an advertisement, with instructions to insert it in the
newspapers of this city, setting forth that A.T. Stewart & Co.,
having decided to discontinue their dry goods business offer
for sale their stocks of merchandise and mill properties.*
—*New York Times,* APRIL 16, 1882

THE OLD STEWART BUILDING

*The fate of the Stewart Building at Broadway, Chambers and
Reade streets in which the wholesale business of A.T. Stewart
& Co. has been transacted for so many years has at last been
settled. It is not to be converted into a hotel as has so often
been rumored of late, but is to be transformed into a large
number of offices for business purposes. ... The necessary
changes will be made and these were filed by Judge Hilton, as
attorney for Mrs. C.M. Stewart in the Bureau of Buildings last
Friday.*
—*New York Times,* SEPTEMBER 20, 1882

A.T. STEWART & CO.'S SUCCESSOR

*Former patrons of the great retail store of the late firm of A.T.
Stewart & Co. need have no hesitancy in continuing their
patronage at the same establishment. Mr. E.J. Denning, the
present proprietor, has adopted most of the judicious methods of his successful predecessors and he has retained in
his employ such of Stewart & Co.'s clerks as chose to remain
with him. ... The numerous departments are fully stocked*

with the latest styles of goods of all varieties and colors and low prices.

—New York Times, October 26, 1882

"It makes me sad, very sad to think of breaking up a business like this. Here are men who have grown up from boyhood in the employ of this concern and to sever relations between employer and employees which are almost paternal is really too bad. ... I cannot express the sentiment of sincere regret which arises when I think of breaking up all these old associations. ... For 30 years Mr. A.T. Stewart and myself were just like brothers and the interest that I took in this business was second only to his ... The mere thinking of it kept me awake a good part of last night."

—Henry Hilton, New York Times, April 16, 1882

And so it comes about that the enterprises upon which the rich man depended for future fame have all been more or less blighted. The source of all his wealth, his dry goods business, has disappeared a few years after him; his city may preserve his name, but the principle it represented is gone.

—Brooklyn Eagle, April 15, 1882

The closing of A. T. Stewart & Co. was deeply felt in Garden City, Long Island, the town Stewart had founded as one of the first planned communities for working men and women in the country. Designing and establishing it for his employees to rent homes there, Stewart had built schools, churches, a hotel, and a gas and water works, and had supplied a train route to and from the community. And it was the site where Mrs. Stewart had embarked on her endeavor to build her lasting monument to her husband, the Episcopal Cathedral of the Incarnation. News of the demise of the company left the people of Garden City bewildered. Although Stewart and his wife, Cornelia, had taken great pride and interest in the establishment and growth of the city, residents questioned Hilton's continued commitment to its development given the circumstances surrounding the closing of the Stewart business. According to an April 17, 1882, article in the *New York Times*, "Some in and about the place believe that Garden City will never be what was intended to be by its founder and doubt of its being a success under the management of the estate. Instead of being a working man's paradise its residents are well-to-do people and it is believed by some that the estate will eventually determine upon individual ownership. Many arrive at this conclusion from the fact of the abandonment of a number of Mr. Stewart's enterprises and the fast closing up of the affairs of the vast estate."

GARDEN CITY

The closing of the great house of A.T. Stewart & Co., or, in other words, the withdrawal from business of Judge HILTON has already produced some speculations in the public mind as to the future of Garden City. ... Before his death Mr. STEWART had decided to make Garden City a sort of American Oxford— a place where all possible educational facilities, from primary school to the fully equipped university, could be provided. ... Garden City is now a town of modest and attractive cottages, occupied to a very large extent by people who have been drawn to the place by the educational opportunities offered to their children. ... The town and the houses and railroads therein belong to the ESTATE. No man can buy a house or a foot of land from the ESTATE, and whoever lives in Garden City lives under the direct rule of the ESTATE. ... The closing of the business of A.T. STEWART & Co. has undeniably alarmed those Garden Citizens whose faith in the ESTATE is not immovable. ... Now, if Judge HILTON is determined to rest from his labors in New York, may he not also determine to rest from his labors in Garden City? A.T. STEWART & Co. may vanish from the face of the earth, but the ESTATE will carry out its vast and far-reaching purposes."

—EDITORIAL, *New York Times*, APRIL 18, 1882

BUSINESS IN STEWART'S STORE
Consolidation Of The Firms Hitherto Conducting The Trade

By an arrangement perfected during the present week, the firms of Groocock, Sylvester & Hilton and Edwin J. Denning, who succeeded to, and have for some time conducted, respectively, the wholesale and retail business of the late firm of A.T. Stewart and Co. have consolidated their interests. The two departments will continue, nevertheless, to be conducted independently of one another. The wholesale firm will be known as Groocock, Sylvester & Hilton and the retail as E.J. Denning & Co.

—*New York Times*
November 25, 1882

As in all things previous, Cornelia Stewart remained stoic during the liquidation of her husband's business. The same woman who at first was struck down physically and emotionally in sorrow by the theft of her husband's remains had by 1882 outwardly appeared to be enjoying her well-appointed lifestyle. Many believed that she had long ago obtained—surreptitiously and without Hilton's involvement or approval—the remains of her husband's body from those who had stolen it and had found a sanctified final resting place for him at the Cathedral of the Incarnation in Garden City.

———

All of it taken together—Hilton's egregious business ineptitude, his public relations blunders, and his cold-hearted behavior in the face of the sensational theft of his benefactor's remains—led, within a mere six-year period, to the demise of the A. T. Stewart empire with which Hilton had been entrusted. Despite his guilt in the liquidation of A. T. Stewart & Co. and despite the low esteem with which Judge Henry Hilton was regarded in the business community and in the general public, the sale of the company netted him approximately $5.5 million.

BAG OF BONES

In which, in 1881, Mrs. Stewart, without Henry Hilton's approval, makes arrangements with men claiming to be the grave robbers for the return of her husband's remains. On a deserted road in New York's Westchester County, two wagons cross paths, one containing an emissary from Mrs. Stewart with a twenty-thousand-dollar ransom and the other driven by unidentified men who exchange a burlap bag of bones for the ransom money and ride off. The bones are taken by train to Garden City, where they are placed in the crypt at the Cathedral of the Incarnation.

Throughout the hot August month of 1881, during J. M. Fuller's excavation at Cypress Hills Cemetery and the ongoing pursuit of A. T. Stewart's body, the widow Stewart remained inconspicuously silent. As far as anyone could tell, Cornelia Stewart remained secure in the knowledge that her husband's remains were safe and sound in the crypt she had built for him in Garden City's Cathedral of the Incarnation.

Mrs. Stewart had begun plans for building the magnificent cathedral in honor of her husband in 1877. The cornerstone of the Episcopal church was laid on June 28 of that year, and it was officially opened on April 9, 1885, in an extraordinary religious ceremony. The deed to the property and buildings was ultimately signed over to the church. The cathedral was a replica of a thirteenth-century Gothic structure, with all the elaborate and picturesque architecture associated with the European medieval period. Built of brown sandstone, the ornate structure included a more than two hundred foot spire that dominated the Garden City skyline.

> *Dear Sir*
>
> *Having, as you are aware, begun the erection of a church edifice in Garden City, L. I., intended to be an enduring memorial of my dear deceased husband, and intending to present it when completed to the corporate body known as the Cathe-*

dral of the Incarnation in your diocese, to be held on a perpetual trust for the purposes of the corporation and for the use of the Protestant Episcopal Church, I have to request that you will perform the ceremony of laying the corner-stone.

I may here, and in this connection it seems proper I should, add what has already been stated to you personally, as the Bishop of the diocese and head of the corporation referred to, that it is also my intention, upon the consecration of the building and its occupation as the cathedral church, to provide a suitable fund by way of endowment for its permanent maintenance as such, also furnish a residence to be occupied by the Bishop, and in other ways make the edifice and its appendages in every aspect appropriate and complete for cathedral purposes.

The building has progressed already so far that it is desirable the corner-stone should be laid at an early day, and I trust you will give the subject your early consideration.

— LETTER FROM CORNELIA M. STEWART TO BISHOP A. N. LITTLEJOHN,

JUNE 19, 1877

An event without a parallel in the history of Christianity dawned upon the American Church last week, in the laying of the corner-stone of the cathedral of the Incarnation, at Garden City, in the Diocese of Long Island. For many months the construction of a beautiful and magnificent church edifice has been going on quietly in that favored spot. No one dreamed of the plans that were here silently working, and how far-reaching and grand they were. Indeed, now, only she whose heart is equal in the largeness of its liberality to the responsibility of her great wealth, and the confidential friend of him whose memory she thus nobly perpetuates, are aware of what is yet to be done in that place, and thence throughout the diocese, for the glory of God and the good of His Church.

If the possession of wealth is a great blessing, the ability to use it rightly is a greater blessing still. If wealth brings

great enjoyment, the disposition to dispense it well must bring a greater satisfaction and delight. There were those who sneered, when Mr. Stewart died, at the fact that he had made no large charitable bequests. They little knew what were his plans, or how faithfully and wisely and industriously those to whom he entrusted them would carry them out.
—*Churchman*, Vol. 36, July 7, 1877

George W. Walling, the former New York City police superintendent, reported in his 1887 memoir, *Recollections of a New York Chief of Police*, that despite ongoing investigations, A. T. Stewart's remains had been recovered in late 1880 or early 1881. According to Walling, they were recovered through the clandestine efforts of Cornelia Stewart, not through any investigations by the likes of private detectives like J. M. Fuller, the New York City police force, or even Judge Henry Hilton. This explained Mrs. Stewart's calm demeanor.

Walling spent nearly forty years in the New York City Police Department involved in many of the city's most scandalous crimes—the Stewart grave robbery among them. The police superintendent from July 1874 until June 1885, Walling had a reputation as a tough, honest law enforcement officer. There was no reason to believe he wasn't telling the truth as he knew it in his book.

A CITY'S GREAT SENSATIONS
TOLD BY THE VETERAN CHIEF WALLING
The Notorious Crimes Of The Past Fifty Years Which Have Startled The Metropolis

Recollections of a New-York Chief of Police" is the title of a somewhat voluminous publication, soon to be issued from the press by George W. Walling, the veteran ex-Superintendent of

Police. The book covers 40 years of the criminal history of the metropolis, and depends for its interest upon a rehearsal of the most prominent and sensational crimes of the last four decades, together with the histories of the participants. Its aim is to be interesting, and though it assumes to be simply an unvarnished statement of facts, the facts are nevertheless eked out in places, as in the A.T. Stewart grave robbery, with the imagination necessary to form a proper literary conclusion.

—*New York Times*
October 30, 1887

The *New York Times* cast a dubious eye on Walling's claim regarding the recovery of Stewart's body. "The account cannot be relied on as entirely authentic because it is fragmentary at best and Walling had little to do with the case and knew not very much about it. ... As to whether the remains were or were not actually returned, those in possession of the facts still refuse to say," the *Times* reported.

Still, as much as there was no one to support Walling's claim, there was also no one willing to officially dispute it. If anything, Cornelia Stewart's own peaceful disposition through the ordeal demonstrated the fact that her beloved husband's body had been recovered. With or without Walling's claim, there was nothing else to go on except rumor and speculation since everyone truly connected with the case was not talking. If, as the saying goes, "Dead men tell no tales," then in the matter of A. T. Stewart, those remotely connected to dead men told no tales, as well.

Shortly following the January 1879 in which former New York postmaster Patrick Jones reported to the press that he had been contacted by Stewart's grave robbers, Mrs. Stewart's public demeanor changed dramatically. Without discussing any details, Cornelia Stewart told friends and family, with great certainty, that the body of her beloved husband had been returned and placed in the family vault in the basement of the Cathedral of the Incarnation in Garden City. If it was *her* contention that such was the case, then who was to doubt her, with or without corroborating evidence? Walling's book illustrated to disbelievers *how* the body was returned.

———◆•••◆———

There is no doubt that the remains of *someone* were carefully placed in the crypt at the Cathedral of the Incarnation sometime in late 1880 or early 1881, but there is no complete record of whose remains or exactly when. According to two accounts, those of George Walling in his 1887 memoir and Herbert Asbury in his 1927 book, *The Gangs of New York: An Informal History of the Underworld*, Cornelia Stewart undertook the retrieval of her husband's bones in late 1880 without Judge Hilton's involvement. Each source claims she was able to get her husband's remains back after paying a twenty thousand-dollar ransom.

> *"But the distracted widow and her relatives, without the consent of Judge Hilton, opened negotiations on her own account."*
> —GEORGE W. WALLING, *Recollections of a New York Chief of Police,*
> 1887

> *"Mrs. Stewart, who had been fearfully upset by the theft of her husband's body, approached the ghouls on her own account through General Jones and Romaine wrote that he would return the corpse for one hundred thousand dollars. Mrs. Stewart favored the immediate payment of this sum, but General Jones countered with an offer of twenty thousand dollars, which Romaine accepted."*
> —HERBERT ASBURY, *The Gangs of New York:*
> *An Informal History of the Underworld, 1927*

Walling maintained that the piece of velvet cloth sent to Jones as proof that the mysterious Romaine was indeed in possession of Stewart's body was a perfect match to the missing section of velvet cut from the lid of Stewart's coffin. The coffin plate that was also returned as proof by the robbers was also identified as authentic. Garden City resident William Blodgett claimed that he saw men carry a coffin into the crypt at the Cathedral of the Incarnation. According to Blodgett, after that, a guard was stationed outside the crypt. Why else would a guard be placed there if it wasn't to protect the recovered remains of A. T. Stewart?

Clearly, if Mrs. Stewart, through her secret negotiations, had been able to recover her husband's body, it would not have behooved anyone involved to have the details of the talks made public. If she did pay a handsome ransom for the return of the body, it would have opened the flood gates for other like-minded ghouls intent on making a small fortune by stealing the remains of the wealthy.

———

Neither Walling nor Asbury identified how Cornelia Stewart contacted the grave robbers, who they were, or the exact date that the exchange took place. Neither revealed who conducted the negotiations on Mrs. Stewart's behalf after attorney Patrick Jones opened communications, but it was assumed that Jones acted as the go-between. According to Walling's account, the robbers instructed Mrs. Stewart to have one man, a person of her own choosing, whom she trusted implicitly, drive a wagon out to a lonely deserted road in New York's Westchester County.

Both Walling and Asbury opined that the wagon driver was more than likely one of Mrs. Stewart's nephews, although he remained unnamed. The robbers provided Mrs. Stewart a map showing the route that her lone emissary had to follow. According to the grave robbers' instructions, the emissary was to continue driving along the deserted Westchester road, being watched by the robbers. If they were satisfied that the driver was alone and not being followed, they would catch up with the wagon along the route, and the exchange would be made. Stewart's emissary should have the agreed upon ransom, which was speculated to have been twenty thousand dollars—a far cry from the $200,000 the grave robbers had originally demanded.

"He was to leave New York City at ten o'clock at night alone, in a one-horse wagon, and drive into Westchester County along a lonely road. ... If the man was acting in good faith, and was

not accompanied or followed by detectives, he would be met and given further directions. ... A young relative of Mrs. Stewart undertook the hazardous errand, and drove out into the country."

—GEORGE W. WALLING, *Recollections of a New York Chief of Police,*
1887

Around 3 a.m., Walling and Asbury claim, a masked rider approached and signaled Stewart's emissary to drive his wagon down a dark and deserted lane. About a mile down the lane, a horse and buggy was stationed in the middle of the lane, blocking travel any farther. Two masked men climbed out of the buggy holding a burlap sack and approached the wagon. In Walling's rendition, a verbal exchange took place.

Walling's description of the exchange only further fueled speculation that he had taken great liberties with his story, since there was no way he could have known the extent of any conversation that took place.

———

According to Walling's rendition:

"A masked man promptly appeared, and brought forward a bag to his buggy, saying, 'Here 'tis, where's the money?'

'Where is the proof of identity?' asked the messenger, as the bag containing the mortal remains of A. T. Stewart was lifted into the buggy.

'Here!' said the other, holding up an irregular bit of velvet, and opening a bull's-eye lantern upon it with a click. The piece was compared with a bit of paper of the same shape which the New Yorker had brought with him to this lonely spot.

'Come, hurry up!' was the command.

The messenger obeyed by producing the money, and the robbers retired a few feet and counted it by the light of their lantern."

———

Asbury's account was similar, sans the dialogue:

"Two men clambered and approached him. Both were masked, and one carried a heavy gunny sack. A triangular strip of velvet was offered to the messenger as proof of the identity and the money was promptly paid over, whereupon the ghouls dumped the gunny sack into the wagon and drove northward in their own vehicle. The messenger hurried back to the city with the bones of the merchant rattling in the sack beneath his feet."

The bag of bones was reportedly taken to a secure location, where it was loaded into a trunk and transported by train to Garden City. By the time of the alleged recovery in late 1880 or early 1881, A. T. Stewart's remains had been relegated to a mere pile of bones. The bones were then deposited into a coffin that was placed inside the crypt beneath the foundation of the Cathedral of the Incarnation.

Asbury wrote that the bones "remain to this day and for many years were protected by a hidden spring which, if touched, would have shaken a cluster of bells in the church tower and sent an alarm throughout the village."

Despite the possibility that Stewart's remains had been recovered, others continued to come forward and say they had them. In 1884, Lewis Sweigels, a professional grave robber who had once been implicated in an attempt to rob the grave of Abraham Lincoln, told the Chicago police that he and two others—a man named Larry Gavin and a New York City saloon keeper named Coffee had stolen Stewart's body. At the time of his admission, Sweigels was serving time in the Chester, Illinois, State Penitentiary for an unrelated crime. According to Chicago Police Chief William McGarigle, Sweigels promised to return Stewart's remains in exchange for a pardon and a percentage of any reward associated with the return of the remains. He was issued a pardon and reportedly formed a partnership with McGarigle and several Chicago detectives for the expressed purpose of returning the body and cashing in. Reportedly, the group had several meetings in New York with either Hilton or one of his representatives. McGarigle confirmed that negotiations were conducted, but he denied that there was any partnership with Sweigels. In an article published in the *New York Times* in April 1884, McGarigle said he became disenchanted with the convict's claim when Sweigels was unable to produce Stewart's remains. McGarigle admitted to reporters that he had been duped.

THE STEWART GRAVE ROBBERY
A Story From Chicago About The
Restoration Of The Body

Chicago, April 6. The *Inter Ocean* publishes an interview with an unnamed detective, who claims that in the Summer and Fall of 1882 Chief of Police McGarigle, of Chicago, and two or three detectives held negotiations with the notorious Lewis C. Sweigels, then serving a term for robbery in the Chester (Ill.) Penitentiary under an assumed name. Sweigels, who was known to be a professional grave robber, and was concerned in the attempt to rob the grave of President Lincoln, told a very complete, circumstantial and consistent story of the robbery of A.T. Stewart's grave. ... Sweigles promised to restore the body only on condition of his pardon from the penitentiary and receiving part of the reward.

—*New York Times*
April 7, 1884

In 1885, New York attorney Bernard Cowen revealed that he had a client named Terrence H. Forrest who spoke to him about a cemetery next to Grace Episcopal Church on Broadway, not far from where Stewart built his Cast Iron Palace. As told by Forrest, during the excavation and building of Stewart's store, graves at the cemetery had been dug up and coffins and bones were coldheartedly hauled away with the other debris.

Forrest maintained that in 1874, two years before Stewart's death, two unidentified Irishmen came to New York to pay a visit to their father's grave at the church cemetery only to discover that it had been dug up during the Stewart excavation, with no word of where it had been taken. When they tried to reach Stewart for an answer, they were rebuffed. When they asked the contractor, they were told the graves had been summarily removed on Stewart's direct orders. When they went back to confront Stewart again, they were thrown out of his offices. As the two men were leaving, they vowed revenge on Stewart.

"Mark you Stewart, your bones will never rest. You'll get the same treatment!" they reportedly vowed.

According to Forrest, the two young Irishmen were the ones who stole Stewart's body. Forrest was adamant about his claim and revealed to Cowen that the two young men were relatives of his, so he knew the story was founded in truth. Forrest said he let the two men bury Stewart's remains on his farm in Amityville. Cowen reported that he never had the opportunity to verify Forrest's story.

———

George Walling's story of the return of Stewart's remains was recounted in a variety of respectable magazines, journals, and newspaper. A November 1888 issue of *Chambers's Journal* reported, "The agreed ransom was handed over. The mortal remains of the deceased millionaire were lifted on to the buggy of Mrs. Stewart's representative, and he started on his homeward journey. Twenty-four hours later, his gruesome burden was transferred at dead of night, and with a privacy in singular contrast to the pomp and circumstance of its first burial, to its permanent resting-place in the crypt of the Cathedral. The wandering bones found rest at last, never, it is hoped, to be again disturbed."

Chambers's Journal also perpetuated the speculation that Stewart's remains were now watched over by some sophisticated alarm system. According to the *Journal,*

"Any such disturbance would indeed be hazardous, for the remains now lie in the silent guardianship of Science. If any modern ghoul should once more attempt to violate their resting-place, an electric current will flash an instant message to the tower above, and the bells will sound a tocsin such as shall rouse the heaviest sleeper from his slumbers, and call every man in Garden City to lay hands upon the rash invader."

Robbing Graves for Ransom

Grave robbing for purposes of mere plunder are not uncommon, and in some States whose citizens have not risen to the realization of the necessities of medical science the colleges carry on a brisk trade in cadavers which keeps the resurrectionists occupied on dark nights. But grave robbery as a means of extorting blackmail is a comparatively new notion. The first successful attempt of the kind was that of the rogues who carried off the body of A.T. Stewart. Whether a ransom has been paid and the body recovered is a mystery which puzzles society. Mrs. Stewart, at all events, was not averse to paying a good round sum to recover it, as the most important feature of the Cathedral at Garden City.

—Brooklyn Eagle
January 7, 1882

In April 1885, regardless of whether anyone believed that A. T. Stewart's remains had been recovered or not, eighty-three-year-old Cornelia Stewart, the ailing widow of the millionaire merchant, closed the book on the sordid tale of her husband's grave robbery by officially dedicating the Cathedral of the Incarnation in Garden City. Stewart's crypt was located in the deepest recesses of the magnificent structure. Nearly one thousand people traveled great distances to take part in the dedication ceremony. Ten train cars of enthusiastic well-wishers, businessmen, politicians, lawyers, judges, and other professionals and their wives and children, many of them Episcopalians, made the trip down on a special train from the Long Island City station. By the time they arrived for the opening service at eleven o'clock that morning, most were unable to get near the cathedral, never mind get inside and take a seat. The police had barred the three entrances to the elaborately constructed house of worship. The cathedral was already surrounded by hundreds of worshippers and curiosity seekers.

Construction of the cathedral took nine years and cost approximately $3 million. H. C. Harrison, the noted English architect, designed the church. According to Harrison, the building itself was smaller than most cathedrals, but he attempted to overcome the limitation of its size by providing an overabundance of detail. It was, according to Harrison, a stunning example of "pure floriated Gothic."

The cathedral erected by his widow will be the only monument to him, and the irony of the fate even here provokes a ghastly smile. The mausoleum which was to contain his body will be the center of popular interest as Mrs. Stewart hoped it would be; but the interest will reside in the doubt whether his remains are really deposited there or not.

—*Brooklyn Eagle*
April 15, 1882

MEMORIAL TO THE MERCHANT PRINCE

In which one thousand people travel to Garden City, Long Island, to take part in the April 1885 dedication ceremony of the Gothic-style Cathedral of the Incarnation—the huge, ornate, and costly memorial Cornelia Stewart has built for her husband. Construction of the cathedral takes nine years and costs approximately three million dollars. On May 22, 1885, Cornelia Stewart signs over the deed of the great cathedral and all of its adjacent buildings and schools to the Episcopal church for one dollar.

In March 1885, a *New York Times* editorial attempted to calm the nerves of Garden City residents who feared that, with the closing of the A. T. Stewart & Co, business would come an end to the development of their beloved community.

"At last those who put their trust in the ESTATE are to be rewarded," the *Times* editorial proclaimed. The much anticipated Cathedral of the Incarnation, nine years in the making, would finally open in an elaborate ceremony, the editorial promised. "The unbelievers who have mocked at the ESTATE and said that it would never open the cathedral will be put to shame."

Despite the long delay in the construction of the magnificent edifice, the *Times* scolded Garden City doubters for not understanding the intricacies of building a structure the size, scope, and magnitude of the Cathedral of the Incarnation. The nine years it took to construct the ornate building was nothing compared with European cathedrals that sometimes took "five hundred years to build." The *Times* added that "even at the end of that time they leave a tower or something else unfinished."

Instead of doubting the intention of the governing body of the estate (with Henry Hilton at its head), the people of Garden City should have been "full of admiration and gratitude" that the estate had undertaken to build the cathedral within a mere ten-year span.

The grand opening of the cathedral was set in stone for April 9, 1885, and the residents of Garden City had only Judge Henry Hilton to thank.

AT LAST

For several years thoughtless and wicked persons waited for the completion of the cathedral and professed to believe that 'in a few weeks' or 'next Spring' the building would be finished or consecrated. When they found that they were wrong they suddenly lost all belief in the ESTATE, and proclaimed that it never meant to finish the cathedral. ...

The result is that to-day Judge HILTON ... has completed and opened the Garden City Cathedral.

—New York Times
March 20, 1885

It looked as though Cornelia's face had been painted on a crumbling slab of alabaster calcite, which might have been all right if, whoever had drawn it on, had done it correctly. They didn't. One eye was larger than the other. The lips were too big and too red. The mouth was lopsided, teetering between a smile and a frown. There were two big rosy cheeks, each perfectly round and red, but also of a unequal size. The eyebrows were drawn on in bold, black strokes careening upward and out, their ends hidden under the jet-black ringlets of her ill-fitting wig. From where one might suspect her ears were located, hidden beneath the thick fake hair, dangled long, shimmering silver earrings whose ends disappeared into the thick red fox fur collar of her otherwise dark coat.

Cornelia Stewart seemed oblivious to her clownish appearance and simply pursed her lips into what might have been construed as a wistfully bemused smile, her blue watery eyes looking out over the elaborate church altar with the perplexed stare of someone who might have been watching a circus roll into town. She blinked constantly as if it was too much to take in all at once, her eyes darting back and forth nervously, her head never moving except for a slight palsy shake.

It was a cold day in April 1885. A slight drizzle was falling outside, and gusts of cloudy breath were visible from the mouths of the hundreds of men, women, and children who had gathered outside one of the church's three entrances. A cold wind swept across the cathedral lawns, the grass damp and still thin and dark brown with no signs of turning green. The trees were as barren as they had been in the middle of December. Nearly one thousand people had traveled great distances to take part in the dedication ceremony. Ten cars of enthusiastic well-wishers, businessmen, politicians, lawyers, judges, and other professionals and their wives and children, many of them Episcopalians, had made the trip down on a special train from the Long Island City station. By the time they arrived in Garden City for the opening service at 11 o'clock that morning, most were unable to get near the cathedral, never mind get inside and take a seat. The three entrances had been barred by police details, the place already surrounded by hundreds of devout worshippers and curiosity seekers.

Everything, including the glass used for the windows, was English except the organ and the coat of arms of the late Mr. Stewart. The cathedral was, by all architectural and design standards, built with a "sumptuousness and thoroughness of detail which can only be secured by the lavish use of money." For Cornelia Stewart, money was no object.

THE STEWART MEMORIAL
THE NEW CATHEDRAL AT GARDEN CITY
Bishop Littlejohn To Open The Building To-Day—The Two Schools Established By Mrs. Stewart

It has remained for the widow of a New York millionaire, who gained his wealth in the most respectable and prosaic of employments, to revive the chantry on American soil. ... The chimes that sound from the tall steeple of the "cathedral" at Garden City, Long Island, came to America in the same year that Mrs. A.T. Stewart caused ground to be broken for a great memorial to the greatest merchant in the "dry goods trade." ... Nine years have passed and now the chantry, or mortuary chapel, has become a good sized church with appointments for the Bishop and clergy of Long Island, a famous organ built by Mr. Hilborne L. Roosevelt. ... If anybody wants to know what "pure floriated Gothic" is, according to the most approved views of English architects, a visit to Garden City is all that is necessary to his enlightenment.

—*New York Times*
April 9, 1885

The church chimes began to peal. Outside, people moved closer and closer toward one of the entrances to try to look inside or just to hear Episcopalian Bishop Abram N. Littlejohn deliver the opening service and blessing of the new cathedral. Littlejohn was a stout, balding man, his hair brushed from the back to front, barely covering his ears in feathery white curls. He had a commanding presence with his back straight and the bulk of his body pushing forward from his steadfast spine like a barrel concealed in a white linen smock and purple robe. He had a booming voice and spoke with conviction and precise elocution. He had been the bishop of the Protestant Episcopal Diocese of Long Island since 1869.

———————

Mrs. Stewart established two other memorials in Garden City in memory of her husband—the cathedral schools of St. Paul and St. Mary. The three-story St. Paul's was established in 1877, reportedly on the advice of Henry Hilton. It was a school exclusively for boys. St. Paul's was made of brick and stone, done in English Gothic design, with ornate porches of carved stone, a clock and bell tower, and a copper spire.

It combines all the best features of modern collegiate edifices in this country and Europe. ... Every part of the building is fireproof; it is thoroughly ventilated and supplied with gas and water in every room ... steam heating apparatus furnish a uniform temperature throughout the edifice. ... The different stories are connected by an elevator. ... The course of instruction in this school is designed to cover six years and to prepare boys for admission to college, scientific schools or other higher institutions of learning.

—*New York Times*
April 9, 1885

The St. Mary's School, which formally opened in 1877 as well, was designed to provide young women and girls, according to the *New York Times,* a "thorough education in every department, and to develop such qualities of mind and heart as will form accomplished Christian women."

Cornelia Stewart was the driving force behind them all. Her memorials to her husband were the Cathedral of the Incarnation, with its magnificent spire, the small seminary, the lavish bishop's residency, and two schools. She was even further instrumental in persuading the Diocese of Long Island to move its formal headquarters to Garden City from Brooklyn, lured there in no small part by the exquisite cathedral and buildings placed at its disposal.

In a 1998 *New York Times* article, Natalie Naylor, director of the Long Island Studies Institute at Hofstra University, said, "Garden City would be a very different place had it not been for her. Cornelia Clinch Stewart's role has not been given the credit it should have. She was able to do it with his money and as a monument to him. Bringing the Episcopal Diocese from Brooklyn, which was the third largest city in the country, made a difference in terms of the character of Garden City."

The two schools, which remained integral parts of the Garden City community for decades, were ultimately closed in 1993 due to financial difficulties. Following Mrs. Stewart's death in 1886, her heirs formed the Garden City Company to oversee the management of the community. After this move, residents for the first time were able to purchase homes in Garden City rather than simply rent them from the Stewart estate as they had previously done.

> *"That move was one of a series of circumstances that kept Stewart's project from failing. ... The project could have faltered after they both died. ... Those formative years, from 1893 to 1919, were solely credited to the Garden City Company's incredible talent to doing the right thing."*
>
> —JOHN ELLIS KORDES, LOCAL HISTORIAN,
> *New York Times,* NOVEMBER 15, 1998

It was cold and damp inside the cathedral. Most of those with reserved seating in the front rows of the long wooden pews facing the bronze lectern kept their coats, furs, jackets, and long, dark capes on. Cornelia Stewart stood with the congregation as the organist, George W. Morgan, played the "Hallelujah Chorus," on the cathedral's magnificent organ, rapidly blinking her eyes and staring straight ahead with a bemused look on her face. Except for being seated in a place of honor at the very front of the church, she looked like any old woman of means: thin and gaunt, stoop-shouldered, her face badly painted on, her head weighted down by the ill-fitting curly black wig, and a large, wide-brimmed black hat with a sheer black mourning veil pulled up to reveal her face. Her frame was cloaked in a long, black wool coat with a red fox fur collar, her pale hands hidden within a black fur muffler from which hung a string of dark rosary beads.

Life alone had been mostly good for eighty-three-year-old Cornelia Stewart. She could be thankful for many things, most of all the vast fortune her husband had left her. Since his death nine years earlier, she had lived alone in one of the most elegant mansions on Fifth Avenue in New York City, where her every need was tended to by a battery of servants. Even the vast fortune bequeathed to her was taken care of by Judge Henry Hilton, a trusted friend. Her children had passed away, so the entire fortune had come to her.

Cornelia had no mind for business. She was glad Hilton oversaw her husband's vast dealings. Her only concerns had become her vast collection of wigs and cosmetics. The cosmetics, hundreds of exotic ointments, potions, creams, elixirs, and lotions, all promised endless youth and beauty, and all of them, no matter how unusual or expensive, had failed miserably for her as her tired, wrinkled, pinched face attested. No amount of cosmetics could turn back the clock, a fact she still refused to believe as she spent more and more on acquiring the most elaborate creams and ointments in the hope of uncovering the youth she so desired.

———•····•———

Seats in the cathedral had been reserved for family and close friends. In the front pew to the right of the center aisle sat Judge Henry Hilton and his wife; the former New York governor R. E. Fenton and his wife; Brooklyn Mayor Seth Low and his wife; Prescott Hall Butler and his wife; the Rev. J. B. Wetherill and his wife, a grand-niece; John Hughes, a son-in-law of Judge Hilton's; and Mrs. Stewart's three maiden sisters, Emma, Anna, and Julia Clinch.

The service was conducted by the Rev. G. R. Vandewater of St. Luke's Church, Dr. J. Carpenter Smith of Flushing, New York, and the Rev. Dr. Snively of Brooklyn. Following the service, Bishop Littlejohn took his place at the lectern and opened his manuscript, beginning with a text of Isaiah from the Bible. Littlejohn looked over the gathering from his perch atop the ornate brass lectern and turned his gaze to Cornelia Stewart.

Before proceeding to any other thought I stop here on the threshold of my subject to give utterance to what, next the reverent worship of Almighty God, is the strongest impulse in all hearts at this moment," Littlejohn said.

As we look about us on this rare scene of architectural beauty, these lines of grace, these rich traceries in wood and stone, yonder uplifted arches, floating in air like ascending hymns arrested in their flight to the skies; these windows glow-

ing with a light that is religious but not dim ... the story of the incarnation of the Son of God, from the world's morning to its evening; that organ of exquisite modulation and mighty compass, combing the sublime diapason of the sea with the softest note of a bird warbling in the air; yonder monumental spire, whose chaste, serene beauty charms in sympathetic fellowship the rays of rising and setting suns, and the nightly gleam of the far-away stars—as we look upon all this our hearts with spontaneous unanimity unite in a loving and grateful tribute of admiration to her who, moved by tender remembrances of the departed, by a desire to do the most enduring good in her generation, has consecrated her wealth to make here the place of God's feet glorious. That she may live to gather some of the fruit to grow upon this tree of her planting, that peace and happiness may be the portion of her declining years, and that, at the last, when her face shall be turned to the rest that remained for the people of God in the temple not made with hands, the recollection of this pious work for the living, this enduring memorial of her beloved dead, may bring with it the benediction of Almighty God, the redeeming presence of His everlasting Son, the sure comfort of the Holy Ghost—this is the prayer trembling on all lips at this moment and struggling for utterance with the impatient fervor of a long pent-up emotion.

Littlejohn thanked Henry Hilton, but not by name.

And then only second to this feeling toward our venerated benefactress is that which we cherish toward him who is so generally known as her chosen friend and advisor. The informing, directing mind in this work from the beginning he has put upon everything that we see in the impress of his ripe judgment, his cultured sense of the beautiful, and, where it may be had, the congenial vesture of the useful, his vigilant, painstaking care extending to all details. Gladly do we avail ourselves of this first appropriate occasion thus publicly to

*record our estimate of his elevated and comprehensive views
from the start and our gratitude for his invaluable services in
bringing thus far on the way to its consummation this magnificent scheme of affiliated Christian institutions. It is our ear-
nest wish that he may find some part of his reward for these
years of watchful, responsible labor in the success of what he
has done so much to establish. Nor must we fail to suitably
remember the architect of this structure, him whose mind conceived, whose pencil drew, and whose eye watched over the
slow elaboration of these forms of living peace.*

Hilton was seated next to Mrs. Stewart in the front row at her right
hand, a position he had occupied for the past nine years. Conspicuous by its absence was any mention of the late A. T. Stewart's remains
or the crypt far below the cathedral, where his body was reportedly
interred.

GARDEN CITY'S CATHEDRAL
A GREAT CROWD AT THE OPEN-
ING SERVICES
Bishop Littlejohn Pays A Warm Tribute
To Mrs. Stewart's Generosity And
Mr. Hilton's Judgment

The Cathedral of the Incarnation, in Garden City, Mrs. A. T.
Stewart's costly memorial to her millionaire husband, was
opened for public worship yesterday. Enough people waited
around its elaborately carved doors for admittance to have
filled the Roman Catholic cathedral in this city. Ten car loads
of enthusiastic Episcopalians, many of them business and professional men, with their wives and children made an early
breakfast and took a special train from the Long Island City
station. Eleven more cars, filled with devout worshipers from

Brooklyn, joined them. ... The appointed hour of public service passed and still nearly 1,000 people, who had traveled miles to participate in it, had not been able to get near either of the three entrances.

—*New York Times*
April 10, 1885

A two-hundred-foot spire was built on the Gothic brownstone cathedral, making it, at the time, the tallest building on Long Island. An enormous stone tower hovered over the entranceway to the cathedral, and atop it was a brilliant brass cross. Dozens of stone buttresses were built off the main tower, and the angular roof line and variety of conical spires piercing the sky were adorned with a wide assortment of stone gargoyles, copper- and brass-covered towers, and elaborately carved stone pinnacles.

The massive front doors of the cathedral were carved with depictions of the saints, and a series of enormous, meticulously designed stained-glass windows began in the cathedral's vestibule and continued down the length of the vast building. All of the windows contained full figures of saints and apostles, each telling a particular biblical story and each perfectly and precisely drawn down to the most minute detail. Overhead hung a series of elaborate brass chandeliers that lit the way down the aisles of the cathedral. On either side of the aisles were rows upon rows of carved wooden pews lined with purple velvet cushions with gold braid. Huge octagonal mahogany bays were built along the length of the building to house the organ and choir sections that overlooked the congregation seating.

The altar at the front of the cathedral included eight sculptured white marble panels, each separated by columns with huge black stone columns at the corners. Two statues in white marble, one depicting Hope leaning on an anchor and the other of Religion carrying a replica of the cathedral, adorned the front of the church. Toward the front of the altar were two bronze lecterns, the right-hand lectern adorned with an intricately designed eagle, the base of it showing Christ surrounded by a group of children. The lectern on the left included a winding shaft of leafs with a group of men and women gathered at the base of it. The stone floor leading up to the lecterns had a colored, inlaid marble coat of arms of the Episcopalian Diocese of Long Island, and the vestibule was adorned with an elaborate marble depiction of the Stewart coat of arms.

Beneath the main chapel in the basement was the mortuary chapel, and connected to it was a prayer room featuring finely carved wooden pews. The mortuary chapel and prayer room were separated from the rest of the cathedral by two pillars of white carved marble closed with a massive and gleaming brass gate.

Thirteen narrow stained-glass windows ran the length of the basement. The windows included a series of coats of arms, crests, and the likenesses of several bishops of the Episcopal Church. In the center of the basement was a huge marble urn inscribed with the words: "In Memoriam." Across from the urn were dressing rooms for the bishop and other clergy. An elaborate iron and brass circular staircase led from the upstairs chapel down to the basement and dressing rooms. Most of the basement was devoted to classrooms for Sunday school.

On April 17, 1885, nearly a week after the grand opening of the cathedral, Bishop Littlejohn presided over a special Episcopal convention at the Church of the Holy Trinity in Brooklyn to consider accepting the new cathedral in Garden City. Close to one hundred clergy and laypeople took part in the convention. The convention not only had the task of accepting the new structure but also of coming to some agreement on the conditions Mrs. Stewart had placed on the magnificent and generous gift she had offered. Along with giving the new cathedral to the Episcopal Church, Cornelia had stipulated that the church would have to agree to make Garden City the seat of the diocese and that the bishop would have to establish his residency in the home built for him in Garden City. The delegates quickly adopted resolutions to accept the cathedral and all the conditions Mrs. Stewart had attached. The headquarters of the diocese would be in Garden City henceforth.

On May 22, 1885, Cornelia Stewart signed over the deed of the great cathedral and all of its adjacent buildings and schools to the church for one dollar. The deed was immediately placed on record. The deed forbid the church incorporators to convey, lease, or mortgage any of the property. Consecration services for the cathedral were scheduled for June, and it was Stewart's wish to have the recorded deed placed on the altar during the consecration ceremony.

SERVICES OF CONSECRATION
Ceremonies To Take Place At The Cathedral Of The Incarnation

The Cathedral of the Incarnation at Garden City, Long Island, which was built by Mrs. A.T. Stewart as a memorial to her husband, will be solemnly consecrated on Tuesday morning next, in the presence of the clergy and laity of the Diocese of Long Island, the clergy and laity of the Episcopal churches in other dioceses, and such of the general public as see fit to attend. ... Bishop Littlejohn, of the Diocese of Long Island, will officiate. ... The ceremonies will include the formal presentation of the cathedral to the Bishop ... and the placing on the cathedral altar of the deeds of conveyance of the church property with documents assuring to the diocese a perpetual endowment of the cathedral.

—*New York Times*
May 27, 1885

On June 2, 1885, the official service of consecration was held. The seating capacity of the cathedral was estimated at 1,500, and more than two hundred more chairs were located along the aisles and the back and sides of the church to accommodate the multitude of guests, including clergy, dignitaries, and invited guests. Hundreds more gathered outside the cathedral trying to catch a glimpse of the services inside and listen to the music and choir. Unlike the April grand opening, which was cold and rainy, June 2 was a warm summer day. The flowers were blooming and the trees and finely manicured lawns were green and vibrant.

Inside, Cornelia Stewart, dressed in a modest black silk dress with hat and veil sat in the front pew with Henry Hilton once again at her side. Immediate family members and friends sat in the pews behind and beside her. Bishop Littlejohn sat in a chair along the altar. A cadre of Episcopal bishops from Pennsylvania, Massachusetts, New Jersey, and Illinois occupied places of honor in seating along the front altar. With them were representatives of St. Stephen's, Trinity, Hobart, and Columbia Colleges, and Lehigh University.

Following the recital of the Twenty-fourth Psalm ("The earth is the Lord's, and the fullness thereof; the world, and they that dwell therein"), a frail Cornelia Stewart, leaning on Henry Hilton's arm for support and using a cane, made her way slowly up to the altar, where she presented Bishop Littlejohn the deed to the property. Stewart's voice was too weak to address the bishop, so, in her stead, Hilton read the formal presentation of the conveyance of the property. With the deed, Hilton told the congregation, was a bond providing for an annual endowment to the estate of fifteen thousand dollars to be applied to the maintenance of the cathedral, building, and grounds. Quite literally, the deed was done. Had it taken place anywhere other than within the solemn, foreboding cathedral, the audience might have cheered and clapped. As it was, there were audible sighs and murmurs, many in the vast audience nodding their heads in silent approval.

Following the presentation and acceptance of the deed, Assistant Bishop Potter delivered a sermon based on the Bible's "First Chronicles"—"The palace is not for man, but for the Lord God." Potter defended the construction of the massive and costly cathedral in the face of complaints that the money could have been better spent on hospitals, colleges, and libraries rather than such an ornate palace of worship. According to Potter, "Only active Christianity could bring home to men the great fact of the brotherhood of humanity."

It was the duty of Christians to worship in the finest places they could build, Potter proclaimed, celebrating the idea that "here was a church home to which the common people might freely come on an equality with the grandest in the land."

THE GIFT OF MRS. STEWART
FORMAL PRESENTATION OF THE GARDEN CITY CATHEDRAL
Great Throng Witness The Transfer To The Church Of Property Which Cost Over $2,000,000

From all the paths men and women walked past the lines and within the guarded doors of the cathedral, which was to pass by legal gift from Mrs. A.T. Stewart to Bishop Littlejohn for the Diocese of Long Island. The gathering had assembled to witness the gift and service of consecration by the Bishop. ... Judge Hilton ... presented him with the deed to the property, which, for $1, to be paid, conveyed to the church through him, the edifice and grounds on which $2,000,000 had been spent.

—*New York Times*

June 3, 1885

In December 1885, Henry Harrison, the much heralded architect of the Cathedral of the Incarnation, sued Cornelia Stewart for more than ninety-five thousand dollars he claimed was due him for his professional services. Harrison, a resident of Connecticut, brought suit against Mrs. Stewart in the United States Circuit Court. According to Harrison, he was employed by Mrs. Stewart in 1876 to design and prepare plans and drawings for the cathedral, and he claimed he was also hired as the superintendent to oversee the construction of Mrs. Stewart's memorial.

The services he rendered to her in the design and construction of the cathedral, according to Harrison, were valued at approximately $111,000. According to Harrison's suit, he had spent nearly $3,000 of his own money on the project that was never reimbursed, bringing the total amount owed to him to $114,000. Harrison claimed that Mrs. Stewart had only paid him about $18,000 of that amount. According to Harrison, when he demanded the remaining amount due, his request was refused.

According to lawyers for Mrs. Stewart, Harrison had not been Mrs. Stewart's architect for several years, and he had been paid for his architectural designs and plans. Stewart's attorney, Horace Russell, maintained that Mrs. Stewart had only employed Harrison for his architectural work and not as superintendent of the construction.

The case was later settled out of court.

———•••———

At the end of the service of consecration, Henry Hilton escorted the ailing Cornelia Stewart to her waiting carriage. He then made his way through the vast crowd to his own carriage. Hilton always appeared to walk as if someone or something was chasing him, periodically looking over one shoulder or the other, imagining the sound of footsteps behind him as if someone was following close at his heels. Someone was. It was Time, and it was catching up to him.

EXPIRATION DATE

In which Cornelia Stewart dies on October 25, 1886, leaving behind a will that bequeaths nearly half of the remaining Stewart estate to Judge Henry Hilton. Stewart heirs seek to have the will voided, claiming fraud by Hilton. The case lingers in the courts for the next seven years before being resolved. In the end, Hilton's attempts at replicating his benefactor's retail business success all fail. Hilton dies, and the once great Stewart fortune is gone.

Cornelia Stewart died at her palatial mansion on the corner of Fifth Avenue and Thirty-fourth Street on October 25, 1886, at the age of eighty-four. The cause of death was pneumonia.

She had spent the summer, as she always had, at Saratoga and returned to New York City on September 1. She returned home suffering from a cold. Her ill health forced her to cancel many planned engagements until finally, on the Saturday before her death, when she seemed to regain her strength, she arranged to meet with Judge Hilton and make plans for the week ahead. But by Sunday morning her cold had worsened, and her family physician, Dr. J. C. Minor, was called to the mansion to attend to her. Dr. Minor diagnosed her illness as pneumonia and advised her, because of her advanced years, to take every precaution. She remained bedridden, running a high fever, and had difficulty breathing. One of her grand-nieces and two of her servants stayed up all night at her bedside. By the next morning, her condition had grown far worse. She died around 9:30 on Monday morning surrounded by her grand-niece, Mrs. J. B. Wetherill, her two servants, and Dr. Minor.

Following her death, Judge Hilton was summoned. He gave strict orders that no one except close friends and immediate family were allowed into the house. A private detective was stationed at the front door. Several family members of Mrs. Stewart's and Hilton's were summoned to the mansion to pay their respects. Hilton had previously telegraphed Bishop Littlejohn, who was at an Episcopal convention in Chicago. Littlejohn had returned from the convention early to be at Stewart's side. A private service was arranged to be held at the mansion at 11 a.m. on Thursday with Bishop Littlejohn officiating. After the private service, the body was taken by train to the Church of the Incarnation in Garden City, where a public ceremony was held.

MRS. A.T. STEWART DEAD
HER FRIENDS AND RELATIVES
STARTLED BY THE NEWS
The Millionaire's Widow Succumbs
To Pneumonia After Only Two
Days Of Illness

Mrs. Cornelia M. Stewart, widow of Alexander T. Stewart, died suddenly yesterday at her home. ... Whatever the cause, it was found on Sunday morning that she had caught cold and she began to show symptoms of serious illness. ... Everything that could be thought of was done for her, but toward night it began to look as if the chances of recovery were exceedingly small. ... Early yesterday morning she became rapidly worse and at 9:30 o'clock she died, very peacefully, surrounded by those who had sat up with her and her physician. ... Those who visited the house were Prescott Hall Butler, whose wife is a grandniece of Mrs. Stewart; the Rev. J. B. Wetherill, husband of another grandniece; Mrs. John Hughes, a daughter of Judge Hilton; Judge Smith, husband of Mrs. Smith, and Mrs. Stewart's three maiden sisters.

—*New York Times*
October 26, 1886

A large crowd gathered in front of the Stewart Marble Mansion on Fifth Avenue the morning of the private funeral. Dark embroidered shades were drawn on every window. A police guard surrounded the mansion. No one except family and invited guests were allowed inside for the service. When her coffin was carried out into the main hall, about two hundred former A. T. Stewart & Co. employees, along with Mrs. Stewart's household staff, were allowed to pay their respects. Stewart's servants were deeply upset. Many of them had been with her all their lives. She had been an employer as well as a friend.

Cornelia Stewart had lived out the remainder of her life since her husband's death in 1876 quietly, shunning publicity, with her only extravagance being her dresses and cosmetics. She wore expensive gowns and dresses, and kept rooms filled with toiletries and cosmetics. Relatives and friends gathered in the hall after the employees paid their last respects. Bishop Littlejohn said a brief prayer. The coffin was chestnut, covered with black silk, and the six handles were silver. The plate on the coffin read simply: "Cornelia M. Stewart, Died October 25, 1886. Aged 84 years and 5 months."

The coffin rested in the center of the great mansion hall surrounded by lilies, roses, and palms. At the head of the coffin was a large cross made from ivy with a wreath of lilies on it. There were also two baskets filled with roses. The service was limited to several prayers. Former Judge Horace Russell told reporters that Mrs. Stewart had been opposed to ostentation during her life and that her wishes were to keep her funeral simple, plain, and private.

"Nothing would have disturbed her more while living than the thought that an unusual display should be made over her when dead," Russell told reporters.

In keeping with Mrs. Stewart's wishes, there were no pallbearers. The undertakers' employees carried the coffin out through the wide front door and down the steps to the hearse and slid the coffin inside. Twenty carriages were lined up on the street waiting to follow the procession to the train station. A special train of seven cars had been prepared to carry the body and mourners to Garden City for the burial ceremony.

At Garden City, the coffin was taken to the Cathedral of the Incarnation and carried to the front. Family and friends followed the coffin into the church and took their reserved seats at the front. About 1,500 people gathered in the cathedral for the burial service, which was conducted by Bishop Littlejohn. Following the service, the coffin was taken to the crypt. Only relatives and several close friends were allowed to accompany the body. Cornelia Stewart's coffin was placed in a lead-lined casket that was put inside another chestnut box, which then was placed in the crypt beside the remains of her husband. A huge marble slab was placed on top of the crypt, and a three-thousand-pound marble urn was set on top of the slab.

"Mrs. Stewart died in the belief that she was to be placed beside her dead husband's corpse. But, as a matter of fact, the magnificent cathedral in Garden City stands over that which in name only is the grave of A. T. Stewart. And that is what his riches brought him."

—LOUIS MEGARGEE, *Seen & Heard,* VOL. 1, 1901

MRS. STEWART'S FUNERAL
SIMPLE SERVICES IN THE
GARDEN CITY CATHEDRAL
A Few Friends And Relatives
Follow The Dead Woman From The
City—The Will Still Unopened

A crowd gathered as early as 9 o'clock yesterday morning in front of the house in which Mrs. Stewart lay dead. A belief seemed to be quite generally held that when the body of Mrs. Stewart was placed in the coffin, the big double doors would be thrown open to the public. It required the influence of the police to convince many persons that the funeral would be private. ... It was 2:35 o'clock when the special train of seven cars, including two parlor coaches, pulled out from the station. ... The run to Garden City was made without a stop in 45 minutes. ... Ex-Judge Russell said yesterday that the contents of the will would not be made public until it was presented for probate. It is thought likely that it will be offered to-morrow.

—*New York Times*
October 29, 1886

Cornelia Stewart was dead and buried. Since her husband's death in 1876, she had endured not only the theft of his remains, which were held for ransom, but also a seemingly endless string of civil litigation in the courts over her husband's will and the millions it included. The stress of it all overwhelmed her at times, affecting her physical as well as mental health. According to some reports, gossip mostly, perpetrated by anonymous servants, she had lost her mind to the point that she would dress up each night in her finest gowns and jewelry, lighting every lamp in the Marble Mansion, pretending to entertain imaginary guests—bowing and curtsying—and carrying on lengthy conversations with ethereal high-society ghosts.

"Meanwhile, Mrs. Stewart sat at her 34th Street window, increasingly reclusive, absorbed with the dream of restored youth, watching the comings and goings at Mrs. Astor's house across the street."
—Wayne Craven, *Gilded Mansions: Grand Architecture and High Society*, 2009

Still, despite rumors of her failing mental and physical condition, Cornelia Stewart managed to complete at least one of her husband's most prized projects—Garden City—the planned community that he had envisioned and begun in 1869. She completed the construction of the $3 million monument to her husband, the Cathedral of the Incarnation, as well as the St. Paul's School for boys and the St. Mary's School for girls. It was not an easy task.

She was not able to save the Working Women's Hotel, nor was she able to save her husband's vast retail empire. Yet, the realization of the hotel as well as the retail business were in the hands of Henry Hilton, and so she could not be held accountable for their demise. And, at least in her own mind, and reportedly through her own pains, she was able to negotiate for the return of her husband's remains and inter them safely in the cathedral in Garden City.

There were many people inside the Stewart family as well as outside who believed that Hilton's Svengali-like hold over Mrs. Stewart and the family fortune was twofold. First, as one rumor had it, Hilton was, in fact, the illegitimate son of A. T. Stewart. One Philadelphia periodical, *Seen & Heard,* published by newspaperman Louis Megargee in 1903, wrote that American publisher G. W. Childs (1829–1894), who co-owned the *Philadelphia Public Ledger* newspaper, once said, "Why there is nothing at all wonderful in the fact that he should have favored his own son over all others, even though that son was illegitimate."

Such speculation would answer why Hilton was able to obtain most of Stewart's fortune following his death and the remainder of it following the death of Cornelia Stewart. There was no proof offered to corroborate this rumor.

The second most prevalent rumor was that Hilton was holding A. T. Stewart's remains and had promised Cornelia Stewart their safe return and burial in Garden City's Cathedral of the Incarnation if she acquiesced to his demands. Hilton knew full well Mrs. Stewart's grief over the theft and her desire to have the remains recovered at any cost—even at the price of the entire Stewart fortune. This rumor also went uncorroborated.

"Hilton became her ruler, and the manner in which this man gradually absorbed the enormous fortune that Stewart left behind him, until the widow was almost without ready money to supply the needs of the palatial residence which had become a burden to her, passes belief. And since then, and almost even to the present day, the Hilton harpies have been snarling over the remains of the Stewart fortune, until they have come to be looked upon in the public eye as even more infamous than the ghouls who stole the bones of the dead millionaire."

—Louis Megargee, *Seen & Heard by Megargee,* Vol. 3, 1903

The reading of Cornelia Stewart's will took place in late October 1886 and was filed in probate court in early November. Only Henry Hilton was privy to the contents of it. The reading of the will set off another firestorm of litigation that would last until 1893 when all the stipulations in the will were finally resolved.

STEWART HEIRS IN COURT
SEEKING TO HAVE THE WIDOW'S WILL DECLARED VOID.
Charges Made Against Ex-Judge Hilton In The Complaint Filed By P. H. Butler, An Heir At Law

A complaint has been filed in the County Clerk's office by Prescott Hall Butler, who is about to bring suit in the Supreme Court to set aside the will of Cornelia M. Stewart. The complaint is perhaps one of the largest ever filed. ... The alleged codicil in the will, the complaint says, giving Mr. Hilton this trust, was obtained by fraud and was part of a scheme or contrivance on the part of this defendant. ... It is also claimed that the defendant never filed an inventory of about $20,000,000 worth of property including a large and valuable collection of works of art.

—*New York Times*
February 19, 1887

Mrs. Stewart made the will in July 1877. Subsequently, several codicils or additions were made to it. According to the *New York Times,* Henry Hilton, along with Charles Clinch and Sarah Smith, the children of Mrs. Stewart's deceased brother, James, received the bulk of the estate. Charles Clinch and Sarah Smith were to receive an estimated $4.6 million each. Hilton, on the other hand, was awarded, in trust, an estimated $9.2 million.

The entire Stewart estate was estimated at approximately twenty million dollars, substantially less than the reported forty million dollars that A. T. Stewart had left to his wife upon his death. The decline in the Stewart fortune was attributed to the transfer of the retail business to Hilton, the building of the Garden City cathedral and schools, and various gifts and homes that Mrs. Stewart reportedly gave to relatives. No mention of the fate of either the Marble Mansion or Stewart's huge, expensive art gallery was made in the will. Mrs. Stewart had planned on bequeathing the mansion and its notable collection of paintings and sculptures to New York City as a gift of a sustaining fine arts museum. She entrusted her plans to Hilton, who, as he had previously done to many of the Stewarts' requests, never carried them out.

"The curious members of New York's money-oriented society wondered why the widow Stewart was wandering around in the marble barn, virtually alone, and who would be given the house in the end."
—MOSETTE BRODERICK, *Triumvirate: McKim, Mead & White: Art, Architecture, Scandal, and Class in America's Gilded Age,* 2010

The *New York Times* reported the bequeathed legacies, both actual and estimated, as: Sarah N. Smith, actual, $250,000; Cornelia S. Butler, actual, $200,000; Lawrence Butler, actual, $100,000; Charles Butler, actual, $50,000; Kate A. Smith, actual, $200,000; Louise Smith, actual, $100,000; Ellen Smith, actual, $100,000; Bessie Smith, actual, $100,000; James Smith, actual, $100,000; Rosalie Butler, actual, $50,000; Helen Butler, actual, $50,000; Virginia Butler, actual, $50,000; Maxwell Butler, actual, $50,000; Prescott Butler, actual, $50,000: household servants, actual, $25,000; Henry Hilton (in trust), estimated, $9,262,500; Charles J. Clinch, estimated, $4,631,250; Sarah N. Smith, estimated, $4,631,250; total, $20,000,000.

Along with receiving the largest share, Hilton was named as executor of the estate, overseeing the Marble Mansion on Fifth Avenue as well as the complete Stewart art holdings. And what of the will's amendments?

In May 1878, an amendment was added revising the legacy given to Henry Hilton. He was to be given half of the estate to be held in trust for completion of work on the Garden City cathedral and schools as deemed necessary. The codicil also stipulated that any heir who contested the will would forfeit his or her claim to the estate.

In July 1878, another amendment was added, authorizing Hilton to manage the money bequeathed him in the trust as he saw fit and without substantiating any of his expenditures.

A third amendment was added to the will in May 1882 giving Sarah N. Smith a one-half share of the interest in the estate left to Charles J. Clinch and adding a $25,000 legacy for her household servants.

The fourth and final codicil was added in November 1885, and it again increased the share of the estate left to Hilton, absolving him of any obligation to use any of the nearly ten-million-dollar trust fund he had been bequeathed in conjunction with Garden City, the cathedral, or the schools. Since the cathedral and schools had been deeded over to the Episcopal Church's Diocese of Long Island, they were no longer Hilton's responsibility.

So far as the public is concerned, this is the end of the Stewart estate.

—*New York Times,* NOVEMBER 2, 1886

The luxurious Marble Mansion remained vacant for a short period of time, and finally in 1890, it was rented to the New York City Manhattan Club, a noted Democratic organization, which remained there until 1899. In 1901 it was sold to a private corporation and was subsequently razed to make room for the Knickerbocker Trust Company, one of the largest banks in the country at the time. The Stewart art holdings contained in it—consisting of some 240 paintings, statuary, and sculptures reportedly worth four million to five million dollars—were auctioned off in February 1887.

THE STEWART COLLECTION
It Is To Be Sold At Auction In February

All doubt about the disposition of the paintings and other art treasures at the A.T. Stewart mansion has been settled by an order from the Executors to sell them at public auction. ... Many of the paintings and other articles have never been seen, even by the most frequent visitors to the Stewart gallery.

—*New York Times*
December 17, 1886

"Hilton's main force was audacity."
—Louis MEGARGEE, *Seen & Heard,* VOL. 1, 1901

The series of lawsuits, brought by heirs of the estate, contesting Cornelia Stewart's will dragged on for years. Newspaper coverage of the lawsuits only further sullied Hilton's already tarnished reputation. Reports exposed a sordid assortment of Hilton's shenanigans. A June 20, 1888, *New York Times* article reported that an examination of the A.T. Stewart & Co ledgers showed that Hilton had paid himself about $5.5 million over a six-year period based on company profits, interest on capital, and guaranteed commissions. Payments he made to himself depleted the company's working capital to the point that it was barely able to function.

It appeared that Judge Hilton was in the habit of drawing out of the business about all of his credits ... making the total yield of the business to him as income on his capital, profits and commissions $5,490,615.75. He withdrew capital from the business during the closing months of the partnership until toward the end it was reduced from about $8,170,000 to about $3,300,000.
—*New York Times,* JUNE 21, 1888

Other public revelations demonstrated Hilton's abuse of Cornelia Stewart. In an incident in 1880, made public in a *Times* article published in April 1889, Hilton had Mrs. Stewart sell her Chemical Bank stock to him for $190 per share. The stock was worth $1,700 per share at the time, and the value of it increased to $2,100 per share in 1885 and $3,000 per share in 1888. According to the newspaper account, "The point of the inquiry was to show that when in 1880 Judge Hilton allowed Mrs. Stewart 190 for 100 shares of that stock, he knowingly took care of himself at her expense."

Going as far back as 1877, at the time Stewart's body was stolen, Hilton had been the brunt of public ridicule and the object of scorn because of his many manipulations. *Puck,* the humor magazine that began publishing in New York in 1876, lambasted Hilton for his ridiculous and boorish behavior regarding the Grand Union Hotel incident in 1877.

"He made Stewart's Grand Hotel in Saratoga ridiculous by excluding one of the leading bankers of the world because he was a Jew," *Puck* proclaimed.

The magazine berated him for his handling of the Working Women's Hotel, exclaiming, "He excited the laughter of the whole country by his absurd management of the Woman's Home which Stewart built."

But the magazine aimed its most profound attack on Hilton for his handling of the Stewart grave robbery.

For common decency's sake, if they are not found soon, Mr. Judge Hilton ought to cut his throat and give his own bones to that grand mausoleum—for a mausoleum without bones is a farce. ... He has got Stewart's millions and in common decency he can offer a few thousands for the old man's bones. ... Puck's advice to Mr. Henry Hilton is "Remember A.T. Stewart—his grave is empty now. Put yourself in his place!"

In January 1890, the Stewart heirs settled out of court, although some particulars of the litigation were not completely settled until 1893. The heirs, it was reported, were disheartened to discover that by the time the case was settled, most of the Stewart fortune was gone.

According to reports in the *New York Times*, "The settlement of the litigation is much more advantageous to Judge Hilton than had been popularly conjectured." Hilton was able to hang on to a vast majority of the wealth bequeathed him by Cornelia Stewart.

FINAL VICTORY FOR MR. HILTON
Litigation Over A. T. Stewart's Estate
Believed To Be At An End

The decision of Chief Justice Daly of the Court of Common Pleas Thursday, in the action brought by Alexander Stewart to eject Henry Hilton from the realty of Alexander T. Stewart, was a victory for Mr. Hilton. ... Lawyers believe that this decision undoubtedly ends all litigation over the property inherited by Mr. Hilton and the decision is of sufficient significance and weight to debar any suit in the future.

—*New York Times*
November 4, 1893

Despite Hilton's victory in the courts, his ultimate handling of the once great retail empire built by Stewart ended in disaster. He tried to replicate the vast success of his benefactor, but all of his business endeavors and those of his sons were costly and abysmal failures. He formed Hilton, Hughes & Co. to oversee Stewart's once vast and thriving retail empire, but the more Hilton established business corporations to further the retail trade, the more significant his losses became. This, however, did not curtail Hilton from buying splendid hotels and extravagant homes and lavishing himself and his family with other luxuries—all at the expense of the dwindling Stewart fortune. The downward financial spiral was unstoppable.

Trying to keep the retail empire running, Hilton was forced to borrow money and then was unable to meet his outstanding debts. By 1898, just a year before he died, most of the Stewart fortune was gone. Having accepted the fact that he could not replicate the success of Stewart, Hilton turned the operations of the company over to his sons until finally Albert Hilton was placed in charge. In January 1899 Albert Hilton filed for bankruptcy, claiming he owed more than twelve thousand creditors approximately $2.5 million. Henry Hilton had financed his son's business venture to the tune of $4 million, it was revealed in court documents.

All good things and bad must come to an end. Henry Hilton died at Woodlawn Park, his summer home in Saratoga, New York, on August 24, 1899. He was seventy-eight years old.

For a man upon whom fortune had smiled, Hilton was never able to achieve the success that his benefactor, Alexander T. Stewart, had. From the time Stewart died in 1876 and the subsequent death of his widow, Cornelia, in 1886, Hilton had been plagued by lawsuits over the Stewart will and suffered one humiliating loss after another in his various business ventures.

HENRY HILTON IS DEAD
SUFFERED A RELAPSE AND EXPIRED AT
SARATOGA YESTERDAY
Once Had Stewart Millions
Was The Merchant's Sole Advisor,
But Could Not Retain The Wealth
After Stewart's Death

SARATOGA, N.Y., Aug. 24—Ex-Judge Henry Hilton of New York died at 5:30 o'clock this afternoon at his Summer home, Woodlawn Park, after a long illness. He suffered a relapse this afternoon. ... Funeral services will be held and the remains taken to Greenwood.

—*New York Times*
August 25, 1899

Hilton's funeral service was held on August 27 at the Bethesda Episcopal Church, and he was buried at Greenwood Cemetery in New York. It was truly the end of the A. T. Stewart saga.

Henry Hilton, to all appearances, was only what Stewart and Stewart's fortune made him. ... In this decade, and in the next decade, marked by the failure of Hilton, Hughes & Co., made notable by the rapid dissipation of one of the greatest fortunes ever amassed by trade. ... Firm after firm that was heralded as the successor of A.T. Stewart took up portions of the gigantic business enterprise, only to fail, and so aid in the destruction of the treasure hoard. ... Money was squandered fast that more had to be borrowed to conduct the immense business now going to wreck. ... In 1898 the son of Mr. Hilton confessed in court that he owed his father some $4,250,000—one of the last remnants of the vast Stewart estate.

—*New York Times*
August 25, 1899

Stewart's original department store, the Marble Palace, at 280 Broadway, was purchased in 1917 by the *New York Sun,* which remained there until 1966. It is today primarily referred to as "The Sun Building." The building was declared a national landmark in 1965.

John Wanamaker, the Philadelphia-based retail executive, bought Stewart's Cast Iron Palace in 1896, and he turned it into one of the leading department stores in New York City. Wanamaker's closed down its operations at that location in 1954, and two years later, Stewart's Cast Iron Palace burned down during a two-day fire.

Nothing but crumbs of A. T. Stewart's vast empire remains. The retail business is gone from the American landscape. Hardly a soul remembers its existence. His once palatial home, the Marble Mansion, was torn down. His vast art collection was sold off. The building that housed what is considered one of the country's first retail department stores, the Marble Palace, still remains, but not a trace of its retail operations can be found. The great Stewart fortune—gone too.

The only thing that does endure is Garden City and the Church of the Incarnation, where the remains of Cornelia Stewart are buried. The bones of A. T. Stewart, America's "Merchant Prince," also reportedly buried in the Stewart family vault there, have never been positively identified. The identity of the Stewart grave robbers has also never been uncovered. Rumor and speculation still permeates this enduring New York mystery.

No one knows for certain whose bones are buried in the cathedral vault. Fittingly, one persistent rumor, circulated among inhabitants of Garden City, is that the burlap bag that held Stewart's bones was purchased at the A. T. Stewart department store.

ACKNOWLEDGMENTS

I wish to thank my agent, Tris Coburn; my editor at Lyons Press, Keith Wallman; Will Staples for his faith in this and all projects associated with it; my wife, Julia Lee; and my boys, Nate and Andrew.

CHAPTER SOURCES

CHAPTER 1: COUNTER CULTURE

Alden, Henry Mills, Thomas Bucklin Wells, and Lee Foster Hartman. *Harper's Monthly,* Volume 104. New York: Harper & Brothers, 1902.

Ashpis, Hannah Miriam. "Alexander Turney Stewart." n.p., 1939.

Barnum, P. T. *Successful Men and How They Become So.* The Minerva Group Inc., Athena Books, 2004.

Barth, Gunther. *City People: The Rise of Modern City Culture in Nineteenth-century America.* New York: Oxford University Press, 1982.

Bennett, James G., *The New York Herald,* 1846.

Brockett, Linus Pierpont. *Men of Our Day.* Philadelphia: Zeigler, McCurdy & Co., 1868.

Browne, Junius Henri. *The Great Metropolis: A Mirror of New York.* San Francisco: H. H. Bancroft & Co., 1869.

Burrows, Edwin G., and Mike Wallace. *Gotham: A History of New York City to 1898.* New York: Oxford University Press, 1999.

Cantor, Jay E. "A Monument of Trade: A. T. Stewart and the Rise of the Millionaire's Mansion in New York." Winterthur Portfolio, Vol. 10, 1975, University of Chicago Press.

"Career of the Merchant Prince—He Dies at His Residence in Fifth Avenue Surrounded by His Friends." *New York Times,* April 11, 1876.

Chambers's Journal of Popular Literature. Edinburgh and London: W. & R. Chambers, 1876.

Chambers's Journal of Popular Literature, Science, and Arts, Vol. 57. Edinburgh and London: W. & R. Chambers, 1880.

Condra, Jill. *The Greenwood Encyclopedia of Clothing through World History: 1801 to the Present.* Westport, CT: Greenwood Publishing Group, 2008.

Domosh, Mona. *Invented Cities: The Creation of Landscape in Nineteenth-Century New York and Boston.* New Haven, CT: Yale University Press, 1998.

Elias, Stephen N. *Alexander T. Stewart: The Forgotten Merchant Prince.* Westport, CT: Praeger, 1992.

Fanebust, Wayne. *The Missing Corpse: Grave Robbing a Gilded Age Tycoon.* Westport, CT: Greenwood Publishing Group, 2005.

Fischler, Marcelle S. "An Immigrant's Vision Created Garden City." *New York Times,* November 15, 1998.

"Forbes Ranks Richest Americans Ever." *USA Today.* September 21, 1998.

Gray, Christopher. "Streetscapes/The A. T. Stewart Department Store: A City Plan to Revitalize the 1846 'Marble Palace.'" *New York Times,* March 20, 1994.

Hallberger's Illustrated Magazine, Vol. 1. Stuttgart: E. Hallberger, 1876.

James, Henry. "A Small Boy," *A Small Boy and Others* (1913). London: Gibson Square Books Ltd., 2001.

Kessner, Thomas. *Capital City: New York City and the Men Behind America's Rise to Economic Dominance, 1860–1900.* New York: Simon and Schuster, 2004.

Kramer, Rita. "Cathedrals of Commerce." *City Journal,* Spring 1996.

"Making of America Project." *Harper's Magazine,* Vol. 57, 1878.

Miller, Frederic P., Agnes F. Vandome, and John McBrewster, eds. *Alexander Turney Stewart.* Beau Bassin, Mauritus: VDM Publishing House Ltd., 2010.

Morris, Charles. *Men of the Century.* Philadelphia: L. R. Hamersly & Co., 1896. *New York Herald,* 1846.

Rather, John. "A Village Planned by a Merchant Prince." *New York Times,* October 18, 1998.

Resseguie, Harry E. "The Decline and Fall of the Commercial Empire of A. T. Stewart." *The Business History Review,* Vol. 36, 1962.

Rich Men of the World, and How They Gained Their Wealth. Jesse Haney & Co., American News Co., 1867.

Stately Homes in America: From Colonial Times to the Present Day. New York: D. Appleton and Company, 1903.

Stoddard, William Osborn. *Men of Business.* New York: Charles Scribner's Sons, 1893.

Stories of Remarkable Persons. Edinburgh and London: W. & R. Chambers, 1878.

Supplement to the *Hartford Courant,* September 18, 1858.

Thayer, William Makepeace. *Turning Points in Successful Careers.* New York: Thomas Y. Crowell & Company, 1895.

Walling, George Washington. *Recollections of a New York Chief of Police.* New York: Caxton Book Concern, Ltd., 1887.

Whitten, David O., and Bessie Emrick Whitten. *The Birth of Big Business in the United States, 1860–1914.* Westport, CT: Greenwood Publishing Group, 2006.

CHAPTER 2: THE CAST IRON PALACE

"The Art Gallery. A List of Pictures in Mr. Stewart's Collection." *New York Times,* April 12, 1876.

Berger, Molly W. "The Rich Man's City: Hotels and Mansions of Gilded Age New York." *Journal of Decorative and Propaganda Arts,* Vol. 25, 2005.

Burrows and Wallace. *Gotham: A History of New York City to 1898.*

Craven, Wayne. *Gilded Mansions: Grand Architecture and High Society.* New York: W. W. Norton & Company, 2009.

Devens, Richard Miller. *Cyclopædia of Commercial and Business Anecdotes.* New York: D. Appleton and Company, 1868.

Domosh. *Invented Cities.*

———. "Shaping the Commercial City: Retail Districts in Nineteenth-century New York and Boston." *Annals of the Association of American Geographers,* Vol. 80, No. 2, 1990.

Eggener, Keith. *American Architectural History.* New York: Routledge, 2004.

Elias. *Alexander T. Stewart.*

Harper's Magazine, Vol. 34. Harper's Magazine Co., 1867.

Heidler, David Stephen, Jeanne T. Heidler, and David J. Coles. *Encyclopedia of the American Civil War: A Political, Social, and Military History.* New York: W. W. Norton & Company, 2002.

Homberger, Eric. *Mrs. Astor's New York: Money and Social Power in a Gilded Age.* New Haven, CT: Yale University Press, 2004.

Hubbard, Elbert. *A. T. Stewart.* Whitefish, MT: Kessinger Publishing, 2005.

King, Ross. *The Judgment of Paris: The Revolutionary Decade That Gave the World Impressionism.* London: Bloomsbury Publishing, 2006.

Kramer, Ellen W. "Contemporary Descriptions of New York City and Its Public Architecture ca. 1850." *Journal of the Society of Architectural Historians,* Vol. 27, No. 4, 1968.

Miller, Michael. *The Bon Marché: Bourgeois Culture and the Department Store, 1869–1920.* Princeton, NJ: Princeton University Press, 1994.

Morris Jr., Seymour. *American History Revised: 200 Startling Facts That Never Made It into the Textbooks.* New York: Random House Digital Inc., 2010.

Nation, Vol. 13. The Nation Company, 1871.

Nevius, Michelle, and James Nevius. *Inside the Apple: A Streetwise History of New York City.* New York: Simon and Schuster, 2009.

Putnam's Monthly, Issues 1–6. New York: G. P. Putnam & Co., 1853.

Resseguie, Harry E. "Alexander Turney Stewart and the Development of the Department Store, 1823–1876." *The Business History Review,* Vol. 39, 1965.

———. "A. T. Stewart's Marble Palace—The Cradle of the Department Store." *New York Historical Society Quarterly* Vol. 48, Issue 2, 1964.

———. "The Decline and Fall of the Commercial Empire of A. T. Stewart."

Rich Men of the World, and How They Gained Their Wealth. Jesse Haney & Co., American News Co., 1867.

Richmond, John Francis. *New York and Its Institutions, 1609–1871: A Library of Information, Pertaining to the Great Metropolis, Past and Present.* New York: E. B. Treat, 1871.

Smith, Mary Ann. "John Snook and the Design for A. T. Stewart's Store." *New York Historical Society Quarterly* Vol. 58, Issue 1, 1974.

Stately Homes in America: From Colonial Times to the Present Day. New York: D. Appleton and Company, 1903.

Weisman, Winston. "Commercial Palaces of New York: 1845–1875." *Art Bulletin* Vol. 36, No. 4, 1954.

CHAPTER 3: CAVEAT EMPTOR

"Alexander T. Stewart." (Editorial). *New York Times,* April 11, 1876.

"Alexander T. Stewart. Arrangements for the Funeral." *New York Times,* April 13, 1876.

American Magazine, Vol. 1. Crowell-Collier Pub. Co., 1876.

"A. T. Stewart's Funeral. Services at Church and House." *New York Times,* April 12, 1876.

"A. T. Stewart's Will. Full Text of the Instrument." *New York Times,* April 15, 1876.

Beckert, Sven. *The Monied Metropolis: New York City and the Consolidation of the American Bourgeoisie, 1850–1896.* Cambridge, UK: Cambridge University Press, 2001.

Burrows and Wallace. *Gotham: A History of New York City to 1898.*

"The Business to Be Continued. An Important Statement by Judge Hilton." *New York Times,* April 15, 1876.

Calhoun, Charles W. *The Gilded Age: Perspectives on the Origins of Modern America.* Lanham, MD: Rowman & Littlefield Publishers Inc., 2006.

"Career of the Merchant Prince—He Dies at His Residence in Fifth Avenue Surrounded by His Friends." *New York Times,* April 11, 1876.

Cashman, Sean Dennis. *America in the Gilded Age.* New York: New York University Press, 1993.

"The Dead Millionaire. Mr. Stewart's Life and Death." *New York Times,* April 12, 1876.

"Death of A. T. Stewart. Career of the Merchant Prince." *New York Times,* April 11, 1876.

Elias. *Alexander T. Stewart.*

Fanebust. *The Missing Corpse.*

Herald of Health, Vols. 27–29. M. L. Holbrook, 1876.

"Incidents of Mr. Stewart's Life. His Early Mercantile Career." *New York Times,* April 12, 1876.

King, Greg. *A Season of Splendor: The Court of Mrs. Astor in Gilded Age New York.* Hoboken, NJ: John Wiley & Sons, 2008.

"The Merchants' Tribute. Meeting of Dry Goods Men." *New York Times,* April 13, 1876.

"Monopoly and Competition." *New York Times*, April 12, 1876.

"Mr. Stewart's Property. The Assessed Valuation of His Personal Property and City Real Estate." *New York Times*, April 11, 1876.

"Preparations for the Funeral. The Arrangements Not Complete." *New York Times*, April 12, 1876.

"Saratoga's Public Benefactor. Mr. Stewart's Death Profoundly Lamented at the Springs. *New York Times*, April 11, 1876.

Schechter, Harold. *The Whole Death Catalog: A Lively Guide to the Bitter End.* New York: Random House Digital Inc., 2009.

"The Stewart Estate." *New York Times*, April 17, 1876.

Trachtenberg, Alan. *The Incorporation of America: Culture and Society in the Gilded Age.* New York: Hill and Wang, 1982.

Warehousemen and Drapers Trade Journal, Vol. V. n.p. 1876.

Weil, Francois. *A History of New York.* New York: Columbia University Press, 2004.

Weymouth, Lally, and Milton Glaser. *America in 1876: The Way We Were.* New York: Random House, 1976.

"The Will Discussed at the Clubs and Hotels." *New York Times*, April 12, 1876.

CHAPTER 4: A PROBLEM WITH HOTELS

Britten, Evelyn Barrett. *Chronicles of Saratoga* (radio program), 1959.

Burrows and Wallace. *Gotham: A History of New York City to 1898.*

"Cincinnati Hebrews Indignant: Special Dispatch to the New York Times." *New York Times*, December 19, 1878.

"Common Sense about the Women's Hotel." *New York Times*, June 11, 1878.

"Description of the Hotel. The Most Complete and Elegant Structure of the Kind in The World …" *New York Times*, April 3, 1878.

"The Feeling in Chicago. Judge Hilton's Conduct Pronounced Unprecedented …" *New York Times*, June 22, 1877.

"The Hebrew Controversy. Judge Hilton's Determination Unalterable …" *New York Times*, July 19, 1877.

"The Hebrews Excited. Donations by Mrs. Stewart to Jewish Charitable Institutions." *New York Times,* December 17, 1878.

Higham, John. "Anti-Semitism in the Gilded Age: A Reinterpretation." *Mississippi Valley Historical Review,* Vol. 43, No. 4, 1957.

"Hilton vs. Seligman." *New York Times,* June 20, 1877.

"Hotel Discrimination. The Right to Refuse Applicants." *New York Times,* June 20, 1877.

"An Interview with Mr. Hilton. So Urgent Invitations Sent to Hebrews ..." *New York Times,* July 19, 1877.

"Jewish Clothiers of One Mind. They Will Trade No More with A. T. Stewart & Co ..." *New York Times,* June 22, 1877.

"Jewish Merchants Combining. They Are Determined to Deal No More with A. T. Stewart & Co ..." *New York Times,* June 20, 1878.

"The Jewish Question ..." *New York Times,* June 23, 1877.

"Judge Hilton and the Jews. An Offensive Charge in a Jewish Paper ..." *New York Times,* January 20, 1878.

"Judge Hilton and the Ladies. A Public Meeting of Women to be Held ..." *New York Times,* June 2, 1878.

"Judge Hilton's Course Sustained. Mr. Seligman Has Himself to Thank for the Exclusion ..." *New York Times,* June 21, 1877.

"Judge Hilton's Position. The Step He Has Taken Was Forced upon Him." *New York Times,* June 20, 1877.

Marcus, Jacob Rader. *United States Jewry, 1776–1985.* Detroit: Wayne State University Press, 1989.

"Mr. Jesse Seligman's Opinion. He Thinks the Warm Weather Has Affected Hilton's Brain ..." *New York Times,* June 20, 1877.

"Mr. Seligman's Friends. Letters of Sympathy to the Bankers Action ..." *New York Times,* June 21, 1877.

"Mrs. Stewart's Charities. The Donations to the Hebrew Societies." *New York Times,* December 18, 1878.

"Mrs. Stewart's Gifts. Popular Jewish Sentiment Compels Their Rejection." *New York Times,* December 19, 1878.

"Not Only for the Women. A White Elephant to Be Made Profitable ..." *New York Times,* May 26, 1878.

"Opinions of Jews in This City ..." *New York Times,* June 20, 1877.

"Removal of the Stewart Wholesale Store ..." *New York Times,* November 13, 1878.

"A Reply to Judge Hilton ..." *New York Times,* June 20, 1877.

"Resenting Their Insult. They Are Determined to Deal No More with A. T. Stewart ..." *New York Times,* June 22, 1877.

Resseguie. "The Decline and Fall of the Commercial Empire of A. T. Stewart."

Scobey, David. "Anatomy of the Promenade: The Politics of Bourgeois Sociability in Nineteenth-century New York." *Social History,* Vol. 17, No. 2, 1992.

"Scolding Judge Hilton. The Women's Great Mass Meeting ..." *New York Times,* June 5, 1878.

"Selecting Their Guests. The Grand Union Restrictions ..." *New York Times,* June 20, 1877.

"A Sensation at Saratoga ... No Jews to be Admitted ..." *New York Times,* June 19, 1877.

"The Stewart House in Chicago ..." *New York Times,* December 20, 1877.

Stradling, David. *Making Mountains: New York City and the Catskills.* Seattle: University of Washington Press, 2007.

"They Decline the Gift. Judge Hilton and the Jews." *New York Times,* December 23, 1878.

"The Unjust Judge." *New York Times,* June 6, 1878.

"The Walls of Division. Why They Should Not Be Set Up ..." *New York Times,* June 24, 1877.

"A Woman's Hotel No More. The Park Avenue Opened ..." *New York Times,* June 9, 1878.

"The Women's Hotel Open. A Great Enterprise Begun ..." *New York Times,* April 3, 1878.

"Women's Suffrage Association. The Ladies Have More to Say about the Woman's Home ..." *New York Times,* June 7, 1878.

"Working Women's Hotel. Grand Legacy from Mr. Stewart ..." *New York Times,* November 12, 1877.

"The Working Women's Hotel. To Be Opened on Tuesday Evening ..." *New York Times,* March 24, 1878.

CHAPTER 5: THE GHOULS STRIKE

Asbury, Herbert. *The Gangs of New York: An Informal History of the Underworld.* New York: Basic Books, 2001 (originally published in 1927).

"A. T. Stewart. The Millionaires' Body Not Recovered." *Brooklyn Eagle,* November 9, 1878.

Burrows and Wallace. *Gotham: A History of New York City to 1898.*

"The Cemetery Robbery. Mr. Stewart's Body Not Found." *New York Times,* November 9, 1878.

"The Cemetery Robbery ... Mrs. Stewart Offers a Reward of $25,000 ..." *New York Times,* November 9, 1878.

Elias. *Alexander T. Stewart.*

Fanebust. *The Missing Corpse.*

Ferrara, Eric. *Gangsters, Murderers & Weirdoes of the Lower East Side.* Lulu.com, 2008.

"The Ghouls. Additional Details of the Stewart Grave Robbery." *Brooklyn Eagle,* November 8, 1878.

"Ghouls in New York City. A. T. Stewart's Body Stolen." *New York Times,* November 8, 1878.

"The Grave Desecrators. Tracing the Robbers of Mr. Stewart's Grave." *New York Times,* November 10, 1878.

"How Grave Robbers Work. Special Dispatch to the New York Times." *New York Times,* November 13, 1878.

Kannard, Brian. *Skullduggery: 45 True Tales of Disturbing the Dead.* Nashville, TN: Grave Distractions Publications, 2009.

"A New York Sensation. A. T. Stewart's Remains Carried Off." *Montreal Gazette,* November 8, 1878.

Riis, Jacob August. *The Making of an American.* New York: Macmillan, 1904.

"The Robbers of the Tomb. A Rumor That Mr. Stewart's Body Found ..." *New York Times,* November 11, 1878.

"Searching. Are the Brooklyn Police on the Track of A. T. Stewart's Remains." *Brooklyn Eagle,* November 9, 1878.

Shultz, Suzanne M. *Body Snatching: The Robbing of Graves for the Education of Physicians in Early Nineteenth Century America.* Jefferson, NC: McFarland & Company, 2005.

"Startling. The Late A. T. Stewart's Remains Stolen." *Brooklyn Eagle,* November 8, 1878.

"The Stealing of A. T. Stewart's Body." *Brooklyn Eagle,* November 8, 1878.

"Stealing the Body of a Dead Millionaire." *Boston Globe,* November 8, 1878.

"Stewart's Stolen Body. The Prospect of Its Recovery." *New York Times,* November 14, 1878.

Walling. *Recollections of a New York Chief of Police.*

CHAPTER 6: THE BEST DETECTIVE TALENT

Anbinder, Tyler. *Five Points.* New York: Simon and Schuster, 2001.

Asbury. *The Gangs of New York.*

Buk-Swienty, Tom. *The Other Half: The Life of Jacob Riis and the World of Immigrant America.* New York: W. W. Norton & Co., 2008.

Burrows and Wallace. *Gotham: A History of New York City to 1898.*

Cook, John Douglas, et al. *The Saturday Review of Politics, Literature, Science, and Art,* Vol. 46. John W. Parker and Son, 1878.

Craughwell, Thomas J. *Stealing Lincoln's Body.* Cambridge, MA: Harvard University Press, 2009.

Elias. *Alexander T. Stewart.*

Fanebust. *The Missing Corpse.*

Ferrara. *Gangsters, Murderers & Weirdoes of the Lower East Side.*

"The Grave Desecrators. Tracing the Robbers of Mr. Stewart's Grave ..." *New York Times,* November 10, 1878.

"Is Stewart's Body Found? Indications Pointing That Way ..." *New York Times,* November 13, 1878.

Lardner, James, and Thomas Reppetto. *NYPD: A City and Its Police.* New York: Macmillan, 2001.

"Mr. Walling's Trip to New Jersey ..." *New York Times,* November 15, 1878.

Nash, Jay Robert. *Bloodletters and Badmen.* New York: M. Evans, 1973.

Nation, Vol. 29, The Nation Co., 1879.

Nation, The Nation Co., July–December, 1879.

"Searching New Jersey." *New York Times,* November 11, 1878.

"Seeking for the Ghouls. Mr. Stewart's Body Likely to be Recovered ..." *New York Times,* November 12, 1878.

Smith, Alfred Emanuel. *New Outlook,* Vol. 68. Outlook Publishing Co., 1901.

Walling. *Recollections of a New York Chief of Police.*

CHAPTER 7: THE SEARCH CONTINUES

Asbury. *The Gangs of New York.*

"The A. T. Stewart Outrage. No Further Disclosures." *New York Times,* November 18, 1878.

"A. T. Stewart's Body Found. The Guilty Persons All Known." *New York Times,* November 15, 1878.

Burrows and Wallace. *Gotham: A History of New York City to 1898.*

"The Cemetery Robbery. Two of the Ghouls Arrested." *New York Times,* November 16, 1878.

Christian, George. (Diary entry). *Evening Star,* December 15, 1873.

"Closing on the Ghouls. Successful Efforts to Catch Them." *New York Times,* November 17, 1878.

"Dr. Douglass Not Dr. Christian ..." *New York Times,* November 24, 1878.

Fanebust. *The Missing Corpse.*

"The Grave Robber Christian. He Turns Up in the Stewart Case." *New York Times,* November 21, 1878.

"The Grave Yard Robbers. Still Searching for the Thieves." *New York Times,* November 23, 1878.

"How Grave Robbers Work. Special Dispatch to the New York Times." *New York Times,* November 13, 1878.

"No Further Arrests Made ..." *New York Times,* November 24, 1878.

"A Possible Clue to the Stewart Grave Robbery." *Brooklyn Eagle,* November 18, 1878.

"Stewart. Contradictory Reports about the Missing Body." *Brooklyn Eagle,* November 15, 1878.

"The Stewart Resurrection Case." *Brooklyn Eagle,* November 15, 1878.

Walling. *Recollections of a New York Chief of Police.*

"Working Up a Fine Clue ..." *New York Times,* November 18, 1878.

CHAPTER 8: VREELAND AND BURKE

"Another Clue Pointing to New Jersey." *New York Times,* November 19, 1878.

Asbury. *The Gangs of New York.*

"A. T. Stewart's Body Found. The Guilty Persons All Known." *New York Times,* November 15, 1878.

"The Body Said to Be Under Guard." *New York Times,* November 19, 1878.

Burrows and Wallace. *Gotham: A History of New York City to 1898.*

"The Case of Vreeland and Burke ..." *New York Times,* November 21, 1878.

"The Cemetery Robbery. Two of the Ghouls Arrested." *New York Times,* November 16, 1878.

"Closing on the Ghouls. Successful Efforts to Catch Them." *New York Times,* November 17, 1878.

Fanebust. *The Missing Corpse.*

"The Grave Yard Robbers. Still Searching for the Thieves." *New York Times,* November 23, 1878.

"Henry Vreeland Discharged." *New York Times,* December 4, 1878.

Lardner and Reppetto. *NYPD.*

"Light at Last. The Police Clearing Up the Stewart Mystery." *Brooklyn Eagle,* November 18, 1878.

"Not Found. The Stewart Mystery Still Unsolved." *Brooklyn Eagle,* November 16, 1878.

"Search for the Robbers. No Further Arrests Made." *New York Times,* November 22, 1878.

"The Stewart Grave Robbery." *New York Times,* November 28, 1878.

"The Stewart Mystery." *New York Times,* November 25, 1878.

"The Stewart Mystery. The Police Still Looking ..." *New York Times,* November 25, 1878.

"Stewart's Grave Robbers. All But One of Them Arrested." *New York Times*, November 20, 1878.

"Stewart's Stolen Body. Capt. Byrnes Corroborates the Times Statement ..." *New York Times*, November 19, 1878.

"Still in the Dark." *Brooklyn Eagle*, November 19, 1878.

"Two Prisoners in Court. The Extraordinary Story Told by Capt. Byrnes ..." *New York Times*, November 19, 1878.

"The Village of Chatham Excited. Looking for Mr. Stewart's Remains ..." *New York Times*, November 20, 1878.

"Vreeland and Burke Committed. Capt. Byrnes Formal Complaint ..." *New York Times*, November 20, 1878.

Walling. *Recollections of a New York Chief of Police.*

CHAPTER 9: KEEPING UP WITH THE JONESES

"A. T. Stewart. The Reported Recovery of His Body." *Brooklyn Eagle*, January 16, 1879.

"A. T. Stewart's Body." *Brooklyn Eagle*, August 14, 1879.

"The Body of A. T. Stewart. New Stories Concerning the Grave Yard Robbery ..." *New York Times*, August 14, 1879.

Burrows and Wallace. *Gotham: A History of New York City to 1898.*

Caldwell, Mark. *New York Night: The Mystique and Its History.* New York: Simon and Schuster, 2005.

"Eighteen Acres under One Roof." *New York Times*, December 27, 1878.

Fanebust. *The Missing Corpse.*

Gilfoyle, Timothy J. *City of Eros: New York City, Prostitution, and the Commercialization of Sex, 1790–1920.* New York: W. W. Norton & Co., 1994.

"The Hebrews Excited. Donations by Mrs. Stewart to Jewish Charitable Institutions." *New York Times*, December 17, 1878.

"Mr. Alexander T. Stewart. An Undertaker Tells the Police a Story." *New York Times*, December 3, 1878.

"Mrs. Stewart Not Deceived. A Statement Concerning Her Husband's Body by Her Family Physician." *Brooklyn Eagle*, August 19, 1879.

"Mrs. Stewart Not Misinformed." (Letter to the editor). *Brooklyn Eagle,* August 19, 1879.

"The Recovery of Stewart's Body." *Brooklyn Eagle,* January 16, 1879.

"The Search for Stewart's Body: Special Dispatch to the New York Times." *New York Times,* December 12, 1878.

"The Stewart Grave Robbery. A Number of Detectives Withdrawn from the Case." *New York Times, November* 26, 1878.

"Still Looking for Stewart's Body." *New York Times,* December 11, 1878.

"Tracing a Dead Body." *New York Times,* December 13, 1878.

"An Unpunished Crime. Anniversary of the Robbery of Stewart's Tomb." *Brooklyn Eagle,* November 7, 1879.

Walling. *Recollections of a New York Chief of Police.*

"What Gen. Jones Says. His Mysterious Correspondence with Romaine ..." *New York Times,* August 14, 1879.

CHAPTER 10: THE MYSTERIOUS PACKAGE

Asbury. *The Gangs of New York.*

Burrows and Wallace. *Gotham: A History of New York City to 1898.*

Fanebust. *The Missing Corpse.*

"A Great Nation in Grief. President Garfield Shot by Assassin ..." *New York Times,* July 3, 1881.

"The Man Who Thought He Knew Who Stole Stewart's Body ..." *New York Times,* August 15, 1879.

"The Newly Aroused Interest in Cypress Hills Cemetery ..." *New York Times,* August 22, 1881.

"Sala's Remarkable Story. An Italian Stone-Cutter's Queer Experiences ..." *New York Times,* August 14, 1879.

"Stewart's Body Sought. An Important Excavation Begun at Cypress Hills ..." *New York Times,* August 21, 1881.

"The Tragedy in the Depot. Guiteau Fires His Cruel Shots from behind the President ..."*New York Times,* July 3, 1881.

Twain, Mark. *The Stolen White Elephant.* Los Angeles: Pub Group West, 1987 (originally published 1882).

CHAPTER 11: THE CYPRESS HILLS CEMETERY INCIDENT

"A. T. Stewart's Remains. The Newly Aroused Interest in Cypress Hills Cemetery ..." *New York Times*, August 22, 1881.

Brooklyn Daily Eagle, August 23, 1881.

Burrows and Wallace. *Gotham: A History of New York City to 1898*.

"The Cypress Hills Search Abandoned." *New York Times*, August 24, 1881.

"Detective Fuller ..." *Brooklyn Eagle*, August 23, 1881.

"Digging. New Yorkers Prospecting for a Soft Spot at Cypress Hills." *Brooklyn Eagle*, August 22, 1881.

Fanebust. *The Missing Corpse*.

"Judge Hilton Co-Operates ..." *New York Times*, August 21, 1881.

"A Permit for an Excavation. The Controller of the Cypress Hills Cemetery Astonished." *New York Times*, August 21, 1881.

"A Ramble in a Cemetery. Introducing a Somewhat Novel Phase of Detective Work." *New York Times*, August 21, 1881.

"The Search Begun. Unexpected Parties Appear on the Scene ..." *New York Times*, August 21, 1881.

"Some Curious Facts for Superstitious People." *New York Times*, August 22, 1881.

"The Story of the Robbery. How the Body Snatchers Secured Mr. Stewart's Remains ..." *New York Times*, August 22, 1881.

CHAPTER 12: GOING OUT OF BUSINESS

"Altering the Stewart Stores ..." *New York Times*, May 5, 1882.

"A. T. Stewart & Co.'s Successor." *New York Times*, October 26, 1882.

"Business in Stewart's Store ..." *New York Times*, November 25, 1882.

"Buyers of the Stewart Business ..." *New York Times*, May 11, 1882.

"The Chicago Trade Branch." *New York Times*, April 16, 1882.

"Considering Garden City's Future ..." *New York Times*, April 17, 1882.

Elias. *Alexander T. Stewart*.

"Garden City." (Editorial). *New York Times*, April 18, 1882.

Kessner. *Capital City.*

Kramer, Rita. "Cathedrals of Commerce." *City Journal,* Spring 1996.

"The Old Stewart Building." *New York Times,* September 20, 1882.

Resseguie. "Alexander Turney Stewart and the Development of the Department Store, 1823–1876."

———. "A. T. Stewart's Marble Palace—The Cradle of the Department Store."

———. "The Decline and Fall of the Commercial Empire of A. T. Stewart."

"Retiring from Business. The Firm of A. T. Stewart & Co. Winding Up Affairs." *New York Times,* April 16, 1882.

"The Stewart Chicago Branch ..." *New York Times,* April 21, 1882.

"The Stock of A. T. Stewart & Co." *New York Times,* April 29, 1882.

CHAPTER 13: BAG OF BONES

Asbury. *The Gangs of New York.*

Burrows and Wallace. *Gotham: A History of New York City to 1898.*

Fanebust. *The Missing Corpse.*

Walling. *Recollections of a New York Chief of Police.*

CHAPTER 14: MEMORIAL TO THE MERCHANT PRINCE

"At Last." (Editorial). *New York Times,* March 20, 1885.

"A Big Cathedral Organ. The Immense Instrument in the Church at Garden City ..." *New York Times,* June 14, 1885.

Burrows and Wallace. *Gotham: A History of New York City to 1898.*

Cantor, Jay E. "A Monument of Trade: A. T. Stewart and the Rise of the Millionaire's Mansion in New York."

"The Cathedral Accepted." *New York Times,* August 17, 1885.

"The Cathedral at Garden City." *Brooklyn Eagle,* March 20, 1885.

"The Cathedral School ..." *Brooklyn Eagle,* June 19, 1879.

Churchman, Vol. 36. Churchman Co., 1877.

"Consecration. Formal Dedication of the Garden City Cathedral." *Brooklyn Eagle,* June 2, 1885.

"Consecration Services. What Judge Hilton Is Reported to Have Said about Them." *Brooklyn Eagle,* May 29, 1885.

Deems, Charles Force, et al. *Frank Leslie's Sunday Magazine.* New York: Frank Leslie, 1885.

"First Service. Opening of the Cathedral of the Incarnation." *Brooklyn Eagle,* April 9, 1885.

"The Garden City Schools. Beginning a Great Work ..." *New York Times,* May 26, 1879.

"Garden City's Cathedral. A Great Crowd at the Opening Services ..." *New York Times,* April 10, 1885.

"The Gift of Mrs. Stewart. Formal Presentation of the Garden City Cathedral ..." *New York Times,* June 3, 1885.

"The Great Cathedral Schools ..." *Brooklyn Eagle,* May 29, 1883.

"Improving Garden City. What Wealth and Taste Have Accomplished." *New York Times,* June 4, 1882.

"Laying a Corner Stone. The Cathedral School for Boys at Garden City." *New York Times,* June 19, 1879.

"Mrs. Stewart's Gift ..." *New York Times,* May 22, 1885.

"Mrs. Stewart's Gift. The Deed of the Garden City Property Placed on Record." *Brooklyn Eagle,* May 21, 1885.

Nevius and Nevius. *Inside the Apple.*

"Services of Consecration ..." *New York Times,* May 27, 1885.

"The Stewart Memorial. The New Cathedral at Garden City..." *New York Times,* April 9, 1885.

"A Suit against Mrs. Stewart ..." *New York Times,* December 29, 1885.

"A University at Garden City ..." *New York Times,* August 1, 1880.

CHAPTER 15: EXPIRATION DATE

Broderick, Mosette. *Triumvirate: McKim, Mead & White: Art, Architecture, Scandal, and Class in America's Gilded Age,* New York: Alfred A. Knopf, 2010.

Craven. *Gilded Mansions.*

Domosh. *Invented Cities.*

————. "Shaping the Commercial City: Retail Districts in Nineteenth-century New York and Boston."

Eggener. *American Architectural History.*

Elias. *Alexander T. Stewart.*

"Final Victory for Mr. Hilton ..." *New York Times,* November 4, 1893.

"Henry Hilton Dead ..." *New York Times,* August 25, 1899.

Megargee, Louis, *Seen & Heard,* Vol. 1, 1901.

————. *Seen & Heard by Megargee,* Vol. 3, 1903.

"Mrs. Stewart Dead ..." *New York Times,* October 26, 1886.

"Mrs. Stewart's Funeral ..." *New York Times,* October 29, 1886.

Resseguie. "Alexander Turney Stewart and the Development of the Department Store, 1823–1876."

————. "A. T. Stewart's Marble Palace—The Cradle of the Department Store."

————. "The Decline and Fall of the Commercial Empire of A. T. Stewart."

"The Stewart Collection ..." *New York Times,* December 17, 1886.

"Stewart Heirs in Court ..." *New York Times, February* 19, 1887.

"The Vanderbilt Palaces. An Interior View of the Great Houses on Fifth Avenue ..." *New York Times,* August 25, 1885.

BIBLIOGRAPHY

A

Alden, Henry Mills, Thomas Bucklin Wells, and Lee Foster Hartman. *Harper's Monthly,* Vol. 104. New York: Harper & Brothers, 1902.

"Alexander T. Stewart." (Editorial). *New York Times,* April 11, 1876.

"Alexander T. Stewart. Arrangements for the Funeral." *New York Times,* April 13, 1876.

"Altering the Stewart Stores ..." *New York Times,* May 5, 1882.

American Magazine, Vol. 1. Crowell-Collier Pub. Co., 1876.

Anbinder, Tyler. *Five Points.* New York: Simon and Schuster, 2001.

"Another Clue Pointing to New Jersey." *New York Times,* November 19, 1878.

"The Art Gallery. A List of Pictures in Mr. Stewart's Collection." *New York Times,* April 12, 1876.

Asbury, Herbert. *The Gangs of New York: An Informal History of the Underworld.* New York: Basic Books, 2001 (originally published in 1927).

Ashpis, Hannah Miriam. "Alexander Turney Stewart," n.p., 1939.

"At Last." (Editorial). *New York Times,* March 20, 1885.

"A. T. Stewart & Co.'s Successor." *New York Times,* October 26, 1882.

"A. T. Stewart. The Millionaires' Body Not Recovered." *Brooklyn Eagle,* November 9, 1878.

"The A. T. Stewart Outrage. No Further Disclosures." *New York Times,* November 18, 1878.

"A. T. Stewart. The Reported Recovery of His Body." *Brooklyn Eagle,* January 16, 1879.

"A. T. Stewart's Body." *Brooklyn Eagle,* August 14, 1879.

"A. T. Stewart's Body Found. The Guilty Persons All Known." *New York Times,* November 15, 1878.

"A. T. Stewart's Funeral. Services at Church and House." *New York Times,* April 12, 1876.

"A. T. Stewart's Remains. The Newly Aroused Interest in Cypress Hills Cemetery ..." *New York Times,* August 22, 1881.

"A. T. Stewart's Will. Full Text of the Instrument." *New York Times,* April 15, 1876.

B

Barnum, P. T. *Successful Men and How They Become So.* The Minerva Group Inc., Athena Books, 2004.

Barth, Gunther. *City People: The Rise of Modern City Culture in Nineteenth-century America.* New York: Oxford University Press, 1982.

Beckert, Sven. *The Monied Metropolis: New York City and the Consolidation of the American Bourgeoisie, 1850–1896.* Cambridge, UK: Cambridge University Press, 2001.

Bennett, James G. *The New York Herald,* 1846.

Berger, Molly W. "The Rich Man's City: Hotels and Mansions of Gilded Age New York." *Journal of Decorative and Propaganda Arts,* Vol. 25, 2005.

"A Big Cathedral Organ. The Immense Instrument in the Church at Garden City ..." *New York Times,* June 14, 1885.

"The Body of A. T. Stewart. New Stories Concerning the Grave Yard Robbery ..." *New York Times,* August 14, 1879.

"The Body Said to Be Under Guard." *New York Times,* November 19, 1878.

Britten, Evelyn Barrett. *Chronicles of Saratoga* (radio program), 1959.

Brockett, Linus Pierpont. *Men of Our Day.* Philadelphia: Zeigler, McCurdy & Co., 1868.

Broderick, Mosette. *Triumvirate: McKim, Mead & White: Art, Architecture, Scandal, and Class in America's Gilded Age.* New York: Alfred A. Knopf, 2010.

Brooklyn Daily Eagle, August 23, 1881.

Browne, Junius Henri. *The Great Metropolis: A Mirror of New York.* San Francisco: H. H. Bancroft & Co., 1869.

Burrows, Edwin G., and Mike Wallace. *Gotham: A History of New York City to 1898.* New York: Oxford University Press, 1999.

"Business in Stewart's Store ..." *New York Times,* November 25, 1882.

"The Business to Be Continued. An Important Statement by Judge Hilton." *New York Times,* April 15, 1876.

"Buyers of the Stewart Business ..." *New York Times,* May 11, 1882.

C

Caldwell, Mark. *New York Night: The Mystique and Its History.* New York: Simon and Schuster, 2005.

Calhoun, Charles W. *The Gilded Age: Perspectives on the Origins of Modern America.* Lanham, MD: Rowman & Littlefield Publishers Inc., 2006.

Cantor, Jay E. "A Monument of Trade: A. T. Stewart and the Rise of the Millionaire's Mansion in New York." Winterthur Portfolio, Vol. 10, 1975, University of Chicago Press.

"Career of the Merchant Prince—He Dies at His Residence in Fifth Avenue Surrounded by His Friends." *New York Times,* April 11, 1876.

Cashman, Sean Dennis. *America in the Gilded Age.* New York: New York University Press, 1993.

Chambers's Journal of Popular Literature. Edinburgh and London: W. & R. Chambers, 1876.

Chambers's Journal of Popular Literature, Science and Arts, Vol. 57. Edinburgh and London: W. & R. Chambers, 1880.

Christian, George. (Diary entry). *Evening Star,* December 15, 1873.

Churchman, Vol. 36. Churchman Co., 1877.

"Cincinnati Hebrews Indignant: Special Dispatch to the New York Times." *New York Times,* December 19, 1878.

"Closing on the Ghouls. Successful Efforts to Catch Them." *New York Times,* November 17, 1878.

"Common Sense about the Women's Hotel." *New York Times,* June 11, 1878.

Condra, Jill. *The Greenwood Encyclopedia of Clothing through World History: 1801 to the Present.* Westport, CT: Greenwood Publishing Group, 2008.

"Consecration. Formal Dedication of the Garden City Cathedral." *Brooklyn Eagle,* June 2, 1885.

"Consecration Services. What Judge Hilton Is Reported to Have Said about Them." *Brooklyn Eagle,* May 29, 1885.

"Considering Garden City's Future …" *New York Times,* April 17, 1882.

Cook, John Douglas, et al. *The Saturday Review of Politics, Literature, Science, and Art,* Vol. 46. John W. Parker and Son, 1878.

Craughwell, Thomas J. *Stealing Lincoln's Body.* Cambridge, MA: Harvard University Press, 2009.

Craven, Wayne. *Gilded Mansions: Grand Architecture and High Society.* New York: W. W. Norton & Company, 2009.

"The Cypress Hills Search Abandoned." *New York Times,* August 24, 1881.

D

"The Dead Millionaire. Mr. Stewart's Life and Death." *New York Times,* April 12, 1876.

"Death of A. T. Stewart. Career of the Merchant Prince." *New York Times,* April 11, 1876.

Deems, Charles Force, et al. *Frank Leslie's Sunday Magazine.* New York: Frank Leslie, 1885.

"Description of the Hotel. The Most Complete and Elegant Structure of the Kind in the World …" *New York Times,* April 3, 1878.

"Detective Fuller …" *Brooklyn Eagle,* August 23, 1881.

Devens, Richard Miller. *Cyclopædia of Commercial and Business Anecdotes.* New York: D. Appleton and Company, 1868.

"Digging. New Yorkers Prospecting for a Soft Spot at Cypress Hills." *Brooklyn Eagle,* August 22, 1881.

Domosh, Mona. *Invented Cities: The Creation of Landscape in Nineteenth-century New York and Boston.* New Haven, CT: Yale University Press, 1998.

———. "Shaping the Commercial City: Retail Districts in Nineteenth-century New York and Boston." *Annals of the Association of American Geographers* Vol. 80, No. 2, 1990.

"Dr. Douglass Not Dr. Christian ..." *New York Times,* November 24, 1878.

E

Eggener, Keith. *American Architectural History.* New York: Routledge, 2004.

"Eighteen Acres under One Roof." *New York Times,* December 27, 1878.

Elias, Stephen N. *Alexander T. Stewart: The Forgotten Merchant Prince.* Westport, CT: Praeger, 1992.

F

Fanebust, Wayne. *The Missing Corpse: Grave Robbing a Gilded Age Tycoon.* Westport, CT: Greenwood Publishing Group, 2005.

"The Feeling in Chicago. Judge Hilton's Conduct Pronounced Unprecedented ..." *New York Times,* June 22, 1877.

Ferrara, Eric. *Gangsters, Murderers & Weirdoes of the Lower East Side.* Lulu.com, 2008.

"Final Victory for Mr. Hilton ..." *New York Times,* November 4, 1893.

"First Service. Opening of the Cathedral of the Incarnation." *Brooklyn Eagle,* April 9, 1885.

Fischler, Marcelle S. "An Immigrant's Vision Created Garden City." *New York Times,* November 15, 1998.

"Forbes Ranks Richest Americans Ever." *USA Today,* September 21, 1998.

G

"Garden City." (Editorial). *New York Times,* April 18, 1882.

"Garden City's Cathedral. A Great Crowd at the Opening Services ..." *New York Times,* April 10, 1885.

"The Garden City Schools. Beginning a Great Work ..." *New York Times,* May 26, 1879.

"The Ghouls. Additional Details of the Stewart Grave Robbery." *Brooklyn Eagle,* November 8, 1878.

"Ghouls in New York City. A. T. Stewart's Body Stolen." *New York Times,* November 8, 1878.

"The Gift of Mrs. Stewart. Formal Presentation of the Garden City Cathedral ..." *New York Times,* June 3, 1885.

Gilfoyle, Timothy J. *City of Eros: New York City, Prostitution, and the Commercialization of Sex, 1790–1920.* New York: W. W. Norton & Co., 1994.

"The Grave Desecrators. Tracing the Robbers of Mr. Stewart's Grave." *New York Times,* November 10, 1878.

"The Grave Robber Christian. He Turns Up in the Stewart Case." *New York Times,* November 21, 1878.

"The Grave Yard Robbers. Still Searching for the Thieves." *New York Times,* November 23, 1878.

Gray, Christopher. "Streetscapes/The A. T. Stewart Department Store; A City Plan to Revitalize the 1846 'Marble Palace.'" *New York Times,* March 20, 1994.

"The Great Cathedral Schools ..." *Brooklyn Eagle,* May 29, 1883.

H

Hallberger's Illustrated Magazine, Vol. 1. Stuttgart: E. Hallberger, 1876.

Harper's Magazine, Vol. 34. Harper's Magazine Co., 1867.

"The Hebrew Controversy. Judge Hilton's Determination Unalterable ..." *New York Times,* July 19, 1877.

"The Hebrews Excited. Donations by Mrs. Stewart to Jewish Charitable Institutions." *New York Times,* December 17, 1878.

Heidler, David Stephen, Jeanne T. Heidler, and David J. Coles. *Encyclopedia of the American Civil War: A Political, Social, and Military History.* New York: W. W. Norton & Company, 2002.

"Henry Hilton Dead ..." *New York Times,* August 25, 1899.

"Henry Vreeland Discharged." *New York Times*, December 4, 1878.

Herald of Health, Vols. 27–29. M. L. Holbrook, 1876.

Higham, John. "Anti-Semitism in the Gilded Age: A Reinterpretation." *Mississippi Valley Historical Review*, Vol. 43, No. 4, 1957.

"Hilton vs. Seligman." *New York Times*, June 20, 1877.

Homberger, Eric. *Mrs. Astor's New York: Money and Social Power in a Gilded Age.* New Haven, CT: Yale University Press, 2004.

"Hotel Discrimination. The Right to Refuse Applicants." *New York Times*, June 20, 1877.

"How Grave Robbers Work. Special Dispatch to the New York Times." *New York Times*, November 13, 1878.

Hubbard, Elbert. *A. T. Stewart.* Whitefish, MT: Kessinger Publishing, 2005.

I

"Improving Garden City. What Wealth and Taste Have Accomplished." *New York Times*, June 4, 1882.

"Incidents of Mr. Stewart's Life. His Early Mercantile Career." *New York Times*, April 12, 1876.

"An Interview with Mr. Hilton. So Urgent Invitations Sent to Hebrews ..." *New York Times*, July 19, 1877.

"Is Stewart's Body Found? Indications Pointing That Way ..." *New York Times*, November 13, 1878.

J

James, Henry. "A Small Boy," *A Small Boy and Others* (1913). London: Gibson Square Books Ltd., 2001.

"Jewish Clothiers of One Mind. They Will Trade No More with A. T. Stewart & Co ..." *New York Times*, June 22, 1877.

"Jewish Merchants Combining. They Are Determined to Deal No More with A. T. Stewart & Co ..." *New York Times*, June 20, 1878.

"The Jewish Question ..." *New York Times*, June 23, 1877.

"Judge Hilton and the Jews. An Offensive Charge in a Jewish Paper ..."
New York Times, January 20, 1878.

"Judge Hilton and the Ladies. A Public Meeting of Women to Be Held
..." *New York Times*, June 2, 1878.

"Judge Hilton Co-Operates ..." *New York Times*, August 21, 1881.

"Judge Hilton's Course Sustained. Mr. Seligman Has Himself to Thank
for the Exclusion ..." *New York Times*, June 21, 1877.

"Judge Hilton's Position. The Step He Has Taken Was Forced upon
Him." *New York Times*, June 20, 1877.

K

Kannard, Brian. *Skullduggery: 45 True Tales of Disturbing the Dead.*
Nashville, TN: Grave Distractions Publications, 2009.

Kessner, Thomas. *Capital City: New York City and the Men behind
America's Rise to Economic Dominance, 1860–1900.* New York:
Simon and Schuster, 2004.

King, Greg. *A Season of Splendor: The Court of Mrs. Astor in Gilded
Age New York.* Hoboken, NJ: John Wiley & Sons, 2008.

King, Ross. *The Judgment of Paris: The Revolutionary Decade That
Gave the World Impressionism.* London: Bloomsbury Publishing,
2006.

Kramer, Ellen W. "Contemporary Descriptions of New York City and
Its Public Architecture ca. 1850." *Journal of the Society of Architectural Historians* Vol. 27, No. 4, 1968.

Kramer, Rita. "Cathedrals of Commerce." *City Journal*, Spring 1996.

L

Lardner, James, and Thomas Reppetto. *NYPD: A City and Its Police.*
New York: Macmillan, 2001.

"Laying a Corner Stone. The Cathedral School for Boys at Garden
City." *New York Times*, June 19, 1879.

"Light at Last. The Police Clearing Up the Stewart Mystery." *Brooklyn
Eagle*, November 18, 1878.

M

"Making of America Project." *Harper's Magazine,* Vol. 57, 1878.

"The Man Who Thought He Knew Who Stole Stewart's Body ..." *New York Times,* August 15, 1879.

Marcus, Jacob Rader. *United States Jewry, 1776–1985.* Detroit: Wayne State University Press, 1989.

Megargee, Louis. *Seen & Heard,* Vol. 1, 1901.

———. *Seen & Heard by Megargee,* Vol. 3, 1903.

"The Merchants' Tribute. Meeting of Dry Goods Men." *New York Times,* April 13, 1876.

Miller, Frederic P., Agnes F. Vandome, and John McBrewster, eds. *Alexander Turney Stewart.* Beau Bassin, Mauritius: VDM Publishing House Ltd., 2010

Miller, Michael. *The Bon Marché: Bourgeois Culture and the Department Store, 1869–1920.* Princeton, NJ: Princeton University Press, 1994.

"Monopoly and Competition." *New York Times,* April 12, 1876.

Morris, Charles. *Men of the Century.* Philadelphia: L. R. Hamersly & Co., 1896.

Morris Jr., Seymour. *American History Revised: 200 Startling Facts That Never Made It into the Textbooks.* New York: Random House Digital Inc., 2010.

"Mr. Alexander T. Stewart. An Undertaker Tells the Police a Story." *New York Times,* December 3, 1878.

"Mr. Jesse Seligman's Opinion. He Thinks the Warm Weather Has Affected Hilton's Brain ..." *New York Times,* June 20, 1877.

"Mr. Seligman's Friends. Letters of Sympathy to the Bankers Action ..." *New York Times,* June 21, 1877.

"Mr. Stewart's Property. The Assessed Valuation of His Personal Property and City Real Estate." *New York Times,* April 11, 1876.

"Mrs. Stewart Dead ..." *New York Times,* October 26, 1886.

"Mrs. Stewart Not Deceived. A Statement Concerning Her Husband's Body by Her Family Physician." *Brooklyn Eagle,* August 19, 1879.

"Mrs. Stewart Not Misinformed." (Letter to the editor). *Brooklyn Eagle*, August 19, 1879.

"Mrs. Stewart's Charities. The Donations to the Hebrew Societies." *New York Times*, December 18, 1878.

"Mrs. Stewart's Funeral ..." *New York Times*, October 29, 1886.

"Mrs. Stewart's Gift ..." *New York Times*, May 22, 1885.

"Mrs. Stewart's Gift. The Deed of the Garden City Property Placed on Record." *Brooklyn Eagle*, May 21, 1885.

"Mrs. Stewart's Gifts. Popular Jewish Sentiment Compels Their Rejection." *New York Times*, December 19, 1878.

"Mr. Walling's Trip to New Jersey ..." *New York Times*, November 15, 1878.

N

Nash, Jay Robert. *Bloodletters and Badmen*. New York: M. Evans, 1973.

Nation. The Nation Co., July–December, 1879.

Nation, Vol. 13. The Nation Co., 1871.

Nation, Vol. 29, The Nation Co., 1879.

Nevius, Michelle, and James Nevius. *Inside the Apple: A Streetwise History of New York City*. New York: Simon and Schuster, 2009.

"The Newly Aroused Interest in Cypress Hills Cemetery ..." *New York Times*, August 22, 1881.

New York Herald, 1846.

"A New York Sensation. A. T. Stewart's Remains Carried Off." *Montreal Gazette*, November 8, 1878.

New York Times, November 15, 1998.

"No Further Arrests Made ..." *New York Times*, November 24, 1878.

"Not Found. The Stewart Mystery Still Unsolved." *Brooklyn Eagle*, November 16, 1878.

"Not Only for the Women. A White Elephant to be Made Profitable ..." *New York Times*, May 26, 1878.

O

"The Old Stewart Building." *New York Times,* September 20, 1882.

"Opinions of Jews in This City ..." *New York Times,* June 20, 1877.

P

"A Permit for an Excavation. The Controller of the Cypress Hills Cemetery Astonished." *New York Times,* August 21, 1881.

"A Possible Clue to the Stewart Grave Robbery." *Brooklyn Eagle,* November 18, 1878.

"Preparations for the Funeral. The Arrangements Not Complete." *New York Times,* April 12, 1876.

Putnam's Monthly. Issues 1–6. New York: G. P. Putnam & Co., 1853.

R

"A Ramble in a Cemetery. Introducing a Somewhat Novel Phase of Detective Work." *New York Times,* August 21, 1881.

Rather, John. "A Village Planned by a Merchant Prince." *New York Times,* October 18, 1998.

"The Recovery of Stewart's Body." *Brooklyn Eagle,* January 16, 1879.

"Removal of the Stewart Wholesale Store ..." *New York Times,* November 13, 1878.

"A Reply to Judge Hilton ..." *New York Times,* June 20, 1877.

Resenting Their Insult. They Are Determined to Deal No More with A. T. Stewart ..." *New York Times,* June 22, 1877.

Resseguie, Harry E. "Alexander Turney Stewart and the Development of the Department Store, 1823–1876." *Business History Review,* Vol. 39, 1965.

———. "A. T. Stewart's Marble Palace—The Cradle of the Department Store." *New York Historical Society Quarterly,* Vol. 48, Issue 2, 1964.

———. "The Decline and Fall of the Commercial Empire of A. T. Stewart." *Business History Review,* Vol. 36, 1962.

"Retiring from Business. The Firm of A. T. Stewart & Co. Winding Up Affairs." *New York Times*, April 16, 1882.

Rich Men of the World, and How They Gained Their Wealth. Jesse Haney & Co., 1867.

Richmond, John Francis. *New York and Its Institutions, 1609–1871: A Library of Information, Pertaining to the Great Metropolis, Past and Present*. New York: E. B. Treat, 1871.

Riis, Jacob August. *The Making of an American*. New York: Macmillan, 1904.

"The Robbers of the Tomb. A Rumor That Mr. Stewart's Body Found ..." *New York Times*, November 11, 1878.

S

"Sala's Remarkable Story. An Italian Stone-Cutter's Queer Experiences ..." *New York Times*, August 14, 1879.

"Saratoga's Public Benefactor. Mr. Stewart's Death Profoundly Lamented at the Springs." *New York Times*, April 11, 1876.

Schechter, Harold. *The Whole Death Catalog: A Lively Guide to the Bitter End*. New York: Random House Digital Inc., 2009.

Scobey, David. "Anatomy of the Promenade: The Politics of Bourgeois Sociability in Nineteenth-century New York." *Social History*, Vol. 17, No. 2, 1992.

"Scolding Judge Hilton. The Women's Great Mass Meeting ..." *New York Times*, June 5, 1878.

"The Search Begun. Unexpected Parties Appear on the Scene ..." *New York Times*, August 21, 1881.

"Search for the Robbers. No Further Arrests Made." *New York Times*, November 22, 1878.

"The Search for Stewart's Body: Special Dispatch to the New York Times." *New York Times*, December 12, 1878.

"Searching. Are the Brooklyn Police on the Track of A. T. Stewart's Remains." *Brooklyn Eagle*, November 9, 1878.

"Searching New Jersey." *New York Times*, November 11, 1878.

"Seeking for the Ghouls. Mr. Stewart's Body Likely to Be Recovered ..." *New York Times,* November 12, 1878.

"Selecting Their Guests. The Grand Union Restrictions ..." *New York Times,* June 20, 1877.

"A Sensation at Saratoga ... No Jews to Be Admitted ..." *New York Times,* June 19, 1877.

"Services of Consecration ..." *New York Times,* May 27, 1885.

Shultz, Suzanne M. *Body Snatching: The Robbing of Graves for the Education of Physicians in Early Nineteenth Century America.* Jefferson, NC: McFarland & Company, 2005.

Smith, Alfred Emanuel. *New Outlook,* Vol. 68. Outlook Publishing Co., 1901.

Smith, Mary Ann. "John Snook and the Design for A. T. Stewart's Store." *New York Historical Society Quarterly,* Vol. 58, Issue 1, 1974.

"Some Curious Facts for Superstitious People." *New York Times,* August 22, 1881.

"Startling. The Late A. T. Stewart's Remains Stolen." *Brooklyn Eagle,* November 8, 1878.

Stately Homes in America: From Colonial Times to the Present Day. New York: D. Appleton and Company, 1903.

"The Stealing of A. T. Stewart's Body." *Brooklyn Eagle,* November 8, 1878.

"Stealing the Body of a Dead Millionaire." *Boston Globe,* November 8, 1878.

"The Stewart Chicago Branch ..." *New York Times,* April 21, 1882.

"The Stewart Collection ..." *New York Times,* December 17, 1886.

"Stewart. Contradictory Reports about the Missing Body." *Brooklyn Eagle,* November 15, 1878.

"The Stewart Estate." *New York Times,* April 17, 1876.

"The Stewart Grave Robbery." *New York Times,* November 28, 1878.

"The Stewart Grave Robbery. A Number of Detectives Withdrawn from the Case." *New York Times,* November 26, 1878.

"Stewart Heirs in Court ..." *New York Times,* February 19, 1887.

"The Stewart House in Chicago ..." *New York Times,* December 20, 1877.

"The Stewart Memorial. The New Cathedral at Garden City ..." *New York Times*, April 9, 1885.

"The Stewart Mystery." *New York Times*, November 25, 1878.

"The Stewart Mystery. The Police Still Looking ..." *New York Times*, November 25, 1878.

"The Stewart Resurrection Case." *Brooklyn Eagle*, November 15, 1878.

"Stewart's Body Sought. An Important Excavation Begun at Cypress Hills ..." *New York Times*, August 21, 1881.

"Stewart's Grave Robbers. All But One of Them Arrested." *New York Times*, November 20, 1878.

"Stewart's Stolen Body. Capt. Byrnes Corroborates the Times Statement ..." *New York Times*, November 19, 1878.

"Stewart's Stolen Body. The Prospect of Its Recovery." *New York Times*, November 14, 1878.

"Still in the Dark." *Brooklyn Eagle*, November 19, 1878.

"Still Looking for Stewart's Body." *New York Times*, December 11, 1878.

"The Stock of A. T. Stewart & Co." *New York Times*, April 29, 1882.

Stoddard, William Osborn. *Men of Business*. New York: Charles Scribner's Sons, 1893.

Stories of Remarkable Persons. Edinburgh and London: W. & R. Chambers, 1878.

"The Story of the Robbery. How the Body Snatchers Secured Mr. Stewart's Remains ..." *New York Times*, August 22, 1881.

Stradling, David. *Making Mountains: New York City and the Catskills*. Seattle: University of Washington Press, 2007.

"A Suit against Mrs. Stewart ..." *New York Times*, December 29, 1885.

Supplement to the *Hartford Courant*, September 18, 1858.

T

Thayer, William Makepeace. *Turning Points in Successful Careers*. New York: Thomas Y. Crowell & Company, 1895.

"They Decline the Gift. Judge Hilton and the Jews." *New York Times*, December 23, 1878.

Trachtenberg, Alan. *The Incorporation of America: Culture and Society in the Gilded Age.* New York: Hill and Wang, 1982.

"Tracing a Dead Body." *New York Times,* December 13, 1878.

"The Tragedy in the Depot. Guiteau Fires His Cruel Shots from behind the President ..." *New York Times,* July 3, 1881.

Twain, Mark. *The Stolen White Elephant.* Los Angeles: Pub Group West, 1987 (originally published 1882).

"Two Prisoners in Court. The Extraordinary Story Told by Capt. Byrnes ..." *New York Times,* November 19, 1878.

U

"A University at Garden City ..." *New York Times,* August 1, 1880.

"The Unjust Judge." *New York Times,* June 6, 1878.

"An Unpunished Crime. Anniversary of the Robbery of Stewart's Tomb." *Brooklyn Eagle,* November 7, 1879.

V

"The Vanderbilt Palaces. An Interior View of the Great Houses on Fifth Avenue ..." *New York Times,* August 25, 1885.

"The Village of Chatham Excited. Looking for Mr. Stewart's Remains ..." *New York Times,* November 20, 1878.

"Vreeland and Burke Committed. Capt. Byrnes Formal Complaint ..." *New York Times,* November 20, 1878.

W

Walling, George Washington. *Recollections of a New York Chief of Police.* New York: Caxton Book Concern, Ltd., 1887.

"The Walls of Division. Why They Should Not Be Set Up ..." *New York Times,* June 24, 1877.

Warehousemen and Drapers Trade Journal, Vol. V. n.p., 1876.

Weil, Francois. *A History of New York.* New York: Columbia University Press, 2004.

Weisman, Winston. "Commercial Palaces of New York: 1845–1875." *Art Bulletin,* Vol. 36, No. 4, 1954.

Weymouth, Lally, and Milton Glaser. *America in 1876: The Way We Were.* New York: Random House, 1976.

"What Gen. Jones Says. His Mysterious Correspondence with Romaine ..." *New York Times,* August 14, 1879.

Whitten, David O., and Bessie Emrick Whitten. *The Birth of Big Business in the United States, 1860–1914.* Westport, CT: Greenwood Publishing Group, 2006.

"The Will Discussed at the Clubs and Hotels." *New York Times,* April 12, 1876.

"A Woman's Hotel No More. The Park Avenue Opened ..." *New York Times,* June 9, 1878.

"The Women's Hotel Open ... A Great Enterprise Begun ..." *New York Times,* April 3, 1878.

"Women's Suffrage Association. The Ladies Have More to Say about the Woman's Home ..." *New York Times,* June 7, 1878.

"Working Up a Fine Clue ..." *New York Times,* November 18, 1878.

"Working Women's Hotel. Grand Legacy from Mr. Stewart ..." *New York Times,* November 12, 1877.

"The Working Women's Hotel. To Be Opened on Tuesday Evening ..." *New York Times,* March 24, 1878.

INDEX

ABOUT THE AUTHOR

J. NORTH CONWAY is the author of seven nonfiction books, including *The Big Policeman* and *King of Heists* (both from Lyons Press); *The Cape Cod Canal: Breaking Through the Bared and Bended Arm;* and *American Literacy: Fifty Books That Define Our Culture and Ourselves.* He teaches at the University of Massachusetts in Dartmouth and Bristol Community College in Fall River.

DISCARD